ELEMENTARY
DISCIPLESHIP

getting back to
the basics of
following Jesus

STEPHEN SAMS AND JOSH ROMANO

FOREWORD BY JIM PUTMAN

LUCIDBOOKS

Elementary Discipleship
Getting Back to the Basics of Following Jesus

Published by Lucid Books in Houston, TX
www.LucidBooksPublishing.com

ISBN-10: 1-63296-370-1
ISBN-13: 978-1-63296-370-3
eISBN-10: 1-63296-384-1
eISBN-13: 978-1-63296-384-0

Special Sales: Most Lucid Books titles are available in special quantity discounts. Custom imprinting or excerpting can also be done to fit special needs. Contact Lucid Books at Info@LucidBooksPublishing.com.

Table of Contents

Foreword   vii

Introduction: Let's Keep It Simple   1

The Crown: Discovering the Greater Kingdom   7
Chapter 1: The King Who Is and Always Was   8
Chapter 2: The Struggle Is Real   15
Chapter 3: The Kingdom Is within Reach   20
Chapter 4: Kingdom People   26
Chapter 5: Kingdom Come   34

The Net: Counting the Cost, Embracing the Call   41
Chapter 6: A Leader Worth Following   42
Chapter 7: A Calling Worth Embracing   50
Chapter 8: A Price Worth Paying   61
Chapter 9: A Commitment Worth Keeping   71

The Gift: Deciding to Follow Jesus   79
Chapter 10: A Simple Question   80
Chapter 11: God's Purpose   84
Chapter 12: Our Problem   90
Chapter 13: God's Payment   95
Chapter 14: Our Part   99
Chapter 15: God's Promise   109

The Bread: Examining and Applying the Bible   115
Chapter 16: Bread: A Family Favorite   116
Chapter 17: Bread Basics: What Is the Bible?   118
Chapter 18: The Spiritual Wellness Tool: A Balanced Diet   128
Chapter 19: A Plan That Works: EAT   132

The Stone: Relating to Others with Love   **139**
    Chapter 20: Drop the Stones   140
    Chapter 21: Take Up Love   147
    Chapter 22: Join Together   155

The Voice: Connecting to God in Prayer   **165**
    Chapter 23: Knowing the Voice   166
    Chapter 24: The Two-Way Interaction: Hearing   172
    Chapter 25: The Two-Way Interaction: Praying   178

The Towel: Becoming a Servant   **187**
    Chapter 26: Serving Changes the Atmosphere   188
    Chapter 27: The How of the Towel   195
    Chapter 28: The Anatomy of a Servant   205

The Fruit: Developing Deeper Roots   **211**
    Chapter 29: Rooted   212
    Chapter 30: Pruned   219
    Chapter 31: Fruitful   226

The Mission: Sharing the Good News   **235**
    Chapter 32: Mission   236
    Chapter 33: Message   251
    Chapter 34: Method   256

Conclusion   266

Recommended Resources   271

Acknowledgments

Thank you to Axis Church for being on the journey with us to be disciples and make disciples. The adventure continues!

Thank you to our families who gave us the time, encouragement, and support to see this project through.

Thank you to the outstanding team at Lucid Press. Your belief in this resource and ability to keep us on task proved so valuable.

Thank you to our illustrator, Courtney Lustig, at Oak + Ink Design Studio for making our elements and tools express exactly our vision.

A special thanks to Nancy Sams who provided delicious lunches and a home away from home every Wednesday so we could write in peace away from the office.

We dedicate this book to our dear friend and sister Sheri, who constantly encouraged us to write until the day she was called home to Jesus.

Foreword

I think that most who look at the American culture would honestly agree that we are in trouble. In part, I believe this is the result of a misguided Christian church. Our responsibility has been to make disciples, and rather than doing that, we have made converts. In a sense, we have taught people to believe they have crossed the finish line when they accept Jesus and that He has an obligation to make them happy on planet Earth from now on.

We have led people to believe that Jesus was obligated to bless their dreams. Many pastors have created formulas (not found in scripture) that guarantee personal happiness and prosperity on planet Earth. The result has been that people believe they have hell insurance. However, they do not reflect the character and priorities of Jesus. Because people have not been discipled, they do not understand the heart of God, the priorities of God, or the cost of living for Jesus.

Most Christians go to church when they have time, but few experience real relationships with anyone in the faith who will hold them accountable, support them when they are struggling, and encourage them to obey Jesus no matter what. In a sense, Christians live in a state of perpetual infancy with little wisdom or purpose.

American Christians have been distracted by the things of the world and have become lukewarm. We do live in an age of information, and some claim that discipleship is merely a transfer of the right information and behaviors, but that still leaves important components out that result in dissatisfaction and spiritual anemia.

Because time is so valuable in our culture, most try to find shortcuts that allow them to accomplish everything their earthly lifestyle demands, and unfortunately, there is little service to others, outreach to the lost, or relationships that get them through tough times. Few parents are discipling their kids to withstand the constant barrage our media, universities, and peers place on them.

Because these churches represent Jesus to the world, most unbelievers believe that Jesus can't really be who scripture says He is because He doesn't even help those who claim Him as their God. They don't know that the scriptures reveal completely different priorities, lifestyle, and results. In order to change things, it will have to start with Christians in churches led by leaders who start a new movement of discipleship.

As we clean the inside of the cup, it will have a profound effect on those who look at the outside. It will take courageous leaders who are willing to challenge a Christian culture that has been brought up to accept and even crave a good show on Sunday and a message that fits into their busy lives. It will take more leaders like Stephen Sams and Josh Romano who will not only teach biblical truth but will model a reproducible lifestyle for all people to follow.

I met Stephen years ago when he attended one of our discipleship trainings at Real Life Ministries. He immediately struck me as a man who was very sure of the goal to make disciples but humble enough to learn better methods to attain that goal. It was apparent that he was a leader who cared deeply for Jesus and for his team as well.

Stephen Sams and Josh Romano are practitioners as it pertains to discipleship and not merely philosophers and theorists. They have developed material that will enable you to have relational discussions that lead to greater maturity. I believe that this book will play a part in recapturing the biblical model of discipleship, and it will give every person a starting place for discussions that lead to life change.

—Jim Putman

Senior Pastor, Real Life Ministries, Post Falls, Idaho
Author, *Church Is a Team Sport, Real-Life Discipleship, DiscipleShift, The Power of Together,* and *Hope for the Prodigal*

Introduction

Let's Keep It Simple

Stephen

Am I the only one who makes things harder than they should be?

Over the years, I have built a not-so-flattering reputation for not reading directions. Christmas toys, furniture, trampolines, you name it, I get an idea in my head about what it should look like, and I go to town. "Only suckers need directions," I reason to myself. I guess what parts should go together. I find bolts that look like they fit. About halfway through, I start to realize that I'm the sucker. The parts just aren't fitting like they should. The unopened directions mock me. Usually, after some prodding from my practical wife, I reluctantly open the directions. There is a picture on the front of the instructions that clearly shows my eventual goal. On page two, there is a list of all the parts and tools I will need to finish my project. Then, there are directions on how to make my project look like the picture. It turns out that it is easier to build something if you have a picture of what you are building, the instructions, and the right tools to get it done.

Why do we make things more complicated than they should be? That is how I feel about discipleship. Yes, discipleship, that often talked about but rarely understood or practiced command of Jesus. What does a disciple look like, and how in the world do we go about making one?

Discipleship was never meant to be overcomplicated. Our goal in this book is to get back to the basics.

1

The basics matter in every area of life. In every sport, the coach will tell the team, "To be successful, we will focus on the fundamentals." Even professional teams understand this. Baseball teams focus on the fundamentals. They practice stepping toward the target when throwing the ball, gripping the bat properly, and shagging balls in the outfield.

Excellent golfers spend hours at the driving range. Even before the Masters Tournament when you might expect these elite athletes to be resting or gathering their thoughts, they are actually on the range correcting the smallest imperfections. I am a very below-average golfer at best, and it amazes me that even the best of the best still think through things like proper stance, grip, and swing.

Before a new CrossFit athlete even picks up a barbell, most boxes require him or her to go through a basic training class, often called "Fundamentals." When Josh and I opened our CrossFit gym in 2013, we did not require a fundamentals class, but it was not long before we realized the importance of making sure every athlete had a basic understanding of proper movement.

In education, you must learn the basics. In math, you need to learn addition, subtraction, multiplication, and division before you can learn to divide fractions or find x. In grammar, you need to learn the parts of speech before you write a novel. In medicine, the aspiring doctor should learn basic anatomy before attempting to pick up a scalpel. Personally, I prefer to have a doctor who knows where my appendix is before trying to remove it. In music, a young musician must learn how to hold the trumpet, position the fingers, and understand good breathing techniques before playing in a recital. The fundamentals matter in every area of life. If the basics matter in sports, academics, medicine, and music, then how much more important are they when it comes to the Christian faith?

It Started with Asking Questions

This book is about understanding and living out the teachings of Jesus. It was born after many, many months of praying and planning and asking the Lord how we could help the people we lead be better prepared. How can we help them know the truth? How do we help them be disciples of Jesus? How do we equip them so they can then help other people become disciples of Jesus?

Jesus commanded us to "go and make disciples...baptizing them...and teaching them" (Matt. 28:19–20). But we noticed that most Christians we encountered struggled to even define *disciple*, much less make one. This both troubled us and motivated us to clearly identify the basic elements of discipleship.

When we launched Axis Church in 2009, we started it with the crazy idea of being a church that would actually follow this most basic command of Jesus. We were motivated to change the perception that church was just a place to go. We were not interested in becoming the next best church show in our city. We did not want to attract attenders. We wanted people to embrace the mission of Jesus.

What we didn't realize at the time was that going to make disciples is a bit of a messy process. We didn't realize how difficult it would be to change people's perceptions about the purpose of a church. We underestimated the amount of time, energy, and effort it would take to make disciples who make disciples. We studied different models. We attended learning communities with other churches who were asking these same questions. We certainly picked up good advice and incorporated some of the principles or practices of others who were doing it successfully. Truth be told, even after all the discovery and training, we still struggled to identify a clear process or strategy we could embrace.

I think that is why it surprised us that, after months of praying and processing, the nine elements we cover in this book emerged so clearly for us during a one-hour conversation. We had two Bibles and a whiteboard. We asked this fundamental question: What were the things Jesus taught during His time on earth over and over again?

We went back to the source. We found our answer in the most obvious place—the very teachings of Jesus Himself. We walked through the pages of the Gospel of John. There it was, chapter after chapter of the basics—the basic elements of being a disciple of Jesus.

The "What" of Discipleship

In our learning process, we found many resources that address the "why" of discipleship. There are countless authors who provide insight into the critical need to reclaim the Great Commission of Jesus. The command to go and make disciples is resurging in the church world today, especially with church planters.

We also discovered many who are leading the way in modeling the "how" of discipleship. The Great Commandment of Jesus to "love your neighbor as yourself" (Mark 12:31) describes the relational aspect of discipleship. We go, and we go in love. Relational discipleship is how Jesus both taught and modeled for His followers.

We believe that this book provides a needed resource for a missing link in discipleship. We were already convicted of the need to make disciples. We were motivated by the why. We were convinced that we should make disciples how Jesus made them, through relationships. But we struggled with the "what." What is the content? What are the fundamentals? What are the things that Jesus taught more than anything else? What are the basic tools that we need in our discipleship toolbox?

We were not looking for a simple pathway to discipleship. We did not want a 12-step process for discipleship. We did not want a class for discipleship. What we discovered were what we believe to be the basic elements of discipleship. They are concepts and tools that every follower of Jesus needs to know, model, and share.

The Nine Elements of Discipleship

Here are the nine elements of discipleship that Jesus taught His apostles. I want you to notice a couple of things as you read through this list: (1) they all come right out of the book of John, and (2) they all have a memory hook. There is an image associated with each element that will easily remind you of the basics.

1. The Crown: Discovering the greater Kingdom
2. The Net: Counting the cost, embracing the call
3. The Gift: Deciding to follow Jesus
4. The Bread: Examining and applying the Bible
5. The Stone: Relating to others with love

4

6. The Voice: Connecting to God in prayer
7. The Towel: Becoming a servant
8. The Fruit: Developing deeper roots
9. The Mission: Sharing the good news

Along with each element, we have provided a tool for you to use both in your personal growth and in your discipling conversations. We want this to be your own discipleship toolbox. Like every good toolbox, it includes tools you will use over and over. The tools are simple, versatile, and durable. The tools are simple because if they are too difficult, you will be easily tempted to leave them at the bottom of the box and never use them. They are versatile, so they can be used in a variety of settings with people who are in different stages of their spiritual journeys or seasons of life. They are durable. They stand the test of time.

Most of these tools are our creation, while others are modifications of tools that others have developed. These are basic tools for your spiritual toolbox that you can pull out at any moment.

What This Book Is and What This Book Is Not

This book is designed to be a look into the fundamentals of the Christian faith. While there are many biblical references and principles, it will not be a deep dive into theology. It is designed to be a handbook that can be used by those who are curious about Christianity and those who are already deeply committed followers of Jesus. It is filled with scriptures, principles, and personal stories.

It is our sincere prayer that you will find this book to be a resource that you use again and again. It is your own personal guide to Elementary Discipleship.

The Crown

Josh

The Word became flesh and made his dwelling among us.
We have seen his glory, the glory of the one and only Son,
who came from the Father, full of grace and truth.

—John 1:14

Chapter 1

The King Who Is and Always Was

A great story always has a great opening. It has the ability to stir our curiosity and raise questions we must answer. It invites us down a path of discovery. It ignites something inside of us that shouts, "Tell me more!"

The same is true of a great movie. True confession: if a movie doesn't hook me in the first 10 minutes, I am cutting my losses and moving on—unless I promised someone I would watch it. Then it is only a matter of time before I slowly slip into the I'm-just-resting-my-eyes mode.

The best kinds of stories not only keep you awake but also pull you right off the edge of your seat into the depth of them. It's almost as if you were the one fighting the villain, overcoming the impossible obstacle, and battling back from defeat.

The Bible does not disappoint when it comes to openings:

In the beginning God created the heavens and the earth.
—Gen. 1:1

If that introduction doesn't stir our imagination, we might need to stop and check our pulse. The very first line of the Bible introduces the central being of all creation, a being who transcends time, matter, and space. He was the one who existed before anything else and was powerful enough to effortlessly set the universe in motion. He was the one who said, "Let there be light" (Gen. 1:3), and there was. He is the one true God.

In the book of John, we get another account of the very beginning.

> *In the beginning was the Word [Jesus], and the Word was with God, and the Word was God. He was with God in the beginning. Through him all things were made; without him nothing was made that has been made. In Him was life, and that life was the light of all mankind. The light shines in the darkness, and the darkness has not overcome it.*
>
> —John 1:1–5

As we observe the early unfolding of this story, God's story, we see that God created humans in His own image. We were created to exist in perfect harmony with God and one another. The Garden of Eden was a picture of God's perfect world. In the garden, there was no sickness, no heartache, and no violence. There was no shame or suffering. There was an overflow of joy, peace, and pure satisfaction. It was a kingdom that God established for His glory and our enjoyment.

To understand the Kingdom we were made for, we must first come to know the One who wears the crown.

From the early pages of God's story, a portrait of who this mysterious King truly is begins to emerge. The first question we must answer is who is this King? Let's look at a few distinctives that separate our King, Jesus, from every being.

The Perfect King

There is a phrase that gets thrown around a lot today. People say something is perfection to indicate something or someone that is ideal. It might be phrased "that person is perfection" or "that meal is perfection" or "this moment is perfection." True perfection, however, doesn't come in human form. We all have faults and imperfections.

There is nothing like writing a book to make you acutely aware of your own imperfection. A friend of mine offered to help edit this book. I was a bit overwhelmed when I got the first draft back. Let's just say, there was a lot of red ink. I thought maybe the red pen she was using leaked, but there was actually just that much that needed corrected and reworked. This book required a lot of red ink.

If you spent any time evaluating my life, you would discover there is a lot red ink there as well. I'm a work in progress. In complete contrast to us, God doesn't have a single red mark on a single page of His eternal existence. He is what the Bible calls *holy*.

He is morally perfect. He has never sinned and will never sin. He has never so much as had an impure thought. He is absolutely pure (1 John 1:5). He is perfectly wise. There are no gaps in His understanding. He knows every star (Ps. 147:4–5). He knows every sparrow (Matt. 10:29). He knows every detail about every person on the planet (Ps. 139). He knows every hair on every head (Matt. 10:30). His every intention is perfect. He is perfect in His execution. He keeps every promise. He is complete perfection.

Not only is our King perfect, He is referred to in the book of James as the *perfecter of our faith*. If God is the perfecter, then I don't have to be. I don't have to be my own perfecter or anyone else's. I can leave the editing to the perfect King.

A Powerful King

Another distinctive of our King is that He is all-powerful.

One of the ways God introduces Himself in the Old Testament is El Shaddai. It means God almighty. He greets Abraham this way:

When Abram was ninety-nine years old the LORD appeared to Abram and said to him, "I am God Almighty; walk before me, and be blameless, that I may make my covenant between me and you, and may multiply you greatly." Then Abram fell on his face. And God said to him, "Behold, my covenant is with you, and you shall be the father of a multitude of nations. No longer shall your name be called Abram, but your name shall be Abraham, for I have made you the father of a multitude of nations."

—Gen. 17:1–5 ESV

Can you imagine the weight of this moment for Abraham? You can bet God's voice didn't crack when He spoke "I am God Almighty!" It's also a safe bet to assume Abraham's heart rate was reading a little on the high end when he looked at his Fitbit. The only thing he could do in the presence of pure power was fall on his face. That seems to be the only option when confronted with the all-powerful—to fall on your face. God is a King of immeasurable power. He is God almighty. He is the King of all kings, the Lord of all lords.

From the first book of the Bible to the last book of the Bible, God's power is demonstrated through wonders, miracles, and supernatural manifestations of His glory. Our King is not a king that can be tamed or controlled. He is a King of unfathomable might. Any other power on earth is not a power that is owned; it is a power that is loaned. The King of the universe is the source of pure power. Look at these words from Revelation:

> And the twenty-four elders who sit on their thrones before God fell on their faces and worshiped God, saying, "We give thanks to you, Lord God Almighty, who is and who was, for you have taken your great power and begun to reign. The nations raged, but your wrath came, and the time for the dead to be judged, and for rewarding your servants, the prophets and saints, and those who fear your name, both small and great, and for destroying the destroyers of the earth."
>
> —Rev. 11:16–19 ESV

A Purposeful King

Power without purpose is a dangerous proposition, but our King does not wield His power aimlessly. He does not assert His power carelessly. He operates with an absolute precision. We see this on a cosmic macro level down to a cellular micro level. From the forces governing our universe to the smallest of carefully crafted systems and cells in our body, there is tremendous evidence of a King who cares about the details.

One of my finest creations, which I admit isn't saying a lot, is a farm table I created for my wife. She was out of town, and I seized the opportunity to travel to Kentucky to my father-in-law's workshop to craft a table as a Christmas gift for her. I guess I should admit that I did have some help. Here's the first thing my father-in-law asked me: "Where is the plan?" I was like, "What do you mean? The plan is we are going to build a farm table." "Yeah, but what are the specs? We need a specified plan."

Who knew? We found a plan online. That plan gave way to a process, which eventually culminated in a finished masterpiece. I swelled with pride. I was so excited to share my gift that I didn't even wait until Christmas for the big reveal.

God, the purposeful King, set out with a plan. His plan led to a creation process, which culminated in a perfectly crafted creation. I love reading the account in Genesis where God looked on the creation process with delight. Each time He crafted something new into the tapestry, He looked on it and "saw that it was good" (Gen. 1:10). At the pinnacle, the big reveal moment, He created a being in His own image, and it was a human being. Genesis 1:31 reports, "God saw all that he had made, and it was very good."

All that God does is purposeful and deliberate. He is a God who sets out with great intention and carries out His plan to perfect, delightful execution.

A Personal King

I recall a conversation I had with a friend a few years back. We were kayaking along a beautiful stretch of the Little Miami River. It was quiet, and we let the current pull us along while we cast fishing lines into the water, hoping for a bite. There wasn't a lot biting that day, but the conversation was worth the trip. We talked about life, which led to talking about God, which happens to be my favorite topic, if you couldn't tell. He told me that he believed in God but saw God more as a distant, impersonal force rather than a relational being. I listened, and I honestly wasn't very surprised by his characterization because it's a pretty common one today. There is this belief that God does His thing off somewhere, and

He doesn't really concern Himself with our affairs down here. He's either too busy or simply doesn't care.

This couldn't be further from the God we read about in scripture. We read about a God who reveals Himself. He interacts with us, He operates on our behalf, He provides for us, He cares for us, and, as crazy as it sounds, He even wants a relationship with us. This stumped King David as he pondered this idea: "What is man that you are mindful of him, and the son of man that you care for him?" (Ps. 8:4 ESV).

Don't worry. We will discuss this more. But for now, begin to consider something that has the power to change the trajectory of your story. The King over everything is a personal King. He knows you by name. He knows how many hairs are on your head. He knows your every thought. He knows when you lie down and when you wake. And He wants you to know Him.

My prayer for you is the same prayer I silently prayed for my friend that day on the river. "God, reveal Yourself. Make Yourself known to him. Create a desire in him to know you more." I hope you'll allow the personal King to do the same for you.

If you are even slightly compelled by this thought, then do what Jesus told His disciples to do in Matthew 6:33: "But seek first his kingdom and his righteousness, and all these things will be given to you as well."

Seek first.

Seek the King.

Seek the Kingdom.

The more you seek, the more you will see.

The more you seek the King, the more you will see the things of the Kingdom flooding into your heart and life. When the King is your primary pursuit, unexpected things begin to happen.

It has been the times in my life when I have chased hardest after God that I have witnessed a far better plan for my life. Opportunities have emerged out of thin air. God has imparted wisdom to me. He has answered prayers that I didn't even think to pray. People around me have experienced breakthroughs. He provided comfort to me through difficulty. I have had the least regrets. Most importantly, the times I have chased hardest after God are the times I have been nearest to the King.

This is my desire for you: Seek more, and you will see more. We have only scratched the surface. There is so much more to learn and discover. It all begins with a desire to want to know Him more.

King David was one who delighted in seeking the true King. I'll leave you with his words: "Taste and see that the LORD is good; blessed is the one who takes refuge in him" (Ps. 34:8).

Questions for Reflection

In what ways have you witnessed the King's power?

How have you witnessed the King's purpose and artistry?

In what ways have you witnessed the King's personal touch?

Will you take some moments to do what it says in Psalm 34:8?

Chapter 2

The Struggle Is Real

I'm not much of an artist. This is not a new self-discovery. Let's just say you wouldn't find me winning any coloring contests. Scribbling has always been more my specialty. In elementary school, I tried to make a clay mug, and I remember my teacher saying, "Well, isn't that something!" He was right. It *was* something. But it certainly wasn't anything close to a mug.

So, as you can imagine, I wasn't totally stoked on my mom's idea of taking a family trip to an art studio for a painting class. I knew it would end badly, but I decided to try to make the most of it. The teacher stood up front and showed us the picture we would be painting: a flower. "Perfect," I thought, "my favorite" (cue sarcasm). It didn't matter anyway, because mine would look a lot more like a paint fight gone bad. As we finished painting, the teacher's assistant came around. Bless her heart, she was the most encouraging woman. After a look at each canvas, she commented, "What a great looking painting."

I couldn't wait to see if she would lie to me or not, because everyone in the class could see that my painting was a very sad looking flower. Sure enough, she said, "What a great looking painting." I laughed and thought, "Compared to what?" Something had gone horribly wrong with my picture. I knew what it should have looked like, but it fell short.

I don't think it takes very long to look at the world we live in and think, "Something is wrong with this picture. Surely this isn't what it's supposed to look like. Everywhere we look, we see violence, hatred, anger, insecurity, brokenness, pain, and evil. We see relationships fall apart; we see disease and natural disasters ravage the lives of real people.

Then we dig a little deeper and discover the same thing within ourselves. We discover that there is something broken *in* us, not just *around* us. We wrestle with jealousy, anger, and selfishness. We know the good we should do, but we often choose the bad. All of that leads us to this question: What's wrong with this picture?

As we go back to the very beginning of God's story, we see the beauty of God's original creation. In Genesis, we get a front row seat as God carefully and intentionally creates the earth, the skies, the oceans, the birds, and all the animals. He envisions every detail. Then He paints humans into the picture and delights in what He has created. Adam and Eve live in perfect unity with God without fear, shame, or guilt. Everything is as it's supposed to be. The picture is perfect. It's beautiful. This garden called Eden is God's ideal for humans flourishing in His presence.

God encourages them to enjoy all He has created and, most importantly, enjoy Him and His goodness with nothing holding them back. He gives them only one warning: "You must not eat from the tree of the knowledge of good and evil, for when you eat from it you will certainly die" (Gen. 2:17).

All of us who have read the story know what happened from there. They ate from the tree—first Eve and then Adam. Both disobeyed God. They sinned against the holy and perfect God. The perfect picture began to change and became corrupted. Shame entered the picture, so Adam and Eve hid from God. They began to see the consequences of disobedience. They were banished from the garden because God and sin can't coexist. The relationship between humanity and God was broken. The natural order of things was disrupted. Disease, disaster, pain, and brokenness fought to overshadow God's goodness.

How could God let all this happen? That's our first reaction, isn't it? Why is God allowing evil to disrupt His perfect creation? That often leads us to wonder this: Why all this suffering around us?

When God created humans who had the power to choose, He created the opportunity for us to rebel against Him. He knew we could reject Him and choose evil instead. It started with Adam and Eve, but the curse of sin carries into all humanity. The Bible reminds us that we all have the same sin problem. We all rebel against God in one way or another. When we rebel, we are choosing to deny His authority as King. Our rebellion gives way to an opposing kingdom. Jesus refers to it as the kingdom of the world. It is a kingdom marked by things that are contrary to God's perfect design.

God's perfect Kingdom was marred by sin, which led to an opposing kingdom. These two kingdoms are in tension. We picture the two opposing kingdoms—the kingdom of the world (KOW) and the Kingdom of God (KOG)—like this:

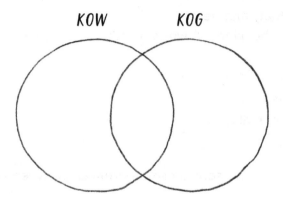

KOW   KOG

The opposing ruler of the kingdom of the world, Satan, holds temporary dominion over this realm. He is not a true king, only a power-hungry imposter. That does not make him any less threatening. We see him show up in the creation story as a serpent, and he still has the same mission that he did then: to bring destruction and devastation to God's creation. He employs a strategy of deceit, just as he did with Adam, Eve, and the fruit. He lies and exploits our human longings. Jesus warns His followers, "The thief comes only to steal and kill and destroy; I have come that they may have life, and have it to the full" (John 10:10). Peter, a follower of Jesus, echoes the sentiment in 1 Peter 5:8: "Be alert and of sober mind. Your enemy the devil prowls around like a roaring lion looking for someone to devour."

The struggle is real, and the stakes are high. The devil's strategy is simple yet effective. It starts with lies, temptations, and half-truths like these:

You will not surely die.

You are missing out.

God is withholding something from you.

Nobody will even notice.

It's harmless, it won't hurt anyone.

There are far worse things.

Lies, temptations, and half-truths give rise to sin, shame, and separation from God and His Kingdom. Ultimately, it leads to devastation, defeat, and death.

Think of the kind of world that's produced by the opposing kingdoms:

Light vs. darkness

Spirit vs. flesh

Good vs. evil

Life vs. death

We visually represent these differences between our world and God's world:

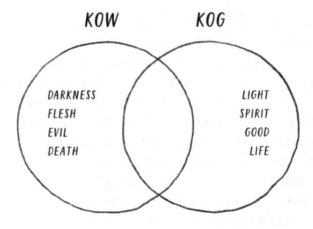

The Apostle Paul captures this idea with powerful imagery:

For our struggle is not against flesh and blood, but against the rulers, against the authorities, against the powers of this dark world and against the spiritual forces of evil in the heavenly realms.

—Eph. 6:12

If we feel as if we are caught between two worlds at war, it is because we are. While it sounds a bit like science fiction, it is anything but.

This is reality. The struggle is real. The stakes are high. But the war is won.

Questions for Reflection

If you could paint a picture of the perfect world, what would it have in it?

What do you see in this world that is most troubling or upsetting to you?

Why do you think the words *flesh*, *darkness*, and *evil* are used to describe the kingdom of the world?

How do you see the struggle unfolding in your own life?

What strategies does the enemy use on you? What lies does he tell you?

What worldly attitudes, actions, or attributes are most tempting for you to fall into?

Chapter 3

The Kingdom Is within Reach

I'll never forget our first trip to the beach with our firstborn. One of the coolest parts about being a parent is getting to experience a new first with your child. I was so excited for Aiden to get his first breath of ocean air, to get that first feeling of sand between his toes, and to get that first glimpse of endless ocean.

He was almost as excited as I was. We talked about it for weeks leading up to our trip to Hilton Head Island. We built up his anticipation and stirred his imagination for our summer adventure. Then came the hard part: getting there. Car rides with young kids are not something that parents dream of, but the destination was worth it. Nine hours of driving, multiple diaper changes, and way too many tears (his and ours) later, we finally made it. And I thought, "The look on his face when he takes in the vast ocean is going to make the long drive a distant memory."

Process number two, getting ready for the beach, was almost as painstaking as the drive down. Sunscreen: check. Way too many items to carry a few short miles along a hot boardwalk: check. Me complaining about not needing all this stuff: check.

We finally made it to the beach. How did Aiden react? Let's just say…not the way I had hoped. For starters, he didn't like how the sand felt. The closer I took him to the water, the higher the decibels of his screaming. At that point, I did what any respectable, grown man would do. I said, "Forget this." My wife stayed, and Aiden and I made the long journey back.

Halfway back, though, he found something that rocked his toddler world: the outdoor showers on the boardwalk. I'm only slightly exaggerating when I say that we spent hours pressing the button and running into and out of the cold shower. People laughed as they walked by, seeing him so enamored with a simple shower. It only took us the rest of the week to graduate from the simple pleasure of the shower to greater joys of the vast ocean.

I believe we, too, are guilty of settling for the simple pleasure of a small shower when we have access to an endless ocean of God's infinite goodness. I fear that we all can be a bit shortsighted when it comes to our pursuits. We pursue short-term pleasure, quick fixes, instant affirmation, personal success, and temporary comforts. God has more in store for us than the temporal pleasures the world could ever offer.

C. S. Lewis speaks of our tendency to settle for less:

We are half-hearted creatures, fooling about with drink and sex and ambition when infinite joy is offered us, like an ignorant child who wants to go on making mud pies in a slum because he cannot imagine what is meant by the offer of a holiday at the sea. We are far too easily pleased.[1]

The apostle Paul affirms this:

For although they knew God, they neither glorified him as God nor gave thanks to him, but their thinking became futile and their foolish hearts were darkened. Although they claimed to be wise, they became fools and exchanged the glory of the immortal God for images made to look like a mortal human being and birds and animals and reptiles. Therefore God gave them over in the sinful desires of their hearts to sexual impurity for the degrading of their bodies with one another. They exchanged the truth about God for a lie, and worshiped and served created things rather than the Creator—who is forever praised. Amen.

—Rom. 1:21–25

---

1. C. S. Lewis, *The Weight of Glory* (New York: HarperCollins, 1949), 26.

C. S. Lewis also captures this longing we all have: "If we find in ourselves a desire that nothing in this world can satisfy, the most probable explanation is we were made for another world."[2]

No matter how we try, we will only be able to find things in this world that temporarily satisfy. When we settle for the things of this world, we are settling for less than God's best. We were made for a better world—a world we can only access through the person of Jesus.

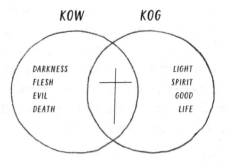

In John, we see the most unexpected thing happen. The King of creation puts on human skin and moves into our world. God Himself steps into the struggle. "The Word [Jesus] became flesh and made his dwelling among us" (John 1:14).

We can't miss the implication of this. God considered us worthy enough to depart His holy and perfect Kingdom, move into our mess and imperfection, and load the struggle onto His own shoulders.

Luke tells about a pivotal moment in the early stages of Jesus's ministry. After a 40-day and 40-night resistance against Satan in the wilderness, Jesus begins His earthly ministry with a powerful proclamation. Walking into a Jewish synagogue, He steps up to the podium and begins reading a scroll from the prophet Isaiah, which declares:

"The Spirit of the Lord is on me, because he has anointed me to proclaim good news to the poor. He has sent me to proclaim freedom for the prisoners and recovery of sight for the blind, to set the oppressed free, to proclaim the year of the Lord's favor."

---

2. C. S. Lewis, *Mere Christianity* (New York: HarperCollins, 1952), 135–136.

Then he rolled up the scroll, gave it back to the attendant and sat down. The eyes of everyone in the synagogue were fastened on him. He began by saying to them, "Today this scripture is fulfilled in your hearing."

—Luke 4:18–21

This is what we call a mic-drop moment: Today, this is fulfilled in your hearing! I (Jesus) am the one the prophet spoke of. The King has come to earth. Good news is here. Freedom is here. Healing is here. The Lord's favor is upon you!

When Jesus steps up to the "microphone" to begin His earthly ministry, His declaration shakes heaven and earth. The Kingdom of God is near, He said. It's within reach. You only need to reach out and take hold of it. He wasn't saying someday or somehow. He was saying that it starts here and now. It comes through Me, He says. What's impossible for you is possible for Me. Through Me, you will have the opportunity to reunite with God. You will be able to see all God's promises fulfilled.

He wouldn't be the first and certainly wouldn't be the last to come with visions of greater things to come, but something was different about Jesus. He didn't just talk a big game; He delivered. People noticed that He spoke as one who actually had authority. He didn't come with empty promises. He backed up His words by healing the sick, casting out evil, rejecting the religious establishment, and giving us a glimpse back into the world we were made for. He even secures our access into it. By coming into our world, sacrificing Himself, dying on a cross, and rising from the dead three days later, He defeats the ruler of the worldly kingdom, conquering evil and death, staking our claim to victory over the present evil world and its hold on us.

So how do we take the next step forward toward the King and His Kingdom? Jesus lays it out for us: "'The time has come,' He said. 'The kingdom of God has come near. Repent and believe the good news!'" (Mark 1:15).

Did you catch the two big action words? *Repent* and *believe. Turn from* the kingdom of the world and *take hold* of the Kingdom of God.

23

Repent

Repentance is a word that gets tossed around a lot among church people. I remember a guy who walked on the streets near my college campus. He wore a heavy A-frame sign around his neck with the words, "Repent or burn." He purposefully provoked people who passed and called them names. As I passed one time, he called me "a child of the devil."

Repentance gets some bad PR, but what if we have mischaracterized it? Jesus called people to repentance, too, but His approach was different. When Jesus spoke of the Kingdom, crowds gathered, and people leaned in. Repentance was the way forward. He didn't swing the word around like a club. Rather, He threw it out like a life preserver to people who were drowning. He said He did not come to condemn the world but to save the world. Repentance is an offer to turn from one way in pursuit of a better way. It is turning from the kingdom of the world in exchange for the Kingdom of God. Repentance is *turning from* the attitudes, attributes, and actions of the kingdom of the world in exchange for the better things of God's Kingdom.

Repentance is being sorry for the ways we rejected and turned from God. It's not just *saying* sorry, it's *being* sorry. There is a difference. As a parent, I have to reinforce this difference time and time again with our four-year-old. I remind him, "If you are *actually* sorry about pushing your little brother over, you won't do it again the next time you get the chance."

Repentance is a commitment to live under the leadership and rule of King Jesus. It isn't just a one-time event; it is a constant realignment with God's desires because His desires are life-giving. It is through repentance that God reclaims us as His own, restores us to the truest best version of ourselves, and repurposes us for His glory.

We can't make our home in both kingdoms simultaneously. Repentance is choosing God's Kingdom as our home. It's rejecting the kingdom of the world. When Jesus commands us to repent, He has our best interest in mind. It is up to us to decide if we want God's best or want to settle for less.

Believe

Since we define repentance as turning from the things of the world, we see this next command to *believe* as turning to God and the things of God. If we aren't careful, we can reduce believing to some internal change in our thinking. When Jesus tells us to believe, He is urging us to buy in.

As an example, I think sugar is bad for me. In fact, I've read loads of research that talks about the destructive consequences of eating too much added sugar. I've even personally experienced how awful I feel when I've had a lot of sugar and wake up with a headache or sick stomach. So I have knowledge about sugar. However, when my wife walks through the door with my favorite type of cake, I can still manage to eat the whole thing without worrying too much about the consequences of eating sugar.

Am I *fully* bought in on the idea that sugar is bad for me? No, because buying in means taking on a new way of living. I'm not here to argue if you should have a piece of cake from time to time; I'm simply pointing out that *belief should lead to buy-in*. This is what we are called to with the Kingdom of God: complete buy-in.

Jesus illustrates this level of commitment when He says, "The kingdom of heaven is like treasure hidden in a field. When a man found it, he hid it again, and then in his joy went and sold all he had and bought that field" (Matt. 13:44).

Believing is taking hold of God's Kingdom. It's more than an internal way of thinking; it's a new mindset that gives way to a new way of living. It's stepping into God's best and experiencing His blessing because that is what we want more than anything else.

So do you want God and His Kingdom? It is only possible when we do as Jesus commands us: *Repent and believe.*

Questions for Reflection

What attitudes, actions, and attributes do you believe best characterize the Kingdom of God?

What are you currently repenting of/turning from?

What are you turning to/believing?

Chapter 4

Kingdom People

My latest TV obsession is the TV show called *Suits*. I am not sure how accurately it depicts the world of courtrooms and lawyers since I'm not a lawyer, but it is entertaining and grips my interest. The show focuses mostly on corporate law, a lot of which seems to be driven by contracts and dealmaking. Contracts are written agreements that bind two parties around certain predetermined requirements. Contracts, however, like anything else, are only as good as the people who sign them and stand behind them.

One of the ways to understand our relationship with God is through the lens of "covenant." God established a covenant with His people. We see it traced from Adam and Eve through Abraham's family line and eventually through the person of Jesus. In each era in history, God identifies a remnant of people to carry out His purpose and receive His blessing. These are the Kingdom people.

What we all know well is that the human agents continue to breach the contract. God uses this contract not as a way to bind them but rather to guide them nearer to His promises and Kingdom realities. But in following their own ways, they defy the contract. There is the old covenant relationship that God sets up with His people prior to Jesus and a new covenant relationship that comes through Jesus. The strength of God's covenant is rooted in the fact that God has established it and stands behind it.

The writer of Hebrews says this of the new covenant relationship God establishes with His people:

This is the covenant I will establish with the people of Israel after that time, declares the Lord. I will put my laws in their minds and write them on their hearts. I will be their God, and they will be my people. No longer will they teach their neighbor, or say to one another, "Know the Lord," because they will all know me, from the least of them to the greatest. For I will forgive their wickedness and will remember their sins no more.

—Heb. 8:10–12

God has established a covenant with us if we choose to enter into it. With our newfound covenant relationship come both rights and responsibilities as citizens of heaven.

Rights

Before we dive deeper on this one, I want to steer us away from the thinking that rights mean something we deserve or are entitled to. In the sense we are using it here, it is not something we have earned or even deserve. In fact, these covenant rights come through God's great mercy and have everything to do with what Jesus did for us and nothing to do with what He owes us.

All of us have breached the contract in one way or another. We are covenant breakers. But it is through Jesus that we become beneficiaries of the Kingdom and its promises. Now, with that in mind, let's look at a few rights God makes available through Christ Jesus our King. We have been granted a right to a royal adoption and a right to a Kingdom inheritance.

Listen to how Paul captures this for the Colossians.

For this reason, since the day we heard about you, we have not stopped praying for you. We continually ask God to fill you with the knowledge of his will through all the wisdom and understanding that the Spirit gives, so that you may live a life worthy of the Lord and please him in every way: bearing fruit in every good work, growing in the knowledge of God, being strengthened with all power according to his glorious might so that you may have great endurance and patience, and giving joyful thanks to the Father, who has qualified you to share in the inheritance of his holy people in the kingdom of light. For he has rescued us from the dominion of darkness and brought us into the kingdom of the Son he loves, in whom we have redemption, the forgiveness of sins.

—Col. 1:9–14

Right to Royal Adoption

One right God extends to His people is a right to be adopted into His royal family. "But you are a chosen people, a royal priesthood, a holy nation, God's special possession, that you may declare the praises of him who called you out of darkness into his wonderful light" (1 Pet. 2:9).

If you spend a moment considering the magnitude of such a promise, it is quite humbling. The King Himself considers us worthy to be part of His very own family. We are adopted.

I have mentioned that I'm a parent of three little boys. You've probably heard people tell you that if you haven't experienced it yourself, it is a unique gift to be a parent. It's not easy, but it is amazing. I will never forget the first time I held both of my newborn infants in my hands. My first thought was this: "Don't drop them." They are a bit slimy and slippery at first. The first feeling that flooded my heart was pride and overwhelming love. The moment I laid eyes on them, I knew I would do anything for them. I had an instant connection that can only be described as a sense of belonging. I knew they were at home with me.

They hadn't done a single thing to earn my affection at this point, but that didn't matter. They were family. This is how God sees His children. He loves us and loves to bless us. He doesn't just tolerate us; He delights in us and wants the best for us.

Jesus makes this comparison in the book of Matthew: "So if you sinful people know how to give good gifts to your children, how much more will your heavenly Father give good gifts to those who ask him" (Matt. 7:11 NLT).

God provides endless gifts to His children. The best part is that they come not out of obligation but out of a lovestruck motivation.

That brings us to another right we have as Kingdom people.

Right to a Kingdom Inheritance

What if you got a call today from a family representative letting you know that you have just received a huge inheritance. A distant aunt you have never met has left you all she had to her name, which is billions of dollars in assets. What would you do first? My guess is that you would not turn it down. True, you didn't earn a penny of it, but your dear auntie left it to you from the goodness of her heart. You would take full advantage of the blessing!

We have an inheritance as God's children. Through a covenant relationship with Him, we have been granted full access to His estate. It contains things far greater than money, gold, or silver. It is not made of temporal things but eternal things. Read how Peter describes it:

> *Blessed be the God and Father of our Lord Jesus Christ! According to his great mercy, he has caused us to be born again to a living hope through the resurrection of Jesus Christ from the dead, to an inheritance that is imperishable, undefiled, and unfading, kept in heaven for you, who by God's power are being guarded through faith for a salvation ready to be revealed in the last time.*
>
> —1 Pet. 1:3–5 ESV

Maybe you don't have a rich aunt. But you do have a heavenly Father who possesses all the riches of the world. He doesn't need a bank account because there is nothing that He lacks. We could never fully grasp the things He has prepared for us, but we can count on it being more than we could possibly envision from our limited human perspective.

Responsibilities

At the time of this writing, Prince Harry and Duchess Meghan were recently wed. Yes, I watched the royal wedding. Yes, my wife forced me. Yes, I found it long but also kind of interesting. What interested me the most was thinking about how this American actress would adjust to the lifestyle of royalty. Sure, she was used to the limelight given her success as an actress, but I wouldn't expect being a duchess to be a walk in the park. Somebody is always watching. If she even stands or scratches her nose the wrong way, it will show up in a magazine the next day. It is a pretty fascinating privilege to be royalty, but it is a privilege that comes with responsibility.

Privileges come with responsibilities. Sometimes we think the word *responsibility* means something restrictive. Being a Kingdom people is not restrictive. It's actually quite the opposite. It's a life of flourishing. We have both Kingdom rights and Kingdom responsibilities.

Here are three of the most critical royal responsibilities.

Be Devoted to the King

There can only be one true King in your life. Sure, you can serve other kings. You can make your career your king. You can make your sport your king. You can make some person in your life your king. You can allow lots of things to rule your world. But anything less than the true King will leave you wanting.

In one of Jesus's teachings, He reminds people that they cannot serve two masters. He was specifically referencing money, but His point was that we are fooling ourselves if we think both God and anything else can share the throne. Eventually, one or the other will be forced out. God will not take the throne by force in our lives. He will not violate our free will. It comes down to our decision. That doesn't mean that we don't enjoy other things; it just means that God holds the highest authority in our lives.

If you want to determine what you are devoted to, ask yourself the following:

What occupies the majority of my time and energy?

What dominates my thinking?

What eats up the majority of my money and resources?

The truth is that the more devoted we are to God, the more we have to offer others. I have found that when God is the object of my greatest devotion, I am actually better equipped as a husband and father. I have more to give to those I lead and care for. I am more productive and efficient and less overwhelmed and burdened. We are at our best when God holds the highest position in our lives.

Wear the Royal Garments

One of my favorite hobbies is working out and training. Stephen and I own a gym with our friend T. J. I spend at least some time at the gym every day. Since I am both a trainer and a pastor, on any given day I have multiple wardrobe changes. The worst is forgetting a change of clothes and being stuck in sweaty gym clothes for the rest of the day, especially if I am going to visit someone. I have experienced this more than once, so now I have several changes of clothes in my car and office. Those old workout clothes stink, and it certainly isn't the best way to represent myself when I show up to a hospital or counseling appointment, ringing in at 10 on the odor scale. The last thing you want to do is to put old clothes back on.

Kingdom people have been given a new set of clothes to wear. Paul writes:

> *Therefore, as God's chosen people, holy and dearly loved, clothe yourselves with compassion, kindness, humility, gentleness and patience. Bear with each other and forgive one another if any of you has a grievance against someone. Forgive as the Lord forgave you. And over all these virtues put on love, which binds them all together in perfect unity.*
>
> —Col. 3:12–14

These might not be the clothes we are accustomed to. In fact, this new outfit might feel downright unnatural at first. We may reach for our old clothes from time to time. Callousness, pride, impatience, and bitterness may be easier for us to wear, but we have a new role that comes with a new responsibility. We are a people of compassion, kindness, forgiveness, and, most of all, love.

Paul's words help me personally and when I talk to other people who are tempted to put the old clothes back on. We are God's chosen people. We don't just have a new set of clothes; we have a new identity. We are chosen. We are children of God. We are loved. Paul doesn't just instruct us what to do; he tells us who we are. If we can readily recall who we are, it will be much easier to know what to wear. When we wear the right garments, we represent best the Kingdom and its King.

Advance the Royal Kingdom

We will discuss this idea in greater detail later in the book, but as Kingdom people, we are Kingdom ambassadors. "Therefore, we are ambassadors for Christ, God making his appeal through us. We implore you on behalf of Christ, be reconciled to God" (2 Cor. 5:20 ESV).

As those who have fixed our attention on the Kingdom to come and devoted ourselves to the King who always has been, we join in the cause of advancing the Kingdom of heaven on earth. We take on the responsibility of ushering the things of heaven to earth.

Jesus challenges us to pray this prayer: Your Kingdom come, Your will be done on earth as it is in heaven.

For Kingdom people, this is more than a prayer. It becomes our marching orders. We see it as our duty to dispense the things of heaven onto the people of earth. We become fighters of injustice. We become peacemakers, joy-bringers, people of great compassion and love. We bless because we were first blessed. We love because we were loved first. As we do these things, we can help heaven advance in the lives of real people.

C. S. Lewis makes this observation:

If you read history, you will find that the Christians who did most for the present world were precisely those who thought most of the next....It is since Christians have largely ceased to think of the other world that they have become so ineffective in this.[3]

---

3. C. S. Lewis, *Mere Christianity* (New York: HarperCollins, 1952), 134.

It is Kingdom people with a high view of heaven who have been most determined to bring heaven to earth. So may our prayer be as Jesus instructed: God, we want more of heaven on earth. We want more of heaven in our families. We want more of heaven in our communities. We want more of heaven in our workplaces. Invade these places with Your presence. May Your rule advance in us, among us, and through us. Amen.

Questions for Reflection

How does it make you feel when you think of yourself as a child of God?

How do you feel when you consider that you get to share in a heavenly inheritance?

How do you view the rights and responsibilities you have as a child of God?

What things, good and bad, have a way of occupying the throne in your life?

Chapter 5

Kingdom Come

My dad is the worst when it comes to spoilers. He has to be on some all-time-greatest list for ruining endings. I can't figure out if he does it on purpose as a way to stick it to us or if he is actually just that excited about the ending that it slips out. For example, he might say something like this: "Have you seen *The Sixth Sense*? You haven't? I just couldn't believe the therapist was dead the whole time, living as a ghost."

Oops, I just did it, too. But if you haven't seen *The Sixth Sense* by now, then I don't know what to say. I pretty much just avoid my dad at all costs if he has seen a movie or knows the ending to a game I DVRed. Even if he doesn't *try* to spoil the ending, the spoiler will inevitably come out.

This spoiler may not come as a surprise, but here is how the story ends for the people of God's Kingdom: God's Kingdom prevails. Good conquers evil. The light of life drives out darkness. Ultimate victory belongs to the people of God. I'm sorry if you haven't made it to the end of the Bible yet, but the conclusion of this true and unparalleled story is just as compelling as the opening.

The last book of the Bible is Revelation. One of Jesus's disciples, John, saw a vision of the end and what is to come. God revealed the vision to him. While I'll admit this book is a bit dense and cryptic, it contains some incredible imagery of what the Kingdom people will one day experience. Check out the vividness of what John saw:

Then I saw "a new heaven and a new earth," for the first heaven and the first earth had passed away, and there was no longer any sea. I saw the Holy City, the new Jerusalem, coming down out of heaven from God, prepared as a bride beautifully dressed for her husband. And I heard a loud voice from the throne saying, "Look! God's dwelling place is now among the people, and he will dwell with them. They will be his people, and God himself will be with them and be their God. 'He will wipe every tear from their eyes. There will be no more death' or mourning or crying or pain, for the old order of things has passed away."

He who was seated on the throne said, "I am making everything new!" Then he said, "Write this down, for these words are trustworthy and true."

He said to me: "It is done. I am the Alpha and the Omega, the Beginning and the End. To the thirsty I will give water without cost from the spring of the water of life. Those who are victorious will inherit all this, and I will be their God and they will be my children. But the cowardly, the unbelieving, the vile, the murderers, the sexually immoral, those who practice magic arts, the idolaters and all liars—they will be consigned to the fiery lake of burning sulfur. This is the second death."

—Rev. 21:1–8

God promises to make all things new. His kingdom will triumph in the end. The promise of God is that the *end is really only the beginning*. The best part of the story unfolds after the final credits on earth. That is when the citizens of God's Kingdom will finally and fully experience all that God has prepared for them, uninhibited by the kingdom of the world that will be overthrown.

Look at just a few things John mentions that we can anticipate.

Total Revitalization

Then I saw a new heaven and a new earth....He who was seated on the throne said, "I am making everything new!" Then he said, "Write this down, for these words are trustworthy and true."

—Rev. 21:1, 5

In the city of Cincinnati, where we live, there once was a territory along the Ohio River with old abandoned factories. Blocks of dirty worn-out buildings lined the banks of the muddy river. Decades of trash had collected there. When I walked through downtown along this route on my way to a baseball or football game, I would hold my breath as much as possible, wondering if maybe I was inhaling something that could do long-term damage. I never could have imagined or envisioned anything different than this useless pile of debris in the middle of our city. What had once been a bustling area of commerce was now a wasteland. The people of Cincinnati just learned to ignore it and not expect anything else.

Then, someone began to envision the potential of the property and how it could be a place that brought people together, a place of community, a place for fun and enjoyment, and a place to enjoy the outdoors and the beauty of the river. Many years ago, a group of people came together with a vision to restore and revitalize that property. Where others saw a dumpsite, they saw a flourishing park. Where others saw a lost cause, they dreamed about what was possible and then set a plan in motion.

Today, that property is Smale Park, one of the city's most prized parks. Joggers run along the scenic river while kids play on a variety of unique playgrounds. Others sit and read among the vast acreage of green space, trees, and flowers. A wasteland was made new.

In Revelation, the promise of God to make all things new is not just a repair job; it's a total revitalization and complete overhaul. It is God setting all things right in the entirety of creation. It's not limited to just the human population. It is God's goodness invading every nook and cranny of the universe.

Personal Restoration

"He will wipe every tear from their eyes. There will be no more death" or mourning or crying or pain, for the old order of things has passed away.

—Rev. 21:4

The good news of God's Kingdom impacts the entirety of creation, but it also has very personal implications for you and me. Not only does God promise to set everything right *around* us, He promises to set things right *within* us. This transformation begins to take root as we give King Jesus full access to our lives in exchange for full access to His Kingdom. We then begin the process of God renovating the inner recesses of our heart and soul, overflowing into the outer workings of our life, behavior, and action.

I'm the kind of person who likes to push the limits. As I get a little older, I'm reminded that I do, in fact, have limits. I have a few injury stories I could tell. What I've learned is that my earthly body has its limits, and I've been good at finding those limits.

We all have physical limits as well as emotional, relational, and spiritual limits. Our bodies are susceptible to disease, aging, and decay. Our minds are riddled by discouragement, fear, doubt, and disappointment. Our hearts are vulnerable to heartbreak and loss. Our will has its limits, and we are prone to sin.

What great hope we have in God's revelation to John! Through the power of our conquering King, we will one day be granted victory over all these things. The curse of sin will finally be broken, releasing us from the struggle.

There will be no more sadness. We will no longer be subject to sin. There will be no more X-rays and MRIs. We won't need those medications anymore. Our allergies won't be an issue. Nobody will ever have a migraine. Cancer and dementia will no longer be something we must suffer through. We will never again have to stand by a loved one's graveside.

That is the guarantee of the God who never fails. That is the personal destiny of those who put their hope in King Jesus.

Permanent Reunion

"Look! God's dwelling place is now among the people, and he will dwell with them. They will be his people, and God himself will be with them and be their God."

—Rev. 21:3

Dorothy was right. There really is no place like home. Sometimes, I wish I could just click my shoes together and go back to the place where I know my soul belongs. Deep inside, we know this world serves only as an Airbnb on our way back home. That's why we often feel out of place, misunderstood, and like a stranger in our own skin. If we see this world as our home, things will never fully add up, and we will be unfulfilled and possibly even miss out on our true destination. Our real home is with God.

Paul acknowledges this feeling in his letter to the Romans:

We know that the whole creation has been groaning as in the pains of childbirth right up to the present time. Not only so, but we ourselves, who have the firstfruits of the Spirit, groan inwardly as we wait eagerly for our adoption to sonship, the redemption of our bodies. For in this hope we were saved. But hope that is seen is no hope at all. Who hopes for what they already have?
—Rom. 8:22–24

Paul lets us in on a little secret. What you truly long for is just over the horizon. Take heart, and hold out hope. By definition, hope is trusting in what we have not yet seen for what we do not yet possess. If we see this world for what it is, a journey home, we can grab hold of life with greater ferocity, travel along with a fuller perspective, and even help some other travelers find their way back home.

When I was a kid, one of my favorite movies was *Homeward Bound*. I'll give you the Cliffs Notes. Three pets go missing from their beloved owners into the wild. They face harsh, natural elements and challenges from wild animals that are seeking to devour them. Since these particular animals can talk, we get an inside look into what they are thinking and experiencing as they try to find their way back home. The movie ends with three exhausted, battered, and beaten animals back in the place they belong, the loving arms of their owners. I would probably lose a little bit of tough guy cred if I admitted that I teared up a little at the end. Why are we moved by stories like this? The reason is because this narrative speaks to an even greater narrative in all of us. It speaks to a creation that is trying to get back where it belongs, in the loving arms of God, the perfect King.

There is a parable Jesus tells about a lost son who demands his inheritance, leaves home, squanders everything he has, hits rock bottom, and realizes there is no place like home. He is hungry, lonely, afraid and full of regret. After a series of bad choices, he makes the best choice he could ever make, to go back home to his father. The story ends with the father running down the road to embrace his lost son. If you've ever lost a child even for a moment, you can appreciate the emotion of this moment when the father was reunited with his son after worrying day and night. He throws a huge reunion party in honor of the son who was lost and is now home again. Jesus compares this to us being reunited with God.

Think about the reunion of God with His children. I can imagine story after story of weary travelers making their way back home to a welcoming party of epic proportion. Imagine the feeling to finally be home once and for all. In part, we can experience that now as we allow Him to travel with us, but one day we will experience it in full.

God promises total revitalization, personal restoration, and a permanent reunion for His Kingdom people. In the meantime, we stay focused and oriented toward God's Kingdom.

The book of Revelation ends with something like a battle cry. It was a greeting among fellow Kingdom travelers. It was called *maranatha*, which in Aramaic meant "Come, Lord Jesus." In a time when the citizens of God's Kingdom faced persecution and pressure from every side, they kept their eyes on the prize. They reminded one another of the most important jewel of hope they had within them. King Jesus is coming back, and when He does, we will finally be home. We will finally be restored to our former glory, and we will finally take hold of His new heaven and new earth.

So may the cry of our hearts be "Come, Lord Jesus."

Questions for Reflection

What do you find confusing about the coming Kingdom? What questions do you still have?

What does hope mean to you?

Why is hope important for Kingdom people?

Where do you put your hope?

The Net

Josh

The next day Jesus decided to leave for Galilee.
Finding Philip, he said to him, "Follow me."
—John 1:43

"Come, follow me," Jesus said, "and I will send you
out to fish for people." At once they left their nets
and followed him.
—Mark 1:17–18

Chapter 6

A Leader Worth Following

I've heard a story about a group of everyday folks who nobody really expected to amount to much, and yet they ended up becoming some of the most influential world-changers in human history. Many of them probably didn't even travel outside of a 100-mile radius, yet their impact has crossed nations and cultures and spanned thousands of years.

One of them worked for the government. He was pretty unpopular because, as a financial collector, he made a living skimming money from people. He was the kind of guy who wouldn't think twice about scamming your grandma. Needless to say, he wasn't invited to many backyard barbecues. Others were fishermen and tradesmen. They weren't the elite of society or rulers of kingdoms. They were living pretty ordinary lives until they met a man named Jesus. That's when things started to move from ordinary to anything but ordinary. Jesus offered them an invitation that changed the course of their lives, along with countless other lives throughout history. Matthew tells us this true story.

While walking by the Sea of Galilee, he saw two broth-ers, Simon (who is called Peter) and Andrew his brother, casting a net into the sea, for they were fishermen. And he said to them, "Follow me, and I will make you fishers of men." Immediately they left their nets and followed him. And going on from there he saw two other brothers,

James the son of Zebedee and John his brother, in the boat with Zebedee their father, mending their nets, and he called them. Immediately they left the boat and their father and followed him.

—Matt. 4:18–22 ESV

If you have ever read the Gospel accounts in the scriptures, you will see the eyewitness testimony of this story. When I read stories like this, I like to insert myself into the story and consider what was going through the minds and hearts of people as they experienced these events unfolding.

I've found myself wondering how these guys could just up and drop everything for a guy they had never really met. Jesus just walks up to them and says "Come follow me," and they drop everything and follow Him. Maybe it's because I grew up in the era of "stranger danger," but really? You guys have zero follow-up questions? You just follow this guy without hesitation?

I can think of a few questions I would have asked:

1. Where are we going?
2. Who did you say you were?
3. What's in it for me?
4. Why us? Why did you pick us? If you haven't noticed, we don't really have the skill set necessary to change the world. We are unpopular, unskilled, everyday sinners.

Perhaps they did ask some questions that just weren't recorded, but either way, I find it interesting that they just up and followed this rabbi. What compelled these guys to follow Jesus in the first place? Why did they trust Him enough to leave everything behind?

Maybe you've heard people say, "You just have to trust." Is it really that simple?

I remember back in my youth group days, we used to talk about trust. We did activities to drive home the point that we just need to trust more. They had us partner up and do blind trust falls into the arms of our friends. Now, if you knew my friends, you know I was just hoping the floor wasn't too hard because there was a strong chance I was going to hit it. Let's just say I didn't have a lot of confidence that they wouldn't seize the opportunity to watch me land on my butt. So I did what any sensible person would do. I constantly turned back to make sure they were still there, and I fell slowly, hoping to catch myself in case anybody tried to pull something. That's when the leader of the activity would call me out and add a blindfold into the equation. "You must be out of your mind if you think I'm putting that on." So while the intent was to help us build a sense of trust, the only thing I learned is that *trust is only as good as the one you give it to.* My middle school friends weren't at the top of my trust list.

It makes sense to me that many of us have trust issues. Most of us have experienced letdowns and disappointments in our lifetime. We have put our trust in the wrong place or have given it to the wrong person. We turned our backs, thinking they would catch us, and the next thing we felt was our head hitting the floor.

Trust is not easy. I want to acknowledge this up front because even the people we should be able to trust have a tendency to let us down. Perhaps a parent abandoned you, broke a promise, or hurt you in some way. Maybe it's someone else you love—someone you thought would always be loyal to you—whom you trusted with your heart, and they managed to break it in the process.

Some of our trust issues stem from the cultural and political climate we find ourselves in. We encounter politicians who overpromise and underdeliver. We are inundated with stories of scandals and lies. We see abuses of power and authority. We feel like everyone has an agenda. We aren't always sure what information or news is reliable. We find ourselves questioning things that we once held as firm truth. Trust can be difficult to muster up, and I believe it is perfectly reasonable to require good reason before we trust.

Trust should be earned. We shouldn't just give it to anyone. Jesus doesn't ask us to blindly follow. He gives us sufficient reason to follow. He proves that He is a leader worth following. Jesus establishes His credibility prior to issuing His call. Jesus stands out as a leader above all leaders. Here are three ways Jesus established His credibility to the people of His day and to us.

Jesus Casts a Vision beyond What's Visible

One of the greatest qualities of true leaders is that they have the ability to see beyond *what is* to *what could be*. They have a sense for what's possible, and they help paint a vivid picture of a better reality.

When I was a kid, I wasn't much of a reader. I was more of a play outside in the mud, ramp my bike, and jump in the creek kind of kid. I have since developed a greater appreciation for reading, but in my younger years, my library consisted of *Where's Waldo? Highlights* magazines, and those Magic Eye books where you had to find the image inside the image. Those books were so rewarding because if you just looked long and hard enough, you could see something that was undetectable at first glance. At first, the picture just looked like a bunch of swirls and crazy shapes, but the trained eye knew how to look deeper into the picture and see what was previously hidden. It was such a sense of accomplishment when you finally discovered what was there. I always wanted to help others see the picture as well.

The best leaders have this quality about them. On the surface, the future may seem unclear or the solution to the problem outside of reach, but true visionaries can shed light on things not yet visible.

There is nobody who can do this the way Jesus can. Here's one of my favorite descriptions Jesus gives of Himself: "I am the light of the world. Whoever follows me will never walk in darkness, but will have the light of life" (John 8:12).

Jesus has this mysterious way of illuminating what was once hidden. Though hope might be buried in the darkness, He has the ability to bring it to the surface. He tells us that we don't have to walk in darkness but that we can have the light of life. This picture of light speaks to Jesus as the hope of the world. Jesus helps us rethink what's possible when we follow Him.

One of Jesus's most famous sermons is found in Matthew 5–7. We see Him draw people into this picture of what could be and should be. It is a small taste of Jesus's teaching and vision casting for a better reality. When Jesus spoke, people leaned in and listened. Everywhere Jesus went, crowds gathered. Houses were filled to standing room only. People gathered around the outside to hear His teachings. Hillsides were lined with people thirsty for the hope and vision He shared. He was offering more than wishful thinking. He was offering something of true substance. One of the things people took note of is captured in the Gospel of Mark. "The people were amazed at his teaching, because he taught them as one who had authority, not as the teachers of the law" (Mark 1:22).

There was something refreshingly different about Jesus compared to the other leaders and teachers of the day. There was true authority in His teaching. There was a sense that He would deliver on His promises. The authority Jesus possessed was an authority that only God could have. It's an authority we can trust to be fully reliable. His vision wasn't wishful thinking; it was based on His divine wisdom. The track record for delivering on His promised vision still sits at 100 percent.

Jesus Calls People beyond Their Capacity

Not only does Jesus cast a vision beyond what's visible, but He helps us discover a calling beyond our human capacity. When you learn how unimpressive Jesus's original followers were, it almost makes you think He forgot to check their résumés before He hired them. Sinners, tax collectors, and fishermen don't exactly fit the description of world-changers in training. It's like these guys were all that were left. That isn't how it happened, though. Jesus handpicked each of these guys. He saw something in them that they couldn't see in themselves. Jesus saw beyond what was to what could and would be, and He sees beyond who we are to who we have the potential to be.

Something I try to remind people of as often as I can is that *God's call does not depend on our capacity.*

That's refreshing for me because I'm not sure I would have made the cut for the pastor short list if that wasn't the case. In fact, it's been the times when I've been most in over my head that I've discovered what I'm made of—or rather *who I'm made by.* These gifts I possess are just that; they are gifts from God. Another way to say it is God is not limited by my limitations.

When we forget that, we either end up playing it too safe or we collapse under the pressure of the call. When you are in over your head, it is better to think, "I can't do this." I know that is not what you were expecting me to say. I bet you even read that a second time to make sure I didn't make a mistake. It's true. We must acknowledge that on our own, *we can't*, but with God, we can.

A great example of someone who was called beyond their capacity is Mary, the mother of Jesus. Imagine that you are in her shoes. Raising the Son of God is kind of a big deal. When the angel came to reveal to Mary what God would do, he reminds her of the most important thing to keep her sights on: "For nothing will be impossible with God" (Luke 1:37 ESV). Then she simply responds: "'Behold, I am the servant of the Lord; let it be to me according to your word.' And the angel departed from her" (Luke 1:38 ESV). That is one epic trust fall if I've ever seen one. You have to respect Mary and her willingness to step into something far beyond her own capacity.

Jesus is a leader worth following because He helps us discover what's only possible when we move beyond our own capacity into His deeper calling.

Jesus Proves Himself beyond a Reasonable Doubt

Some of the best personal stories I know started with this phrase: "Prove it."

I have been both the innovator and the participant of many bad ideas. I seem to gravitate toward friends who like a good challenge thrown their way. As a way of keeping one another honest, which is an important duty in any friendship, we have the responsibility to check one another when we think someone is full of it. Like, hypothetically, if I were to say I would eat the hottest wings on the menu, a good friend would respond by saying, "Prove it." My wife keeps me honest in many ways, but one of the biggest times was when I told her I wanted to go skydiving. I mostly said this to impress her, but she seized the opportunity to call my bluff and bought us two tickets to go skydiving. She jumped first, so there was no way I could chicken out. I proved it and jumped.

Great leaders don't just talk a big game. They prove they can and will deliver when tested. Jesus has proven Himself.

When we read Luke's account of Jesus calling His disciples, we see something pretty remarkable happen. The disciples have been out fishing all night and come up empty. Jesus gives them a command to push off into the deep water. Somewhat reluctantly, they agree, and what happens next changes the trajectory of their lives. They catch so many fish that their nets begin to break and the boat almost capsizes. They are literally brought to their knees in awe of Jesus, who then says they will now be fishing for people. I love this because Jesus establishes His credibility by performing the impossible. His credibility precedes His calling. He proves He is worthy of following in a single moment, and then He proves it over and over throughout the Gospel accounts.

You have heard the old cliché "Talk is cheap." Anybody can say they will do something. We've all met people who talk a big game only to change their tune when it comes down to it. It's the follow-through that really counts when it comes to finding a leader you can trust, and there is no more worthy candidate than Jesus of Nazareth.

Jesus didn't make small claims:

>He told sick people they would be healed.
>He told sinners they were forgiven.
>He said He would give His life as a ransom for many.
>He told people He was the Son of God.
>His greatest claim was that He would come back from the dead.

Any one of those claims begs for someone to call out, "Prove it." Jesus backed up every claim. It is well documented that He didn't just talk about healing the sick; He rolled up His sleeves, reached out His hands, and restored people to health. He didn't just speak of forgiveness as some pipe dream; He actually released people from sin and bondage and transformed their lives. He didn't just act like He would confront evil; He actively drove out darkness at every turn. He didn't just claim to be the Messiah; He was the Messiah. He didn't just teach of sacrifice and love; He embodied them. He touched the untouchable. Loved the unlovable. Welcomed the unwelcomed.

Jesus proved He was who He said He was. The most powerful testament to who He was as a leader and why I have chosen to trust Him with my life is that He first gave His life. I put my trust in a leader who went first. He laid His own life on the line for people who didn't deserve it. He sacrificed Himself so we could have life. If He had given His life on the cross in the way that He did and had *not* risen from the grave, He would have still had my respect, but He wouldn't have proved to be who He said He was.

The truth remains, however, that Jesus died and three days later rose from the dead. His body has never been produced. Eyewitnesses speak of encounters with a risen Jesus, and the movement He set in motion still carries on today despite opposition, persecution, and constant resistance.

Jesus was who He said He was. He has proved it over and over again.

He has earned our trust. There is no leader more worthy of following than Jesus.

Jesus did many other things as well. If every one of them were written down, I suppose that even the whole world would not have room for the books that would be written.
—John 21:25

In His time on earth, Jesus did more to prove Himself than could ever be written. That leaves us with the same decision the disciples once had: Will we follow Him? Do we believe He is a leader worth following?

Questions for Reflection

Do you have trust issues? If so, why?

Do you trust Jesus?

What compels you to put your trust in Jesus?

What is keeping you from placing your trust in Jesus?

Chapter 7

A Calling Worth Embracing

Every person who has ever walked on earth has desired an answer to a very fundamental yet elusive question: What is my purpose? How do I figure out what it is?

Without the concept of a God who creates us, the answer to that question is rather bleak. In that scenario, there really is no purpose to anything. We are all just witnessing some cosmic accident and find ourselves as a random byproduct of impersonal forces and blind chance. Sure, we can create meaning for ourselves, but our purpose amounts to nothing more than our own desires and the things we choose to give importance to.

If you believe in a personal and intentional God, the story reads much differently. Throughout the scriptures, we see God as intimately involved in the life of every person from the very beginning. That means that every life has meaning and purpose. Not everyone discovers or lives out that purpose, but every human life holds inherent meaning.

We see God's care and intentionality in the book of Jeremiah. When He calls the prophet, He reminds him of something significant: "I knew you before I formed you in your mother's womb. Before you were born I set you apart and appointed you as my prophet to the nations" (Jer. 1:5 NLT).

King David appreciates God's intentional nature when he writes these words in his prayer journal:

You made all the delicate, inner parts of my body and knit me together in my mother's womb. Thank you for making me

*so wonderfully complex! Your workmanship is marvelous—
how well I know it. You watched me as I was being formed
in utter seclusion, as I was woven together in the dark of
the womb. You saw me before I was born. Every day of my
life was recorded in your book. Every moment was laid out
before a single day had passed.*

—Ps. 139:13–16 NLT

Scripture after scripture shouts this truth: God made you with
a unique and specific purpose. God makes no mistakes. Lean into
that truth. God has given you a purpose to live out during your days
on earth. This is why Paul writes, "For we are God's masterpiece. He
has created us anew in Christ Jesus, so we can do the good things
he planned for us long ago" (Eph. 2:10 NLT).

Don't miss this. You are God's masterpiece. He created you to
carry out good things for His greater purpose. God wants more for
you and for your life. He wants you to discover why He put you on
this rock, at this time in history. He wants you to find the ways He
has uniquely gifted you and wired you for something larger than
yourself. He wants to see you fully unleashed in this world for His
good.

I'll never forget the first fishing pole I ever received. It was a
yellow Snoopy fishing rod. My dad got it for me so we could reel
in some giant lake monsters. I'm not sure this pole would handle
the things I was dreaming of catching, but regardless, I was on my
way to being a real fisherman. First, I had to practice. This pole was
pretty simple, which was good since I was only in kindergarten. All
you had to do was press the button, release, and cast. Dad put a
metal weight on the end of the line so I could get some real distance.
I'm still not sure how I didn't break something or someone with
that little lead wrecking ball. I must have been out there for hours
just casting that thing. When Dad thought I was at least proficient
enough to not hook him in the mouth with a stray cast, he extended
the invitation I had been waiting for, "Son, are you ready to hit the
lake?" Yes, I was! While I enjoyed casting in the front yard, there
was nothing like the adventure of the lake.

One of the saddest things I see happen to people is when they never realize their God-given purpose and potential. They were made for adventure, and instead, they get lost in the monotony of everyday living only to let life pass them by. They look up one day and realize they have just been standing in the front yard casting this whole time when the invitation has been to join the greater adventure out on the lake. William Wallace, the main character in the *Braveheart* movie, once said, "Every man dies, not every man truly lives."[4]

We have a choice to make. Do we want to exist or truly live? I don't know about you, but we've got one shot at life this side of heaven, and I don't want to spend it casting in the front yard.

It starts with discovering God's desire for us. The invitation Jesus gave to the disciples also speaks to our fundamental desire to discover our calling. "Follow me, and I will make you fishers of men" (Matt. 4:19 ESV).

It's at the crossroads of this choice that we either enter into the adventure we were made for or settle for something less. Let's look at the key components of Jesus's invitation and our unique calling.

Come, Follow Me

One Christmas when Jess and I were dating, I thought it would be a funny idea to show up at her house with a bow on my shirt and tell her that I was her gift for Christmas. I'm not sure what I was expecting, but let's just say she didn't think it was as amusing as I did. Any of you ladies who are reading this already knew that. I can actually feel some of you rolling your eyes as you read it. In my head, it was going to be this great moment with Mariah Carey singing "All I Want for Christmas Is You" in the background. Thankfully, I was smart enough to get an actual gift on top of the lame gesture.

What if I told you that more than anything else, Jesus just wants you? The greatest gift you can give God is yourself. He wants you to

---

4. "William Wallace: 'Every Man Dies, Not Every Man Truly Lives,'" Scotland Welcomes You, https://scotlandwelcomesyou.com/william-wallace/.

come to Him and walk with Him. This is really about choosing Him and then being unleashed by Him to carry out His purpose on earth. However, it's easy to get that turned around and think we have to work or serve or jump through a bunch of hoops, and then we are in. Jesus already knows us. He knows our limitations, our hang-ups, our secret pasts, and our ugly thoughts—and He invites us anyway. The decision is up to us.

I Will Make You

We are called to be with God. We are also called to be shaped by God.

Calling is just as much about becoming who we were always meant to be as it is about living out the purpose we were made for. Everyone wants to change the world, but the first change must happen inside of us.

We watch a lot of HGTV around my house. One of our favorite shows is *Fixer Upper*. It's amazing what the right tool in the right hand can accomplish. The show gives me a lot of false expectations about what I might be able to pull off when it comes to DIY.

Following Jesus takes a lot of trust because it means we hand over the tools of inner renovation to someone who is far more capable than we are. The Christian life was never meant to be a DIY effort. Instead, it's a calling to *rely*. We let God have full access to do in us what we could never do on our own.

I'll be the first to admit that I'm a "fixer-upper." I've got a long way to go, but choosing to follow Jesus means that day by day I allow Him to shape me to be more like Him, because the more I become like Him, the more I have to offer the world.

Fishers of People

I like that Jesus uses what these men already know and unearths a deeper purpose for them as His followers. He uses the imagery of fishing to capture the core of the calling. He said something like this: "You have been fishing for fish, now I will teach you how to catch the hearts of people and draw them back to where they belong with God."

If we believe that our greatest good is only realized in a relationship with God, then we can understand that the noblest of causes is to unite and reunite people with God. In ways big and small, God takes all the things that make us uniquely us and repurposes us for that larger calling. We are collectively a part of something far greater than ourselves when we say yes to this invitation.

So what does that mean for us individually?

I remember going to summer camp as a kid at a local Christian camp.

Every evening we would sit in the little camp chapel. It was actually more of a glorified shed. I'm pretty sure that a strong wind could have brought the whole thing down. We sang songs, which included some sweet motions. After we sang, the pastor talked, we sang some more, and the girls hugged each other and cried. Then, there was an invitation that separated the middle school faith giants from the irreverent kids who were mostly thinking about whether there would be s'mores at the campfire.

The invitation one night was for those who felt the call to full-time ministry or mission work. I slowly sank down in my seat while others filed forward. "Good for them," I thought, "but what about me? What's my purpose? Can God use somebody like me?"

I understand the irony of all of this now. I never thought I would work in a church. There aren't many other people who knew me that would have picked me out of a pastor lineup, and I don't blame them for that. I share this because I believe that those who serve in the church and as missionaries who leave everything should be honored as heroes for what they do and what they sacrifice. But the calling is broader and wider than these two categories of people.

The calling for full-time ministry is not just for church pastors and overseas missionaries. Jesus is calling bankers, politicians, baristas, business owners, mothers, and fathers. He is sending us as missionaries into our everyday contexts to be His *presence* in our neighborhoods, families, schools, and workplaces. That is what it means to be fishers of people. That is our assignment if we choose to accept it.

I have often used four P's to help people discover their unique calling. They are the four P's of purpose—people, place, problem, and passion. This compass tool is useful in determining God's direction for our present and future purpose, as well as directing those around us as they are seeking God's direction.

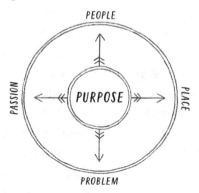

The Passion in You

My oldest son is four as I write this. I've always believed in the power of names, so we named him Aiden, an Irish name that means "little fire." If you happen to know my son, you know that this is the perfect name for him. He has fire in his belly. His passion is already so evident, and my job at the moment is to make sure to contain the fire without snuffing it out. Seriously pray for me. It's a delicate and important process. Something I want more than anything else for my son is that he will channel this passion for God's purpose. I believe it was God who put this passion there to begin with, and it is meant to be used to bring Him glory.

There is a St. Ignatius of Loyola quote that hangs in my son's room. It reads, "Go forth and set the world on fire."[5] This is my constant prayer for him. It is my prayer for you as well. I pray that you will find that spark inside of you and go forth to set the world on fire.

Paul gives his young protégé, Timothy, some critical advice: "I remind you to fan into flame the gift of God, which is in you through the laying on of my hands" (2 Tim. 1:6). When we pursue the passions God places within us, it's like fanning the flame. When

---

5. "Ignatius of Loyola Quotes," Goodreads, https://www.goodreads.com/quotes/78580-go-forth-and-set-the-world-on-fire.

we let these passions sit for too long, like an unattended campfire, eventually they fizzle out. Not every passion comes from God, so we are wise to be discerning to figure out what's from Him and what's not. God has a way of consistently stirring the calling within us when we are doing our best to follow Him.

Find the spark. Fan the flame. Go forth and set the world on fire. What is that thing that stirs deep inside of you? What keeps you awake at night? What makes you feel truly alive? What wild dreams seem too big to even speak out loud? What are the things your heart burns for? What is that thing you could talk about all day?

I remember attending a conference called Passion when I was in college. It was a gathering of thousands of college students from across the United States. It proved to be a catalyst for me in my journey to find purpose. I remember a talk that Louie Giglio gave. I don't remember all the specifics, but I do remember him talking about jeans. It was a strange topic to build a sermon around, but his point was that if you are passionate about jeans, then make the best jeans the world has ever seen. Make them not for you but so you can point to God. Here's the key passage he used: "And whatever you do, whether in word or deed, do it all in the name of the Lord Jesus, giving thanks to God the Father through him" (Col. 3:17).

I believe this is the true difference. When you try to find purpose in yourself or in someone or something else, you always come up short. When you live for the glory of God, everything and anything can be a source of greater purpose.

Do you love being a mom? Be the best mom your kids could ask for, not for personal gain but for God's greater glory. Do you love the sport you play? Play your heart out for God's glory. Reflect His image on the field every time you walk out there. Do you have a heart for kids? Be the best teacher or coach they have ever had. When they ask what makes you special, make sure you tell them that it's Jesus who planted this passion within you. Do you love seeing people live healthy? Bring health and healing in the name of Jesus. Don't leave your passion untapped. Follow the spark. Fan the flame. Go forth and set the world on fire.

The Place Where You Are

I had a friend who always thought purpose was in the next place, next season, or next opportunity. If he could just get there, he would find his purpose. Actually, the truth is, the friend was me. I've thought this way often. "Once I graduate and move to that city, then I will finally be able to live out my purpose. Once I get married and can be a husband, then I will be able to start living my purpose. Once I finally get *that* job, I will be satisfied. Once these kids are out of diapers, I will have more time and get stuff done for God." Dr. Robert Holden calls this *destination addiction.*

There is nothing wrong with a fresh start, and God certainly calls people to specific places at specific times, but what if the place God is calling you to is where you already are? What if you started looking at your current workplace as an opportunity to live with purpose instead of jumping from one job to the next only to be unsatisfied in every place you end up? What if I told you it was possible to make every place a place of purpose? What if every season held its own unique opportunities that you may never get back?

When you always think of being somewhere else, you are least effective where you currently are. What if your calling was closer than you think? What if it is where you already are? How might you live with greater purpose in the place God has you today?

The People Surrounding You

Another way we can live out our purpose is by identifying the people God has surrounded us with. Ironically, the people who are closest to us can also be the easiest to overlook. What if you are meant to play a very specific role in the life of someone around you?

That is something God continues to challenge me on. He keeps showing me that *I'm at my best when I'm bringing out the best in others.* That can be as simple as a word of encouragement in a single moment or a more long-term role such as relationally and spiritually investing in the life of someone who needs to be loved.

There was a well-known Harvard study called the Grant Study.[6] It surveyed the lives of graduates over the course of 75 years to determine if there was a common link to lives that flourished and lives that didn't. What they found is that of the 268 people surveyed, the ones who experienced the greatest success and satisfaction in life had one thing in common—they had someone who cared about them.

Everybody deserves the chance to be loved. Everyone needs someone who cares. Maybe you were meant to be that someone for somebody around you.

The Problem You Can't Ignore

Many people discover their purpose when they collide with a problem.

Another show I watch from time to time is *Shark Tank*. I love seeing people pitch their big ideas to savvy investors. The Sharks are the guys with the money, business background, and experience to decide whose idea is worth investing in.

In one bonus segment of the show, I remember Robert Herjavec telling a group of young entrepreneurs something that struck me, something like this: "Don't start a business. Find a problem, solve a problem."[7]

There is something cool and alluring about starting something, whether that is a business venture, ministry effort, club, or cause. Starting something just to start something is not usually the best motivator. When there's a bump in the road, the efforts built with only good intentions and hopes of success typically crumble.

I like Herjavec's advice because solving a problem carries much greater momentum. There have been many times in history when people have been confronted with problems and have risen up to shine brightly for God.

---

6. George E. Vaillant, Charles C. McArthur, and Arlie Bock, "Grant Study of Adult Development, 1938–2000," 2010, *Harvard Dataverse*, https://dataverse.harvard.edu/dataset.xhtml?persistentId=doi:10.7910/DVN/48WRX9.
7. John Rampton, "8 Characteristics Shared by the 'Shark Tank' Team," *Entrepreneur*, Sep. 6, 2016, https://www.entrepreneur.com/article/281626.

The greatest feats of progress that were achieved were first rooted in a problem that someone or a group of people couldn't overlook.

Throughout the course of history, people who were discontent with the status quo left the greatest marks on our world. We shine brightest for God when we fight for things that matter to Him. History is lined with stories of God's people fighting for injustice, rising up against corruption, dismantling the efforts of evil, and seeking to bring hope for a brighter tomorrow. People who seek to solve the problems of today are the ones who end up leaving the world better than they found it.

So what issue keeps you up at night?

What injustice can you no longer overlook?

What problems, big and small, has God been tugging at you to start solving?

Sink Yourself In

Here is the reality. Discovering your calling won't just happen because you read one chapter in a book. You don't have to and probably won't figure out your life's calling all at once. The way I've tried to stay centered in my calling is by taking things one step at a time. Our life with Jesus is best lived following Him one step at a time. Do these things:

1. Take the next step or perhaps the first step.
2. Don't be afraid to fall. You will fall, but stay close to Jesus, and He will pick you up. Some things can only be discovered when you trust God and step out.
3. Don't try to be somebody else. God created you to be you. Dr. Suess said it well: "There is no one alive who is Youer than You."[8] So live out your journey, not somebody else's.

---

8. "Dr. Seuss Quotes," *Goodreads*, https://www.goodreads.com/quotes/3160-to-day-you-are-you-that-is-truer-than-true-there.

If you are looking for the right place to start, chew on this scripture:

Make a careful exploration of who you are and the work you have been given, and then sink yourself into that. Don't be impressed with yourself. Don't compare yourself with others. Each of you must take responsibility for doing the creative best you can with your own life.

—Gal. 6:4–5 MSG

Begin today. Your calling is worth embracing.

Questions for Reflection

Think about the four P's of purpose:

Who has God surrounded you with?

Where has God placed you?

What passions has God given you?

What problems nag at your heart?

In what ways can you live with greater purpose and calling?

Take some time this week to write out your personal purpose statement in a sentence or two. Will you ask God to help you discover His calling for you?

What does it look like for you to live out Galatians 6:4–5?

Chapter 8

A Price Worth Paying

Ever since I was little, I have been in the trading business. No, I did not trade stocks. It all started with a seemingly insignificant commodity, but to the kids on my block, we might as well have been trading in gold. I'm talking about baseball cards. I'll never forget walking through that checkout line and seeing packages of Topps cards on the shelf. Inside each package was a random assortment of cards with players from each Major League Baseball team.

I've always been a Cincinnati Reds fan, so any card with a Reds player was most valuable to me. I tried to get as many Reds players in my collection as possible, which probably wasn't the best strategy since the cards with the best players were the ones that were actually worth the most. I'm sure I got conned out of some high-value cards such as a rookie card of some big name player for a benchwarmer in a Reds uniform.

After baseball cards came something called Pogs. I promise I'm not making that up. They were these little cardboard chips that had pictures and animation on them. You could match up against someone by putting some of your Pogs and some of theirs in a stack facedown. The best part was when you got a heavy medal paperweight called a slammer that you would throw at a stack of Pogs. Any of them that flipped right side up became your bounty. Sometimes you would lose some of your favorite Pogs, and sometimes you would come out with some of your friend's best Pogs.

Trading is not something we ever really grow out of, but the stakes get a lot higher. Most of life's biggest decisions involve a trade of some kind. In my college finance classes, we talked about something called opportunity cost. The basic idea was that every opportunity has a cost. The opportunity cost is what you give up in exchange for an opportunity.

When Jesus called the first disciples, they had a decision to make. If they were to follow Him, they would need to give up some things. They probably didn't understand what it would mean for them, but Jesus's calling was one they decided was worth it.

We know this because the Gospel accounts show us that "immediately they left their nets and followed him" (Matt. 4:20 ESV). Another version says "at once" they left everything and followed Him. If there was any sense of reluctance, we don't see it. We simply see that they saw this trade was worthy of making.

They left their nets. For a fisherman, that meant they were setting aside the line of work they had been taught their entire lives. These nets represented their income, their security, and their comfort. They were willing to leave those things behind, maybe forever, for Jesus and an unclear future.

Our own calling is no different. Every calling has a cost. Jesus made this clear whenever He was teaching and leading. There would be a price for following Him. It wouldn't be safe, secure, or without challenges, big or small. It wouldn't be the most popular or celebrated choice, and it wouldn't be easy. Please understand that following Jesus means counting the cost and embracing the calling.

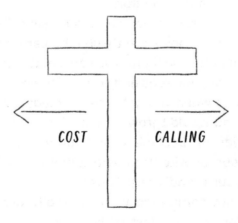

COST   CALLING

As I read some of the teachings that circulate in Christian circles, I'm afraid that some are giving people a false sense about what life in Jesus is really all about. We should be careful not to make promises that Jesus never made. He never promised them power, riches, respect, or adoration. The journey with Jesus was not meant to be a journey of personal gain. Yes, His followers will grow and find true fulfillment, but God's greatest aim is not our personal happiness or personal success. That reduces God to some cosmic genie in a bottle who exists for our purpose. That is completely backward. We exist for His purpose, and it's only when we get our heads and hearts around this that we will ever really know and experience real living.

Maybe this is what Jesus was getting at when he said:

Whoever wants to be my disciple must deny themselves and take up their cross daily and follow me. For whoever wants to save their life will lose it, but whoever loses their life for me will save it. What good is it for someone to gain the whole world, and yet lose or forfeit their very self?

—Luke 9:23–25

The only way we will ever find ourselves and step into our calling is if we are willing to make this critical trade. We give our lives back to God, and in return, we discover true purpose and meaning.

So here's what I want you to do, God helping you: Take your everyday, ordinary life—your sleeping, eating, going-to-work, and walking-around life—and place it before God as an offering. Embracing what God does for you is the best thing you can do for him.

—Rom. 12:1 MSG

I love the visual here of placing your life at the feet of Jesus as your personal offering to Him. If more of us lived this mentality, we would no doubt be less self-focused and more purpose-driven.

So how do we start laying our lives down? How do we begin to step out after Jesus into God's great adventure?

We start by doing what the disciples did. We make a trade. We lay down our nets because every calling has a cost. Here are a few trades we must be willing to make if we are serious about chasing hard after Jesus.

Trading Comfort for Conviction

One of my favorite places to go when I was a college student was called Red River Gorge. It's located in a picturesque region of eastern Kentucky along the Appalachian Mountains. There is a great three-mile round trip hike called Natural Bridge that takes you up to a spot where you can literally see for miles. The hike can be challenging in places, especially if you suffer from fear of tight spaces. I have also taken the hike during the summer, and it was a good thing I packed an extra shirt because I'm a bit of sweater. Once you get to the top, the view makes all the sweat and tight squeezes worth it. As you scan the horizon, you soak up the beauty of mountain ranges, trees, and blue sky. It's one of those places where you are reminded of God's artistry in creation as you simply sit in wonder at the work of His hands.

On a recent trip to the gorge, I noticed a sign I had never seen before as we drove out. It was an advertisement for a chairlift that takes you to the top of the mountain. The slogan read, "Same great view without the sweat." I appreciate the effort to make this view accessible for people who aren't physically able to make the climb, but I found myself shaking my head at the thought of purposefully avoiding the tough climb. It's the climb that makes the view even more breathtaking.

Why are we so tempted to avoid the sweat and struggle of the climb? Maybe it's because we believe that it's only the destination that really matters. I wonder how many of us, if given the option, would choose the path of least resistance? If we could have the blessings of God, the eternal glory of heaven, the deliverance and freedom of God without the costly climb, would we take it? If we are looking for a comfortable ride, the scriptures may prove to be a bit unsettling at times.

C. S. Lewis acknowledged that comfort was not the point:

I didn't go to religion to make me happy. I always knew a bottle of Port would do that. If you want a religion to make you feel really comfortable, I certainly don't recommend Christianity.[9]

Thankfully, God knows what's best, and comfort is not what's best for us. You will see that as you follow Jesus, He continues to draw you out of what's comfortable.

As both a trainer and a pastor, my job is to do this same thing: push people beyond what's comfortable for them. That is not because I like the look of discomfort on people's faces (okay, maybe sometimes). The main reason I seek to push people out of their comfort zone is because that is where growth happens. Growth and progress come through experiencing pain, struggling, and attempting things you have never tried before. The greatest gains come through hard work, sweat, and pain. So if you want to discover your fullest potential in Christ, you have to be willing to trade comfort. When you do, you find that something stronger—conviction—begins to grip your heart. Conviction is the feeling that this is something you must do. When you find conviction, there is very little you wouldn't do. There is no price too high that you are unwilling to pay it.

There is a picture hanging in my office that serves as a reminder to me to continue to break out of my comfort whenever I can. It reads:

The person who risks nothing, does nothing, has nothing, is nothing, and becomes nothing. He may avoid suffering and sorrow, but he simply cannot learn, feel, change, grow or love.[10]

—Leo F. Buscaglia

Trading comfort for conviction is always a trade worth making.

---

9. C. S. Lewis, *God in the Dock* (Grand Rapids, MI: Wm. B. Eerdmans Publishing, 2014), 48.
10. "Leo F. Buscaglia Quotes," *Goodreads*, https://www.goodreads.com/quotes/10522-the-person-who-risks-nothing-does-nothing-has-nothing-is.

Trading Personal Preference for the Greater Good

In the American society I have grown up in, personal preference rules the day. Everything from the meals we eat to the cars we drive can be customized to our specific preferences. Companies work tirelessly to meet our every need and market products that make our lives as convenient as possible.

One of my favorite examples is the Kroger ClickList. If you aren't familiar with that, it's a way for people like me who despise grocery shopping to sit down in the comfort of their own home, click on all the groceries they want, and make somebody else do the shopping for them. Then, they just pull up in their car, and someone else loads their vehicle with all their food for the week while they lean back and listen to their favorite music. What's not to love about that? It's great until you get home and realize that the teenager who picked out your pro-duce was a little less particular than you would have been and made several substitutions because your items were out of stock. Then you grumble and complain that you didn't get exactly what you wanted.

I worry that this mentality can be tough to overcome, even in the church. Sometimes we forget that meeting our personal preferences is not really God's endgame. In fact, personal preference often runs contrary to the greater good. Convenience runs contrary to calling.

I believe many people miss out on the things God is calling them to do, both inside and outside the church, because they don't want to be inconvenienced. They start to develop the mindset that they will only serve or contribute as long as it doesn't impede too much on their schedules or "me time." Ironically, it is usually the people who are most focused on what's in it for them who actually get the least out of it and end up grumbling the most.

I'll admit that I can also be guilty of that. What I've found, though, is the things God calls us to are rarely the most convenient things, and they often come at the least convenient times. We have to be willing to trade our personal preferences for the greater good if we want to step out into our calling. That may be in small ways such as giving up an hour of sleep to serve in some capacity or giving up a portion of our paycheck, or giving up an evening to spend time with someone who needs the company.

I recently got to witness a bunch of young people come together to help meet the need of someone who had a medical bill. It is the times we choose the greater good over personal preference that we find ourselves closest to the heart of God. It is when we lay down the net of convenience that we can more fully take hold of God's purpose.

Here's one of my favorite proverbs: "A generous person will prosper; whoever refreshes others will be refreshed (Prov. 11:25).

I have found this to be true over and over again. It is the times when I focus least on myself that I actually gain the most. It is the times when I set out to be a blessing that I am the most blessed.

Trading Control for Dependence

Another net that we grip tightly to is the net of control. That is one that God continues to press me on. I like feeling a sense of control. That is one of the reasons I've never loved flying in an airplane. I'm not the guy who is breathing heavily into a brown bag, but I'm also not the guy who manages to sleep from wheels up to wheels down on the runway. I took a trip to Florida one time, and I thought the plane was getting ready to land when the pilot pulled the plane up. My heart rate shot through the roof, and I looked around to see if anyone else was alarmed. I just kept giving myself the "be cool, be cool, be cool" pep talk in my head, but the feeling of being completely out of control was more than I could handle. Then I looked over at a lady across the aisle who was dry heaving into a bag, and that about put me over the top. Apparently, there was a plane on our runway, so I'll go ahead and acknowledge that it was the right decision for the pilot to pull the plane up and not land. But without that information, my mind was racing through all the possibilities. I'm much more relaxed when I have the steering wheel in my own hands.

My guess is that many who are reading this feel the same way. You have agreed to follow Jesus wherever He may lead you, but you keep insisting on taking your route instead of His. You may even find yourself questioning why He is leading in a certain direction, or you may even defy His leadership because you think your route is faster or easier. I wonder if God ever shakes His head when we suggest or insist that we know better. One thing I do know, if we find it necessary to grip the steering wheel, we will never be released in the way we could have been if we had let Him drive.

Dependence on God is not an easy adjustment to make, especially in a world that celebrates self-reliance. It is a necessary adjustment to make, though, if we want to live out our calling. There is a song that I have come to love by an artist named Josh Garrels. It's called "Pilot Me." I love how beautifully he captures this idea of dependence on God.

> I will arise and follow you over
> Savior please, pilot me.
> Over the waves and through every sorrow
> Savior please, pilot me.
> When I have no more strength left to follow
> Fall on my knees, pilot me.
> May your sun rise and lead me on
> Over the seas, savior pilot me.[11]

We must get to the place where this is our heart's desire. More than control, we want God's desire to be fulfilled in us and His purpose to be carried out through us. We want Him to pilot us. That can only happen when we lay down control.

Proverbs 19:21 puts it bluntly: "Many are the plans in a person's heart, but it is the LORD's purpose that prevails."

King David also understood the importance of letting God pilot his life when he wrote, "Unless the Lord builds the house, the builders labor in vain. Unless the Lord watches over the city, the guards stand watch in vain" (Ps. 127:1).

The last thing I want is to spend my life laboring and striving in vain. I want God to do the building. I want God to do the piloting. It is then that I can be most confident to arrive where God intended me to go along the journey I was meant to take.

---

11. Josh Garrels, "Pilot Me," *Josh Garrels*, https://joshgarrels.bandcamp.com/track/pilot-me.

As I've been teaching my kids to swim, their tendency is to stay close to the stairs and sides of the pool. It's the best place to hold on. At first, it took every ounce of persuasive strength I have and quite a bit of physical strength to pry those tiny hands off the wall. Slowly but surely, I've shown them that if they hang on to me, we can move out into the deeper water. Even though they aren't skilled enough to swim on their own, I help keep them above the water. It's fun to watch their confidence grow both in themselves and in me.

As I've attempted to live out God's adventure for my life, there are times when I find myself clinging to the wall. He is constantly drawing me out into deeper waters whether that be greater victories, larger influence, bigger opportunities, or crazier dreams. My tendency is to hold on to the wall. But God has taught me that when I finally let go of the wall, He gives me something better to hold on to: Him. That doesn't necessarily mean that I'm venturing into safer territory. God's will often takes us to dangerous places. What is certain is that He goes with us. So no matter how big the risk, God is bigger. No matter how deep the waters, God is taller.

Peter once learned that when he saw Jesus walking on water. It was the middle of the night, the sea was rough, and Jesus decided to catch up to His friends in dramatic fashion. Why wait until morning when you can defy the laws of nature now and walk on water? He walked out to the boat, and the disciples were terrified, as you can imagine, because they thought it was a ghost. Jesus commanded them to not be afraid. Then Peter asked Jesus to invite him out on the water. Jesus called him out by name, and Peter began to step out of the boat. For a few moments, he was actually walking on water. Then he looked around at the wind and waves and began to sink. Jesus grabbed hold of him and then asked him this question: Why did you doubt? I wonder what the other guys in the boat were thinking. Peter did sink, but none of them were even willing to get out of the boat.

It's time to let go of the wall, to step out of the boat, to lay aside our safety, and to take hold of the life of sacrifice. That is where we find our truest meaning and greatest calling. No great accomplishment comes without risk. No worthy cause comes without sacrifice. No great calling comes without cost. You will never find your calling with your feet planted in the boat. God is calling you by name into His adventure.

Jesus traded everything. The price may seem high, but Jesus is not calling us to pay a price He was not first willing to pay.

Jesus gave up comfort. He said, "Foxes have dens and birds have nests, but the Son of Man has no place to lay his head" (Luke 9:58).

Jesus gave up personal preference. He traded heaven for earth. He exchanged the personal privileges of heaven for the sake of humanity.

Jesus gave up control. In the hour of His death, He said, "Father, if you are willing, take this cup from me; yet not my will, but yours be done" (Luke 22:42).

Jesus gave up safety when He laid down His own life for the sake of each one of us.

Jesus's disciples followed in His footsteps. They faced persecution, ridicule, and suffering, all for the sake of advancing His cause. Most of them sacrificed their lives. All of them were willing to give up everything they had because they believed that the price was worth paying. Do you?

Questions for Reflection

What is something you have had to sacrifice for?

What kinds of sacrifices have you made for Jesus?

Has it proved worth it?

What nets do you need to lay down today?

What trades might you need to make?

Chapter 9

A Commitment Worth Keeping

I was intrigued by a headline I came across recently in an opinion piece in the *New York Times*. The headline read, "The Golden Age of Bailing."[12]

Normally, my defenses are elevated when it comes to click bait articles, but it piqued my curiosity, and I clicked. The reason it drew my attention is because I have wondered if this trend of bailing out on commitments really is something that is growing in our generation. We've all received the text: "Sorry I have to cancel, something came up." We've all probably sent that text, too. I know some of you are probably thinking, "What's the big deal with that?" Maybe canceling a coffee date seems small, but what about when it becomes a consistent pattern? What about when your word starts to become diluted because people stop expecting you to show up for things you say you will show up to? What about when those little things give way to bigger things such as bailing on a team you committed to play on, bailing on a job you had a contract for, or bailing on a church because somebody hurt your feelings? The point of the article, which I believe is valid, is that we are far too okay with bailing on things. That may be a trend that is growing, but it is not a new trend.

---

12. David Brooks, "The Golden Age of Bailing," *The New York Times*, July 7, 2017, https://www.nytimes.com/2017/07/07/opinion/the-golden-age-of-bailing.html

Jesus could sniff out a bailer from a mile away. There were many who claimed they wanted to follow after Him, but when it came down to it, He knew their hearts, and they weren't really in it. I respect the fact that Jesus called it for what it was from the beginning. He wanted people to understand the commitment they were making from the beginning so it was a commitment they would keep.

> As they were walking along the road, a man said to him, "I will follow you wherever you go." Jesus replied, "Foxes have dens and birds have nests, but the Son of Man has no place to lay his head." He said to another man, "Follow me." But he replied, "Lord, first let me go and bury my father." Jesus said to him, "Let the dead bury their own dead, but you go and proclaim the kingdom of God." Still another said, "I will follow you, Lord; but first let me go back and say goodbye to my family." Jesus replied, "No one who puts a hand to the plow and looks back is fit for service in the kingdom of God."
>
> —Luke 9:57–62

At first glance, this seems harsh. Burying your father and kissing your family goodbye seem like noble and important things. What Jesus already knew was that these followers never intended to keep their commitment to Him. There would always be something higher on the priority list. There would always be some excuse for why now was not a good time. I think it's worth it for all of us to evaluate our level of commitment. We have to decide if we will let excuses and misplaced priorities take precedent. At some point, we have to come to the decision that Jesus is our foremost commitment.

There are some undeniable qualities that people of commitment possess. These are a few of the things that separate the committed few and the bailers.

1. The committed go all-in.
2. The committed don't look back.
3. The committed see it through.

Go All In

I will admit it, I'm a bit competitive. Whether it is a sport I happen to be playing or family game night, I'm in it to win it. Yes, I'll also admit that I have no reservations taking out a middle schooler in a game of youth group dodgeball. That has been my mentality over the years. I could maybe tone it down a bit for family game night, but the principle of giving it your all is one that I have always bought into. It has been instilled in me from a very young age. I still remember a picture that was on my wall. It had the word *Commitment* on it. Under that word, it read, "All you need to give is all you have."

This is such a simple yet powerful definition of commitment. I wish I could say that it has translated perfectly into my relationship with Jesus over the years. The truth is that when I was in high school, I was "in it," meaning a relationship with Jesus, but I wasn't in it to win it. I was simply in it for the perceived benefits of being in it. I lived my life the way I wanted to live it while training to maintain a somewhat half-hearted commitment to Jesus.

Things shifted dramatically for me in college. God surrounded me with people who embodied commitment when it came to their relationships with Jesus. They showed me what it meant to give all I had when it came to following Him. I remember a transformative moment when I was lying on my bed considering the commitment Jesus made to me. It occurred to me that Jesus gave all He had for me and that because of that, I owed Him all I had. I've since strived more and more for that level of commitment.

There is a time in the Gospels when Jesus is asked what matters most.

> *"Teacher, which is the greatest commandment in the Law?"*
>
> *Jesus replied: "'Love the Lord your God with all your heart and with all your soul and with all your mind.' This is the first and greatest commandment. And the second is like it: 'Love your neighbor as yourself.' All the Law and the Prophets hang on these two commandments."*
>
> —Matt. 22:36–40

We love God with *all* our heart, *all* our soul, and *all* our mind. The essential shift that each of us must determine to make is to move from half-hearted to whole-hearted followers of Jesus. We must get to the place where we can look at Him and say, "I'm all in." I'm ready to give all that I have.

Don't Look Back

One summer we took a trip down to Floyd County, Kentucky. We got the opportunity while we were there to help residents with needed projects and repairs on their homes. I won't forget the day I got to work on Ms. Peggy's house. The truth is that I didn't do much work that day. I just mostly sat and listened to Ms. Peggy talk and share stories about her life and experiences. She may not have had a lot, but one thing she didn't lack was wisdom. She showed me around her small trailer home and took great pride in the things God had provided her. She showed me pictures and other memories. It was when we were standing in the kitchen that something strange caught my eye. There was a grave in Ms. Peggy's backyard. It creeped me out a little bit at first, and I thought, "I've seen this movie before. The one where the sweet old lady isn't who she seems to be." I started to debate if I should ask her the burning question I had. I decided to ask, hoping it was just a pet or something buried out back. "Ms. Peggy, is that a grave in your backyard?" I will never forget her answer: "Oh that's my past buried out there. Sometimes I try to dig it back up, but then I'm reminded that my past is dead and gone. The old me is gone, the new has come." Every day that Ms. Peggy looks out her kitchen window, she is reminded that her past is behind her and there is no turning back.

Maybe that's what Paul was getting at when he told us in Romans that we died to our old life.

What shall we say, then? Shall we go on sinning so that grace may increase? By no means! We are those who have died to sin; how can we live in it any longer? Or don't you know that all of us who were baptized into Christ Jesus were baptized into his death? We were therefore buried with him through

74

baptism into death in order that, just as Christ was raised
from the dead through the glory of the Father, we too may
live a new life.

—Rom. 6:1–4

Paul warns us that if we don't bury our past, our past will bury us. We can't be raised to our new life if we don't bury our old life. We can't move forward if we are constantly looking back. Hebrews 12:1–2 gives us a new fixed focal point.

Therefore, since we are surrounded by such a great cloud
of witnesses, let us throw off everything that hinders and
the sin that so easily entangles. And let us run with per-
severance the race marked out for us, fixing our eyes on
Jesus, the pioneer and perfecter of faith."

We must be consistent in focusing on Jesus. As the old hymn says, "The world behind me, the cross before me; no turning back, no turning back."[13]

Commitment means we go all in. Commitment means we don't look back. Commitment means we see it through.

See It Through

Whenever someone walks though the big garage door of our warehouse gym, it doesn't take me long to figure out who will stick it out and who won't last through the first month. I tell people that CrossFit training is tough but doable. It stretches people to their limits and helps them reach new levels of fitness they never thought possible. What separates those who make it from those who don't might surprise you. It has nothing to do with body type, muscle definition, athletic background, or how in shape they are when they walk through the door. It has everything to do with their attitude.

---

13. S. Sundar Singh, "I Have Decided to Follow Jesus," *Timeless Truths*, https://library.timelesstruths.org/music/I_Have_Decided_to_Follow_Jesus/.

If I can detect determination, I know they will do whatever it takes to succeed. If they like the idea of being fit but don't really want it, then they won't succeed. If they complain or get irritated and pout because they struggle with a certain movement, it's only a matter of time before they quit. If they sell themselves short and unnecessarily stop early because it's hard, I may not even see them back the next day.

I remember a guy coming in one time and telling me that he wanted to sign up because he wanted to go to the CrossFit Games this year. Now to give you some background, less than 1 percent of the worldwide CrossFit population is elite enough to make it to the games. These elite athletes train day and night, year after year, while adhering to a very strict diet. Even the best fall short of getting there after training for the entire year. So when this guy told me that he just learned about CrossFit and wanted to try to go to the games, I started laughing and choking on my coffee. When I regained my composure, I tried to find a less blunt way to say that's not happening. If you dedicated everything to it over time, maybe, just maybe you could qualify. He wasn't satisfied with my answer, so he said, "Well, maybe by next year." I wish I could say that dream came true, but he never even made it to his first session.

Time will tell of our dedication to Jesus. It's no mystery to any of us that life is hard. Living a life of dedication to Jesus is even harder. There will be times when it seems easier to tap out, to turn back, to give up, but what lies ahead will be worth every ounce of sweat and dedication we pour out along the way.

Soak up Paul's words of encouragement:

Not that I have already obtained all this, or have already arrived at my goal, but I press on to take hold of that for which Christ Jesus took hold of me. Brothers and sisters, I do not consider myself yet to have taken hold of it. But one thing I do: Forgetting what is behind and straining toward what is ahead, I press on toward the goal to win the prize for which God has called me heavenward in Christ Jesus.

—Phil. 3:12–14

We keep pressing on because we know the best things are in front of us. We keep pressing on because there is no greater cause. We keep pressing on because there is greater calling. We keep pressing on because it's worth the cost. We keep pressing to take hold of the prize of knowing Jesus more and more. So keep pressing on.

Go all in.
Don't look back.
See it through.

Questions for Reflection

In your own words, how would you describe commitment?

What would you say you are most committed to?

What would you say dominates your time, thinking, resources, and so on?

How would you rate your commitment level to Jesus right now?

What, if anything, keeps you from being fully committed?

What will it take for you to truly go all in?

The Gift

Stephen

For God so loved the world that he gave his one and only Son, that whoever believes in him shall not perish but have eternal life.

—John 3:16

Chapter 10

A Simple Question

When I was a student at Milligan College, I became the youth minister at a church near campus. One Sunday, a woman who was new to our church came up to me and said, "My son wants to become a Christian. Can you come over and talk to him about it?" He looked pretty young, but I said, "Sure." When I got to her home, I sat down with her son and started to share the gospel. I had been a Christian most of my life and was even attending a Christian college, but the truth was I don't think I had ever really shared the gospel with anyone before. I told him that God loves him. He loves him so much that He came into the world and gave His life for him. I told him that Jesus died on the cross for his sins.

Somewhere in the middle of doing my best not to botch the message, this small boy raised his hand. It was just the two of us, but I guess raising your hand seems like the right thing to do when you have a question. I said, "Yes? You have a question?" He said, "How did one man dying save me from my sins?" That seems like such an obvious question, doesn't it? It took me totally off guard. I responded in the best way I knew how. "Well," I said, "in the Old Testament, God demanded a blood sacrifice for the evil doings of His people, the Israelites. So every year, the people brought their best animal to the Temple to be sacrificed by the priest to make atonement for their sins. Jesus is our perfect sacrifice. He shed His blood to redeem us once and for all. Make sense?" His eyes were as big as saucers. It was very clear that it didn't make sense to him at all. This was a defining moment for me. I realized that I was making the most incredible gift ever given too hard to open.

The Best Gift of All

My brother Jonathan was very generous. He was three years older than I. Not only was he older, but he was also much bigger. I always said, "He is a husky, I am a slender." We fought like any brothers do, but our conflicts usually ended quickly. When he got tired of my constant talking, he would just sit on me. Suffocation has a way of ending even the most brilliant rebuttal. Jonathan eventually became an attorney. He was older, he was bigger, and, believe me, he could very effectively plead a case, which, I might add, was very annoying. I was at a significant disadvantage. However, Jonathan was also very generous to me.

I remember one Christmas when I was about 10 and Jonathan was 13. A few days before Christmas, a huge box showed up in our family room behind my mom's chair. I ran over to see whose name was on the box. The tag read, "To Stephen from Jonathan." The huge gift was for me! It had my name on it. Not only that, it was from my husky, future attorney, older brother. I was impressed with the box and more impressed that he would get it for me. The box was so big I could not even get my arms around it to pick it up. The box was so heavy I could barely even push it. I waited anxiously to see what could possibly be inside.

Christmas morning came. I saved the big box for last. I tore into the paper. I opened the box. Do you know what was inside? Another box! I tore the paper off that box. Guess what? I found another box! I tore the paper off that box, and guess what? No, it was not another box. There was balled up newspaper in the box. I sifted through all the paper. "This is getting ridiculous!" I thought. "Did my brother just get me a box of balled-up newspaper?" When I finally got to the bottom of the box, do you know what I found? I found a concrete block. No wonder the box was so heavy. "Is this some sort of a sick joke?" I wondered. "Is my husky brother going to use this as some weapon of torture? Will he hold the block while he sits on me?" Just then, Jonathan said, "Keep looking." Next to the concrete block was a Polaroid camera. I recognized it. It was his prized Polaroid camera. He knew I admired it. He knew how much I would appreciate it. He painstakingly wrapped up the best gift he had and gave it to me. He gave it with love. He did enjoy throwing me off the trail a bit. He purposefully made the gift hard to open. He relished the idea that I would need to work hard to find the prize.

Unquestionably, the most famous verse in the Bible is John 3:16: "For God so loved the world that he gave his one and only Son."

It is such a simple expression that even the smallest child can remember the words. The gift-giver is God. The motive for giving is love. The gift-receiver is the world. The gift is the Son, Jesus.

Why do we make such a beautiful gift so hard to open? How can we share the gift with other people in a way that is both meaningful and accessible?

The Bridge Illustration

After my awkward and revealing encounter with the inquisitive young man who asked, "How did one man dying save me from my sins?" I knew that I needed to find a better and easier way to tell people about the greatest gift of all.

Here I was, a Christian, a preacher's kid, a Christian college student, a youth minister, for goodness' sake, and I wasn't able to clearly share my faith even with a young child. So I set out at that moment to find a way to share my faith so it would be easily understood and true to scripture.

You may be sitting there asking the same question the young boy asked. Maybe you are curious about Christianity, but the idea of someone dying for you on a cross seems confusing. Or maybe you have been in the same situation where someone asked you about what you believe and you had trouble making it simple to understand. It's been more than two decades since that small boy asked me the most basic question. In the years since, I have run into countless Christians who believe that "Jesus loves me this I know, for the

Bible tells me so,"[14] but they have trouble articulating the meaning behind that message.

My encounter with that young man led me to an illustration called the bridge illustration. This illustration isn't original to me. In fact, I don't know who came up with it as a way to understand the gospel, but it has proved invaluable to me. I have drawn it for people on the back of napkins, on the paper that protects the fast-food tray, on notebook paper, and on envelopes. I have shared it with people who are seven and people who are 97. I have shown it to blue-collar workers and white-collar executives. I have drawn it in every one of our Starting Point classes at church and every one of my faith-based classes at a local university where I teach.

I break the bridge illustration down into five big ideas: God's purpose, our problem, God's payment, our part, and God's promise.

---

14. "Jesus Loves Me, This I Know," *hymnal.net*, https://www.hymnal.net/en/hymn/c/51.

Chapter 11

God's Purpose

Every person who has ever been born has looked to the heavens at some point in their life and wondered, "Why am I here? Does my life matter? If there is a God, then does He have a plan for my life?" That's why the number-one-selling Christian book, outside of the Bible, is *The Purpose Driven Life: What on Earth Am I Here For?* by Rick Warren. It's also why one of the top quoted verses is Jeremiah 29:11: "'For I know the plans I have for you,' declares the LORD, 'plans to prosper you and not to harm you, plans to give you hope and a future.'" Everyone wants to know why they are here.

Here is the good news: God loves you, and He wants the very best for you. God has a purpose and a plan for your life. You are not here by accident. You are not a mistake. You are valuable. You are loved.

So what is God's plan for your life? God wants you to know Him, to praise Him, and to have a fulfilling life.

God Wants You to Know Him

When our first son, Benjamin, was born in Dayton, Ohio, I remember the nurse saying something like this: "We need to get him out right away. With every contraction, his heart rate is going down. The cord is wrapped around his neck." It was our first child, so of course we were concerned. The doctor came in and began to try to get him out. I had heard that sometimes doctors use forceps. This doctor used more what looked like a plunger. She stuck this plunger on his little head and pulled with all her might, so much so that when he finally came out, he had a huge sucker mark on his head for about two weeks. The moment he was born was beautiful, but it was also a moment filled with anxiety. He was blue. I like to call him my little Smurf baby. He had been deprived of oxygen. They quickly whisked him off to another area of the birthing center to make sure he was okay. He ended up being just fine, but I will never forget walking down the hall and looking through the window at him as they were working on him. I thought to myself, "I want so much to get to hold you. I want so much to get to know you. I can't wait until there is no glass that separates us and we get to build a lifetime of father-son memories."

You know what? If I, an imperfect father, want so much to get to know my son, how much more do you think your heavenly Father wants to know you and wants you to know Him? He created us so we can be in a relationship with Him, both now and forever. Jesus said, "I have made you known to them, and will continue to make you known in order that the love you have for me may be in them and that I myself may be in them" (John 17:26).

One of the primary purposes for your life is that you would come to know God and have a personal relationship with Him. God is not an impersonal force. He is not a distant God. He did not just create us and leave us.

Here is a principle I have witnessed over the years: What I create, I care about. When you were a child and created a piece of pottery at school, what was the first thing you did? You rushed home to show it to your mom or dad. Even if it was the worst, most lopsided creation ever, you couldn't wait to hear those words, "Wow! It is beautiful." Then you might see it proudly displayed on top of the refrigerator. It has been about 40 years since I created my imperfect artwork, but if I look carefully, I bet I can still find a box called "Keepsakes" and a piece of pottery with my name inscribed on the bottom. What you create, you care about.

God created you. He cares about you so much. You are His handiwork. As imperfect and warped as we can sometimes be, God proudly displays us as His handiwork. More than anything else, He wants a relationship with you. He wants you to know Him.

No matter the circumstances of your birth, you were created by God. No matter what your relationship was like with your father, your heavenly Father loves you deeply. "For you created my inmost being; you knit me together in my mother's womb. I praise you because I am fearfully and wonderfully made" (Ps. 139:13–14).

Psalm 17:8 says, "Keep me as the apple of your eye." Did you even know that was in the Bible? It means that you are protected, cherished, and loved. A literal translation of the Hebrew phrase is "little man of his eye."

My daughter, Rebekah, and I have the same green eyes. All of my other children have their mother's eyes. This is not the only way we are alike: we were both born in June, and we have similar personalities. She's outgoing and has a positive outlook on life. She shares the same calling to serve people in ministry. It is not unusual for someone to come up to us and say, "Oh, she has your eyes!" In a very literal sense, she is the little woman of my eye. Think about this—you are the little man or little woman of God's eyes. He loves you so much.

Isaiah 54:10 says, "Though the mountains be shaken and the hills be removed, yet my unfailing love for you will not be shaken."

This is what the Lord said: "I have loved you with an everlasting love; I have drawn you with unfailing kindness" (Jer. 31:3).

The first, most basic purpose for your life is that you come to know God.

The second purpose for your life is that you praise God.

God Wants You to Praise Him

God created us to praise Him. It may not seem obvious at first, but one of the beautiful things about you is that through you and your life, God receives praise. When you become a Christian, you have the opportunity to spend the rest of your life just thanking Him, worshipping Him, and praising Him.

First Peter 2:9 says, "You are a chosen people...God's special possession, that you may declare the praises of him who called you out of darkness into his wonderful light." There is something amazingly beautiful about that verse. You were created to praise. God deserves your praise. After all, He gave you breath and life. He is so good to us, isn't He? Even when life is hard, I sense God's presence. I see His beauty and creative ability all around me. I sense His comfort and guidance. Life is not always easy, but God is always good.

I am blessed to have grown up in an environment of praise. There was a lot of encouragement in my home as I grew up. My mother was the master at what she called Oreo-cookie encouragement. If she had some correction to give you, she would sandwich it with praise. She would start with praising us, then she would give some words of challenge or correction, then she would end with a little bit more praise. I felt so encouraged that I didn't even realize I had just been given a mid-course correction.

More important than the praise my parents gave me was that I got to witness the praise they offered God. The story of our family has not always been easy. The last few years have been particularly difficult. My mother had a stroke. My father was diagnosed with a rare form of terminal cancer. He was only supposed to live six months. He lived 19 more months. Two months after my father's funeral, my sister was diagnosed with stage four uterine cancer. Like Dad, she lived 19 more months. No one has shaken their fist at God and blamed Him. No one has talked about how unfair life is.

In my Dad's final days in the hospital, even though he was in pain, he still smiled at his visitors. He never complained. He cried when he read the final cards and notes from his grandchildren. He told the nurses, "I am going to heaven. I want you to go to heaven, too." A few nights before he died, through labored breath, my dad asked for his children to be by his side. We had been staying with him in shifts, but he wanted us all there together. We all came. He didn't say anything else. He just wanted us to be there. We did what we always do. We told stories. We laughed. We prayed. We read Bible verses about what Dad was just about to experience in heaven. We sang. We praised.

Some might say, "How can you praise at a time like that? How can you sing?" What else would we do? His entire life's work was focused on praising God. How could we do anything else but praise God in his death?

Listen to the words of King David:

I will extol the LORD at all times;
his praise will always be on my lips.
I will glory in the LORD;
let the afflicted hear and rejoice.
Glorify the LORD with me;
let us exalt his name together.

—Ps. 34:1–3

I am both encouraged and challenged by these verses. Look at the words David uses. I will praise the Lord at *all* times. His praise will *always* be on my lips. Let the afflicted *rejoice*.

It's easy to be negative. It's tempting to have a bad attitude. The easiest thing to do in the world is to be critical and negative. These verses remind us that in good times and in bad times, we reflect the goodness of God's character when we praise.

God wants you to know Him. God wants you to praise Him. God wants you to have a fulfilling life.

God Wants You to Have a Fulfilling Life

God is for you! Does that surprise you? He isn't against you. He isn't just waiting for the moment when you mess up to pounce on you. He is on your team. The Bible calls Him our Abba Father, which is a term of endearment that means "Daddy."

I have four children. It has been a joy to watch them grow. I am on their team no matter what. I want them to have the most fulfilling life possible. A fulfilling life doesn't mean a perfect life. Will they make mistakes? Of course. Will they get hurt? Yes. Will they fall when they ride their first bike? Of course. Will they cry when they get their heart broken? Sadly, yes. Those experiences and more will help shape them, and those experiences are so necessary.

A fulfilling life doesn't mean a life without hardship or pain. A fulfilling life means I want them to be satisfied. I want them to enjoy the best this life has to offer. I want them to love and be loved, to serve and be served.

Guess what? Your heavenly Father wants that for you, too. Jesus said, "I have come that they may have life, and have it to the full" (John 10:10). He wants the best for you.

A fulfilled life means you enjoy the blessings God gives you. A fulfilled life means you appreciate the people around you. A fulfilled life means you fulfill the purpose that God has for you.

Do you know what I have learned about God's purpose? It does not usually come in some dramatic fashion. I have learned that God's purpose for your life does not usually come in a burning bush or a Damascus Road experience. Those things happen from time to time. God's purpose comes in finding fulfillment on the journey.

You have freedom to choose your life's work. You have freedom in Christ to choose where you live. You have freedom to choose who you will marry. But, whatever you do, do it in the name of the Lord Jesus and be thankful. "And whatever you do, whether in word or deed, do it all in the name of the Lord Jesus, giving thanks to God the Father through him" (Col. 3:17).

Josh talked earlier about God's specific calling for your life and how to discover it. But God's general purpose is the same for everyone: come to know Him personally, learn to praise Him always, and find fulfillment in the life He gives you. Sadly, we often decide to choose our own way, and it has led to problems.

Questions for Reflection

Do you find it difficult to explain what it means to be a Christian?

Why do you think we make such a beautiful gift so hard to open?

What keeps you from knowing God more?

Do you find it easier to praise God in the good times or the bad?

Would you describe your life as fulfilling? Why? Why not?

Chapter 12

Our Problem

I was three years old and sleeping in our family's pop-up camper somewhere in the Appalachian Mountains. It was the middle of the night, and I woke up with a sudden urge. Our camper did not have a bathroom, and we were a long way from the bathhouse. I tried to be as quiet as I could as I crawled out of bed and over my oldest brother, Mark. I slowly opened the door to our 1973 Starcraft, which made an annoying creaking sound. I'm sure, despite my best effort, that I woke up the five other cramped inhabitants of our camper. Mom said, "Do you need help?" "No, Mom," I confidently shot back. "I can do it."

It was absolutely dark outside. I can still vividly remember what happened in the moments that followed. My confidence soon melted into embarrassment when, somehow in the darkness, I missed my mark. I ended up with soggy pants and sagging pride. I didn't want to go back into the camper and admit my failure, but I had no choice. A new set of dry clothes was in the cabinet underneath my brother. I mustered the courage to go back inside and said words that would become the punch line for a family story that would be told long into my teenage years. "Oops, I think I missed." No truer words had ever been spoken.

All Have Sinned, Except Jesus

We have a problem. Just because God wants the best, most fulfilling life for us doesn't mean we choose the best, most fulfilling life for ourselves. There is an attitude that too often marks our lives. The Bible calls this attitude sin—rebelling against God's plan for our lives. The word *sin* literally means to "miss the mark."

Isaiah the prophet said it this way: "We all, like sheep, have gone astray, each of us has turned to our own way" (Isa. 53:6). Paul the apostle admitted, "All have sinned and fall short of the glory of God" (Rom. 3:23). There isn't one person, except Jesus, who hasn't missed the mark.

If you don't believe me that all have sinned, then let's just take a walk through some of the most basic commands of God. In the Ten Commandments, God gave the Israelites basic expectations (Exod. 20:1–17). The first four commandments dealt with their relationship with God, and the last six commandments focused on their relationships with one another. Let's just look at a few of them.

Honor your father and mother. Have you ever disobeyed your parents? Did you ever rebel against one of their rules? Did you ever stay out past curfew or sneak out a bedroom window or talk back to them? If you have, then you broke one of the Ten Commandments.

You shall not steal. Have you ever taken something that did not belong to you? Did you ever take something from a store that you did not buy? Did you ever take an answer off a classmate's test in school? Did you ever download a song that you didn't pay for? If you have, then you broke one of the Ten Commandments.

You shall not give false testimony. Have you ever said something that was not true? Did you ever lie on a résumé or application? Did you ever lie to a police officer when he pulled you over for speeding? Did you ever call in sick when you just wanted a day off? If you have, then you broke one of the Ten Commandments.

You shall not murder. I would imagine none of you have broken this commandment. I made this bold assertion once during a sermon. I followed it up by saying, "Because none of you have murdered anyone, let's focus on hate today, because Jesus said if you hate someone in your heart, it is like murder." After the closing song, a man came up to me whom I had never met. He had long hair and tattoos down his arms. He said, "Pastor, you said no one has ever murdered someone. I have murdered someone." I took a step back, literally. I said, "Really? What happened?" He said, "Yeah it was a bar fight. I did my time." So you know what I did? I made him the pitcher on our church softball team. I would whisper to the umpire before the games, "You'd better not miss a call. That dude murdered somebody."

Have you ever killed someone in a bar fight? Did you ever hate someone as Jesus mentioned in the Sermon on the Mount? Did you ever hold a grudge against someone? If you have, then you have broken one of the Ten Commandments.

We could walk through every commandment. Have you ever committed adultery? If not, what about lust? Have you ever misused the name of God or Jesus? Have you ever put anything or anyone else before your relationship with God? If you have, then you have broken one of the Ten Commandments.

"For whoever keeps the whole law and yet stumbles at just one point is guilty of breaking all of it" (James 2:10). Even the best, most pure person you know has broken at least one of the commandments of God. In Romans 3:10, the Apostle Paul writes, "There is no one righteous, not even one."

Every person who is reading this book, including myself, is guilty of sin and missing the mark. That is a problem.

The Penalty for Sin

Our perfect, loving God is serious about sin. The consequences are catastrophic. From the moment Adam and Eve sinned in the garden, God said that the penalty for sin was death.

> The LORD God took the man and put him in the Garden of Eden to work it and take care of it. And the Lord God commanded the man, "You are free to eat from any tree in the garden; but you must not eat from the tree of the knowledge of good and evil, for when you eat from it you will certainly die."
>
> —Gen. 2:15–17

When I first read that, I thought, "They did not die. Adam and Eve went on to have children and grandchildren and have long lives." I have since understood that they did die. They died physically. No, it did not happen immediately, but the process of death started at the very moment of their sin. All of us have inherited the same penalty. The statistics on death are pretty impressive. One out of one of us die.

An even more devastating consequence is that we deserve what the Bible calls a "second death." That is a spiritual death, an eternal separation from our Holy God. Wow! That is serious.

Isaiah and Paul have something to say on this subject. Paul writes in Romans 6:23, "The wages of sin is death." Wages are something you earn. What we have earned for our sin is death. Isaiah 59:2 says, "But your iniquities have separated you from your God."

Our problem is that our sin has left us in dire straits and with a lot of questions.

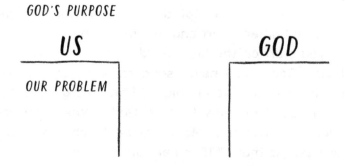

GOD'S PURPOSE

US   GOD

OUR PROBLEM

The great question throughout all human history is this: "How do we get back in a right relationship with God? How do we get to God's side?" The chasm between us is insurmountable. Religious system after religious system started to spring up, and all of them tried to give their own answer to this question. They started on the human side and tried to build their own way back to God through good deeds or religious rituals.

An Islamic center was built in our city, and several years ago I took a guided tour of the facility. A very kind, young woman guided us through each of the areas of the building. She was gracious and hospitable. She explained the purpose of each room and how they use the facility. The tour ended in the large prayer room, which in English is called "a place of prostration." She said, "Can I answer any of your questions?" I raised my hand. I asked, "Is there a salvation concept in the Muslim faith?" Her kind eyes showed a bit of confusion, so I rephrased the question. "How can I get to heaven in the Muslim faith?" She still wasn't quite sure what I was asking. I finally said, "What is expected of those who wish to practice the Muslim faith?" She told us there are five pillars of the Muslim faith: (1) believe in Allah as God and Mohammad as his messenger, (2) perform ritual prayers five times a day, (3) pay alms to benefit the poor, (4) fast during the month of Ramadan, (5) go on pilgrimage to Mecca.

In Hinduism, karma is the result of how you live your life on this earth. Karma affects your future lives. Moksha is the Hindu concept of eternity and is only reached when one has overcome ignorance and desires.[15]

In the instance of both of these major world religions, the emphasis is on human effort and the importance of good deeds.

When you start on the human side, you rationalize to yourself that a loving God would never send someone to hell. When you are on the human side, you think, "If I am just good enough, then maybe I can build my way back to God." When you are on the human side, you wonder, "Maybe going to church or a religious service will get me there." If you are on the human side, you think, "If I just pray more, that will save me." All of these fall short.

Why do they all fall short? Because they don't answer the fundamental question that the small boy asked me that day at his house: "How did one man dying save me from my sins?"

Questions for Reflection

Sin is "missing the mark." What does it mean to miss the mark?

Do you think the penalty for sin is appropriate? Why? Why not?

Why is being a good person or going to church not enough?

---

15. "Moksha," *BBC*, https://www.bbc.co.uk/religion/religions/hinduism/beliefs/moksha.shtml.

Chapter 13

God's Payment

The man-made problem of sin was so deep and the consequences so dire that it required a God-sized solution. Only God could solve our dilemma. Only God could find a way out of this mess. Only God could pay our price. Since the penalty was death. Our loving God looked to earth and said, "I'm the only one who can pay it."

From the very beginning of time, God set a plan in motion to pay for our sins. The very first prophecy in the Bible is found immediately after Adam and Eve sinned and received the death penalty. God, speaking to the deceiver, the serpent, says, "I will put enmity between you and the woman, and between your offspring and hers; he will crush your head, and you will strike his heel" (Gen. 3:15).

This is the first prophecy of the coming Messiah. It is the first prophecy of the virgin birth. It is the first prophecy of the crucifixion. God says something like this to the devil, "Oh you will be able to strike his heel, but he will crush your head. You may think you are winning. You may think you have power. When you strike his heel, you may be under the impression that you struck the final blow. You will be surprised to find out that you are playing right into my hands. Just when you think you have won, you will be surprised to learn that in that very moment, I have defeated death. Through the death of the Son, I provide payment for the sins of the world."

The Apostle Paul said it like this: "The wages of sin is death, but the gift of God is eternal life in Christ Jesus our Lord" (Rom. 6:23).

This very act is what makes Christianity unique. No matter how good you are or how hard you work or how many times you go to church, you cannot pay the penalty. You do not have the resources.

Imagine for a moment that you are a new driver and you get a speeding ticket. It is no ordinary ticket. Let's say you are driving 100 miles per hour in a school zone during school hours. You aren't wearing your seatbelt, and to make matters worse, you are listening to show tunes on your radio (which in and of itself deserves a ticket). You look in your rearview mirror and see the blue shining lights. You are guilty. You don't try to argue. Given the seriousness of the offense, you have to go to court. The prosecutor lays out the case against you. Justice demands a payment for your reckless decision. The judge says, "The penalty you owe for this offense is $10,000." As a high school student, you do not have that kind of money. What will you do? Even if this is your first offense, you have to pay. Even if you were perfect before this, you still have to pay. Even if you promise to never do it again, you have to pay. You would feel helpless.

What would you think if I told you that the judge is your father? As a judge, he says, "You owe $10,000. I know you do not have it, but justice must be served. As your judge, I must enforce this penalty, but as your loving father, I want to pay this great price for you." Just then, the judge stands up, removes his robe, comes down from the bench, and sits next to you as your dad. He pulls out his checkbook and writes a check to the clerk of courts, in your name.

What would you think? How would you feel? Would you accept the gift? His gift for you can also be called His grace for you. Grace is an undeserved gift. You cannot earn it. You do not deserve it. You are guilty. Justice demands a payment. Grace pays the price.

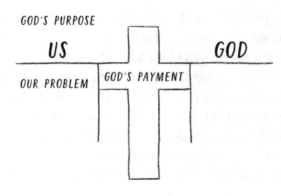

John 3:16 says, "For God so loved the world that He gave His one and only Son, that whoever believes in Him shall not perish but have eternal life." God's love led Him to pay the price for our sin so we will not perish, or die.

There are only two ways to get to heaven.

The Bible describes only two ways to get to heaven. The first is to perfectly follow God's laws and not miss the mark in any area of your life. We have already established that no one is perfect. Paul writes, "There is no one righteous, not even one" (Rom. 3:10). Later in that chapter, he writes, "Therefore no one will be declared righteous in God's sight by the works of the law" (Rom. 3:20). Perfection is a good idea, but it is an impossibility.

The second way is to humbly accept Christ's atoning sacrifice for our sins. Paul goes on to say, "For sin shall no longer be your master, because you are not under law, but under grace" (Rom. 6:14). It is impossible to be perfect. It is impossible to be good enough. I do not deserve God's grace. I do not earn God's grace. I can only humbly accept God's grace or reject God's payment for my sin.

The Bible lays it out beautifully this alternative way.

But now apart from the law the righteousness of God has been made known, to which the Law and the Prophets testify. This righteousness is given through faith in Jesus Christ to all who believe. There is no difference between Jew and Gentile, for all have sinned and fall short of the glory of God, and all are justified freely by his grace through the redemption that came by Christ Jesus. God presented Christ as a sacrifice of atonement, through the shedding of his blood— to be received by faith.

—Rom. 3:21–25

This was God's plan from the beginning. He provided a way for us to be justified and free. Jesus paid our debt.

Isn't it intolerant to say Jesus is the only way?

One day, the disciples were asking Jesus about how to get to heaven. Jesus said, "I am the way and the truth and the life. No one comes to the Father except through me" (John 14:6). Over the years, I have been asked by many people, "Isn't it intolerant to say Jesus is the only way?" It has always been curious to me when people ask that question. It is very popular today to believe that all roads lead to heaven. Many think that as long as you are sincere and a basically good person, then heaven is your home.

Is it intolerant of God to provide a clear path to heaven, or is it loving? If the president of the United States called you on the telephone, invited you to the White House, and gave you specific instructions on how to enter, would you believe that is intolerant or hospitable? Imagine that the president sends you detailed instructions in the mail. He tells you to drive a certain route, enter a specific door, and give an approved password to the doorman. Would it be intolerant of him to do so? What would happen if you decided to take your own path? What if you reasoned, "That is silly and so intolerant of the president. I know what I am going to do. I am going to go to the front lawn. I am going to jump the fence. I am going to sprint as fast as I can across the lawn. I am going to run up the stairs. I am going to demand entrance because I earned it through my own efforts." How is that going to work out for you? Do you know what I would do? I would graciously accept the invitation. I would follow the instructions. I would never think, "I can't believe this intolerant and judging president. How dare he give me such specific instructions?"

The invitation has been given, and here is the only question you need to ask: "Am I willing to follow?" If you are, then read on, because the Bible gives us very clear directions.

Questions for Reflection

Has someone ever paid a debt for you or forgiven you for an offense? How did you feel? Did you find it difficult to receive their grace?

How would you respond if the judge (your father) paid your ticket?

Why do you think people find it difficult to accept God's payment for their sin?

Chapter 14

Our Part

Just because the gift is there doesn't mean everyone receives the gift. When you get a gift from someone, you need to accept the gift.

Imagine that you love this book so much that you want to give me Bengals season tickets. You know how much I love the Bengals. You wrap the tickets up in a nice box and beautiful wrapping paper. You are so excited. You can't wait to give me the gift. With great anticipation, you hand me the box. "Open it! Open it!" you shout. How would you feel if I said, "Thank you so much, but I am busy right now. I will open it later"? How would you feel if a year later you came to my office and saw that same box on my desk? You notice it is not opened. You might ask, "Why did you not open my gift for you?" How would you feel if I said, "I was thinking I would get to it someday"? Would you feel rejected or angry or even hurt?

Here is the principle: just because a gift is given doesn't mean it is received.

The gift of Jesus and His death on the cross for our sins is a gift for everyone, but not everyone opens the gift. Some do not open it because they are too busy. Some do not receive the gift because they believe it is too good to be true. Some do not open the gift because they have doubts. Some do not open the gift because they don't want it.

God has done His part. He paid the death penalty for us. What is our part?

The first and most important step in following Jesus is to believe that He exists and that He paid the price for our sin.

Faith in God and Christ's payment for sin on the cross is the primary condition for salvation. The author of Hebrews writes, "Without faith it is impossible to please God, because anyone who comes to him must believe that he exists and that he rewards those who earnestly seek him" (Heb. 11:6).

Do you believe in Jesus? If you do, then do you know why you believe? If you do not, have you taken time to really research the evidence? Authors Josh McDowell and Lee Strobel do a great job of defending the Christian faith, so I won't try to do that here. But fundamental in becoming a follower of Jesus is to believe that He exists and that He did, indeed, pay for your sin on the cross and resurrect from the dead. Believe that Christmas is about more than a jolly man in a red suit coming down a chimney. It is about God becoming a human, one of us, so we could know Him personally and He could stand in for us as an atoning sacrifice. Believe that Easter is about more than a bunny that rises from a hole in the ground to deliver candy and presents. It is about Jesus rising from the dead on the third day as prophesied in the Old Testament and predicted by Jesus. His resurrection defeated the curse of death and extended to us a promise that because He lives, we will also live.

Is belief in Jesus enough?

Some teach that belief in Jesus is the only step that is required to become a Christian. "After all" they say, "even John 3:16 says 'whoever believes in Him will not perish.'" I remember one of my professors in college saying, "One rule of interpreting the Bible is that not all of God's will is contained in just one verse of scripture." There are other verses that provide us additional instruction. For example, James 2:19 says, "You believe that there is one God. Good! Even the demons believe that—and shudder." Not only do the demons believe; they take it a step further and shudder in fear. The demons believe, but they are not saved. They are not going to heaven because their belief is not a humble belief. They are not going to heaven because their belief is not a surrendering belief. While they know the reality of God, they do not surrender to Him as Lord.

True, saving belief leads us to respond. We respond to Jesus by confessing our faith in Him.

Confession is our ongoing admission of commitment to Christ.

Jesus told His disciples, "Whoever acknowledges me before others, I will also acknowledge before my Father in heaven" (Matt. 10:32).

The Bible instructs us to openly acknowledge our faith in Jesus. When you love someone, you confess that love and stay faithful to that love. Confession is claiming that Jesus is Lord. When you confess your faith, you are telling other people that Jesus is the Lord of your life. You are putting a stake in the ground. You are telling God and others that something is different.

Paul writes:

> *If you declare with your mouth, "Jesus is Lord," and believe in your heart that God raised him from the dead, you will be saved. For it is with your heart that you believe and are justified, and it is with your mouth that you profess your faith and are saved.*
>
> —Rom. 10:9–10

When Jesus died on the cross, He died publically and openly. When you confess Jesus as Lord, you are publicly and openly declaring your faith. Paul told Timothy, "Take hold of the eternal life to which you were called when you made your good confession in the presence of many witnesses" (1 Tim. 6:12). Being a Christian is a personal decision, but it is not a private decision. We are commanded to go into all the world. We are to be Christ's ambassadors. We are light in a room.

We will all, at some point, confess Christ as Lord.

Everyone who has ever lived will one day confess Christ as Lord. "Every knee should bow...and every tongue confess that Jesus Christ is Lord, to the glory of God the Father" (Phil. 2: 10–11 ESV).

At the second coming of Christ, every person will realize that Jesus is Lord and that the Bible is true. For those who did not accept the great gift of Jesus, it will be too late at that point.

Our part is to believe in Jesus, to confess Him as Lord, and then to repent.

Repentance is admitting that you have sinned and pledging that you will try to stay away from that sin.

Repentance is a realization that you are going the wrong direction and you need to turn around and go a different direction. The word *repent* literally means to turn around.

Let's say that my wife and I are driving to a party. I am unclear about the directions. A road turns off to the right, and I pass by the road. My wife says humbly, "Honey, you just missed the turn." I proclaim (in a very manly voice), "Who is driving this car? I know where I am going!" She sits back and thinks, "Okay, we will just see, Mr. Confident." About 10 minutes pass, and I begin to get a sick feeling. I don't want to admit it, but I realize I am lost. I stop at a gas station and ask, "Do you know how to get to this address?" The attendant says, "Sure, go back about 10 minutes and turn on this road. You can't miss it!" I swallow my pride, get back in the car, and say, "You were right. But the attendant said it is very easy to miss!" I turn around and go back the right direction.

Repentance is realizing that you are going the wrong direction in life. It is admitting that you need help to find the way. Repentance is often accompanied by tears. A person sees his or her sin and realizes the need for a Savior. Paul writes that "Godly sorrow brings repentance that leads to salvation" (2 Cor. 7:10). Repentance is not perfection. It is a realization that we are sinners in need of God's grace. Jesus said that "unless you repent, you too will all perish" (Luke 13:3).

Our part is to believe in Jesus, to confess Him as Lord, to repent, and then to be *baptized.*

Baptism is our declaration of faith in Jesus and commitment to Him as Lord.

Admittedly, there is much debate and disagreement in the Christian world about baptism. Some people debate the mode of baptism.

Should baptism be done by sprinkling, pouring, or immersion? Some disagree about the appropriate age for baptism. Should a baby be baptized? How young is too young? Some debate the meaning of baptism. Is baptism simply a step of obedience, or is it a vital part of our response to Christ?

There are many doctrines and church traditions when it comes to baptism. Can we just agree that scripture is more important than church tradition? It is always important to ask the question, "What does the Bible say?" Because there is disagreement, I think it makes sense to simply walk through the scriptures and see what the Bible actually says about baptism.

Baptism is commanded by Jesus.
Just before Jesus ascended into heaven, He gave final marching orders to His disciples. "Therefore go and make disciples of all na-tions, baptizing them in the name of the Father and of the Son and of the Holy Spirit" (Matt. 28:19). There are people who ask, "Do I need to be baptized?" The answer is clearly yes! Jesus told His disciples to go, make disciples, and baptize and teach them. Some people will ask, "Is baptism necessary?" I always answer the same way—every command of Jesus is necessary. Jesus said, "If you love me, keep my commands" (John 14:15).

Biblical baptism was by immersion.
There are four reasons we know this is true. First, the word *baptizo* in Greek means to immerse or dip under. When people in the first century heard the word *baptizo*, a word picture came to their minds. It is what one ship wanted to do to another enemy ship. It wanted to sink it or submerge it. Second, there is not an example in the Bible of someone being sprinkled. Third, church history sheds some light on this as well. It is unclear exactly when the Catholic Church began to practice sprinkling for baptism. But it was not until 1311 at the Council of Ravenna that the church declared there was no difference between sprinkling and immersion. Fourth, the symbolism of a death, burial, and resurrection is best demonstrated in baptism by immersion. Colossians 2:12 says, "Having been buried with him in baptism, in which you were also

raised with him through your faith in the working of God, who raised him from the dead." Peter could have said to repent and run 400 meters. If it was commanded by Jesus, then we would have done it, but it would not have made sense. It is certain that baptism by immersion was the biblical mode of baptism, the practice of the early church, and it made sense that it best represents death, burial, and resurrection.

Biblical baptism was for those who were old enough to believe, confess, and repent.
Again, the Bible must be our rule of faith and practice. While there is some precedent in church history for infant baptism, there is no example of infant baptism in the Bible. The earliest recorded instances of infant baptism were sometime in the late second century. Our part in responding to Christ includes faith, repentance, and confession, and none of those are possible for an infant. Becoming a Christian is a personal decision. No one can make that decision for you.

Biblical baptism marks the beginning of my new life as a Christian.
Just after Jesus ascended to heaven, Peter and the other apostles followed the instruction of Jesus to go make disciples and baptize them. Peter preached the first gospel sermon in Acts 2. Many in the crowd believed in Jesus. The evidence of His crucifixion and resurrection were widely known. The people were convicted when they heard Peter's message. They asked, "What shall we do?" (Acts 2:37). Peter said, "Repent and be baptized, every one of you, in the name of Jesus Christ for the forgiveness of your sins. And you will receive the gift of the Holy Spirit" (Acts 2:38). Three thousand people were baptized that day.

Peter's instruction was simple and meaningful. He did not command something that was difficult or something people had to work to achieve. The people were told to humbly repent and then be baptized. It was meaningful. The very act of being lowered under the water and raised out of the water powerfully demonstrated their spiritual death and resurrection. The result was forgiveness of sins and the gift of the Holy Spirit.

We can see this relationship between baptism and spiritual death and resurrection in several other scriptures. Paul writes:

We are those who have died to sin; how can we live in it any longer? Or don't you know that all of us who were baptized into Christ Jesus were baptized into his death? We were therefore buried with him through baptism into death in order that, just as Christ was raised from the dead through the glory of the Father, we too may live a new life. For if we have been united with him in a death like his, we will certainly also be united with him in resurrection like his. For we know that our old self was crucified with him so that the body ruled by sin might be done away with, that we should no longer be slaves to sin.

—Rom. 6:2–6

These verses describe both the powerful meaning of baptism and the timing of our spiritual death. Paul writes that we "died to sin" (Rom. 6:2). Then he immediately describes the moment that marks that death when he writes, "Don't you know that all of us who were baptized into Christ Jesus were baptized into this death?" (Rom. 6:3). Just as Jesus died, was buried, and raised to new life, so we also die to sin and are raised to new life. Paul goes on to describe the beautiful imagery of baptism when he says, "We were therefore buried with him through baptism into death in order that, just as Christ was raised from the dead through the glory of the Father, we too may live a new life" (Rom. 6:4). Colossians 2:12 similarly reminds us, "Having been buried with him in baptism, in which you were also raised with him through your faith in the working of God, who raised him from the dead." When we are baptized, we are buried with Him and raised to new life. Our baptism marks our new life as a Christian. We have faith in Jesus and His resurrection, we die to our sin, we are buried, and we are raised to walk a new life.

In Galatians 3:26–27, Paul uses a different analogy to describe the same truth. "So in Christ Jesus you are all children of God through faith, for all of you who were baptized into Christ have clothed yourselves with Christ." When were we clothed with Christ? We were clothed when we were baptized, which was preceded by our faith in Jesus.

Many years ago, a teenager, his mom, and stepdad began to come to our church. Chris, the teenager, was confined to a wheelchair. He had a debilitating disease that attacked his muscles. His prognosis was very poor. Despite his inability to move nearly any muscle in his body, his enthusiasm and joy could be clearly seen in his face. After several weeks of coming to church, Chris decided he wanted to be baptized. But then came the question, "How will we baptize Chris with his physical limitations?"

One of our members had a relationship with a local YMCA. We made arrangements ahead of time. After church, we invited people to join us at the Y and celebrate with Chris. We made a plan. Chris had a cloth stretcher that his caregivers used to help move him. We slid that stretcher under him in his chair. Six of us lifted Chris out of the confines of his wheelchair and very carefully walked down the steps of the YMCA pool. When we got into the water, all of us held Chris above the water, wrapped in this stretcher. I asked, "Chris, do you believe that Jesus Christ died for you and rose again on the third day? Do you agree to follow Jesus as Lord of your life?" Chris enthusiastically proclaimed, "Yes I do!" I said, "Upon your confession that Jesus is Lord, I am honored to be able to baptize you in the name of the Father, the Son, and the Holy Spirit, for the forgiveness of your sins and the gift of the Holy Spirit. One, two, three!" We lowered that stretcher together in unison. We buried Chris under the water and raised him to new life. If anyone has ever figuratively thrown their arms in the air in victory, Chris did that day. He could not move, but every fiber of his being celebrated. It wasn't long until Chris passed from this life to his heavenly home where he walked and ran on streets of gold.

Some might ask, "Why would you go to all that effort?" The answer is simple. We are convicted to follow the command of Jesus, the teaching of the apostles, and the example of those first believers.

The Safe Course

Some will ask, "What if I was baptized as a baby? Are you saying I am not saved?" Or "I just believed one day, and I know something changed in me, but I was never baptized. Are you saying I am not a Christian?" Many years ago, I heard a story that really helps illustrate my approach to those and other questions. It is called the "safe course" illustration. There is a woman on a ship. The weather is very stormy. The waves are crashing on and rocking the ship. The woman looks out and notices that there are rocks jutting out from the water everywhere. The woman is fearful that the ship is going to crash into a rock, so she goes to the captain of the ship and says, "Captain, Captain, do you know where all the rocks are?" The captain wisely and confidently replies, "No, ma'am, I don't, but I do know the safe course."

When it comes to our part in receiving the gift of God's salvation, the Bible provides us the safe course. Believe in Jesus and His atoning death on the cross and resurrection from the dead. Confess that belief to people. Repent of personal sin. Be baptized into the death and burial of Jesus. Any practice or experience that is not addressed in the Bible is outside the biblical safe course. As disciples of Jesus, we aren't authorized to speak definitively on anything that is not taught in scripture. So, for my part, I want to be as faithful as I can to what the Bible teaches. My own experiences or church tradition should never take the place of trusting and following the captain.

When we do our part in trusting and following Jesus, God offers us certain promises.

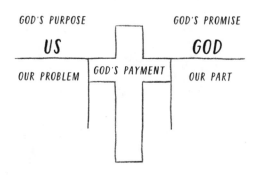

Questions for Reflection

Why is belief in Jesus and His death on the cross the primary condition for salvation?

Why is confession part of our response to Jesus?

What does it mean to repent? Has there ever been a time when you repented?

In your own words, what is the significance of being baptized?

Have you ever followed the biblical "safe course"? If not, what is holding you back?

Chapter 15

God's Promise

There are some God-sized promises for those who become a Christian. They are promises that God gives and God keeps. When you become a Christian, God promises that you will have forgiveness of all your sins. He promises to give you help and guidance every day. He promises that you will be in heaven when you die.

Forgiveness of Sin

Three of the most impactful words someone can utter are "I forgive you." If you owe someone a debt and she says these words, she is indicating that you no longer owe her anything. You are free. If you did something that wounded someone and he says these words, he is telling you that he is releasing you from guilt or fear of retribution. These words are beautifully freeing. Paul tells us that Jesus "has rescued us from the dominion of darkness and brought us into the kingdom of the Son he loves, in whom we have redemption, the forgiveness of sins" (Col. 1:13–14).

When Jesus hung on the cross, He looked at the crowd around Him. He looked into the faces of those who falsely accused Him. He looked into the eyes of those who misjudged Him. He looked into the souls of those who hated Him. He said these beautiful words: "Forgive them."

When you become a Christian, you are forgiven. Your sins are cast into the deepest sea. You don't need to worry about death. You don't need to fear retribution. You can swim freely in the pool of God's refreshing grace.

I used to be under the impression that if I did not ask for forgiveness every night, I was not forgiven. When I was a teenager, I remember going to my parents and asking them about God's forgiveness. I was concerned. I said, "Will God still forgive me if I forget to confess a sin I commit?" They assured me that while it is good to go to God and confess what you have done, God does not wait to forgive you. When Jesus died on the cross, He paid the penalty for the sins of your past, present, and future. His forgiveness is complete.

Hebrews 10 has a lot to say about forgiveness and the impact of the death of Jesus. Hebrews 10:12 says that Jesus "offered for all time one sacrifice for sins." A few sentences later, in verses 17 and 18, it says, "'Their sins and lawless acts I will remember no more.' And where these have been forgiven, sacrifice for sin is no longer necessary." Wow! Those are powerful and freeing words. "Sacrifice for sin is no longer necessary."

God's Help and Guidance in Your Life

I don't know about you, but I need God every day. I need His help. I need His guidance and wisdom. I need His strength to make it through the challenges and pressures of this life. Here is the good news: when you become a Christian, God promises that He will be with you and will be your guide. The final words of Jesus to His disciples are found in Matthew 28:20: "I am with you always." God said in Hebrews 13:5–6, "'Never will I leave you; never will I forsake you.' So we say with confidence, 'The Lord is my helper; I will not be afraid.'"

You are not alone. God gives us help in times of trouble (Ps. 46:1), strength in times of weakness (2 Cor. 12:10), a way out in times of temptation (1 Cor. 10:13), wisdom in times of need (James 1:5), and love always (Rom. 8:38–39). You are a child of God. Do not fear. You are much loved. God is for you!

Heaven

I have performed hundreds of funerals over the years. I can tell you firsthand that there is a big difference between the funeral of a follower of Jesus and the funeral of someone who was not a Christian.

There are similarities. There is sadness at both funerals. There are memories. There are pictures. There is a celebration of life. There is grieving. But I have noticed that the grieving is different.

The most poignant moment in every funeral is the time when friends and family walk by the casket for the final time. It is traditional that the pastor stands at the head of the casket. In that position, I overhear the final messages from a wife to her husband, a child to a parent, or friend to a friend. No matter the situation, I often find myself quietly crying along with the family. I can summarize the difference between the funerals in two phrases: "Goodbye" or "I will see you soon." In 1 Thessalonians 4:13, Paul says that we "do not grieve like the rest of mankind, who have no hope."

Our hope is realized in heaven, which is promised to those who follow Jesus as Lord. When you die, you do not need to fear because you know that your last breath on this earth will be your first breath in heaven. When you die, your loved ones can have confidence that they will see you again. As a child of God, you receive all the benefits, privileges, and promises of God. 1 Peter 1:4 says that we have "an inheritance that can never perish, spoil or fade. This inheritance is kept in heaven for you."

Do you want to go to heaven when you die? If you died tonight, do you know that you would go to heaven? If you are not sure, you can be sure! Follow Jesus as the Lord and leader of your life.

If you make that decision, you don't need to wonder, "Am I in, or am I out?"

Over the years, I have heard many people say, "I do not know for sure if I am a Christian." If they are married, I ask, "Well, do you know that you are married?" With a slight grin, they say, "Of course we do." I continue, "How do you know that you are married?" The husband usually says, "I know because she tells me all the time!" I tell them, "You know you are married because you made a commitment before God and people. You know you are married because you said, 'I do.'"

I will then ask, "Did you love each other before you were married?" "Of course," they say. "Did you love each other after you were married?" "Yes," they proclaim. "What made the difference?

The difference is you entered into a lifelong agreement. You made a commitment to each other."

Have you ever made a commitment to Jesus? Have you ever received the great gift of His love and salvation? The gift is not hard to open.

Where Are You?

So where are you? That is a good question to ask yourself and those you are discipling. Sometimes I ask a person or group to put an X where they think they are on the bridge. Are they right on the verge of crossing? Are they fully on God's side? Are they not interested at all and content to be on the human side? Are they somewhere in the middle?

Another tool we use sometimes with the bridge illustration is to ask a person if they are in one of these categories: Do you *realize* the gift? Are you in the stage of awareness but you just have not yet accepted the gift? Have you *received* the gift? Do you believe the gospel? Have you *responded* to the gift? Have you taken the steps we described earlier? Do you *remember* the gift? Are you a committed follower of Christ and take time to appreciate and remember all He has done for you? Another category is someone who simply *refuses* the gift. Many people Jesus encountered decided to walk away from the gift He offered them.

Conclusion

My encounter with the young boy with the insightful question is not the only time I made the gift hard to open. Several years ago, I had a wise, older elder in my church who was a retired plumber and pipe fitter. He told me that one of his coworkers, Mr. Montgomery, was in the nursing home and near the end of his life. My friend said, "Steve, let's go visit Mr. Montgomery. I want you to share your faith with him. He is not a Christian, and he is at the end of his life."

We drove together to the nursing home and saw Mr. Montgomery lying in his bed. My friend introduced us, and after some small talk, I said, "Mr. Montgomery, you know that I am a pastor. I would like the opportunity to tell you about Jesus and how to become a

Christian. Would that be okay?" Mr. Montgomery's body was failing, but his mind was still very sharp. He said, "Sure, I would like that." So I began to tell him about Jesus and how Jesus saved us by dying on the cross for our sins. I honestly don't remember everything I said that day, but I do remember saying too many words. I saw a familiar, glossy-eyed look in his eyes. My friend must have seen the look also because he finally broke into the conversation. With crystal clarity he said, "Gene, what Steve is trying to tell you is that he and I are going to heaven, and he wants to know if you want to go with us."

Can it really be that simple? The answer is yes! Jesus did the hard part. He died for you and me. He came as a gift to the world. The packaging was not impressive. The gift was not found in a box; it was found in a manger. The packaging was not balled-up newspaper; it was held in swaddling clothes. But the gift was given with great love. The tag read, "To the world, from God."

Questions for Reflection

Which of the three promises (forgiveness, help, heaven) is the most important to you personally?

In what ways do you need God's help today?

Why do you believe some people struggle with this question: "Am I sure I am a Christian?" Have you ever asked yourself that?

The Bread

Stephen

I am the bread of life. Whoever comes to me will never go hungry, and whoever believes in me will never be thirsty.

—John 6:35

Chapter 16

Bread: A Family Favorite

My family still gets together for Sunday lunch almost every weekend at Mom's house. We can easily have 20 to 30 people on any given Sunday. For my mother, it is a three-day process. She buys groceries and prepares the food on Saturday. On Sunday, she puts together the final touches and sets the table. Monday is clean-up day. I don't take this family tradition for granted. The conversation is interesting and, at times, hilarious. The stories help ground us and remind each generation about our heritage of faith. The food is beautifully prepared and delicious! The main dish is different every weekend. It could be ribs or lasagna or pot roast or fried chicken or pork and sauerkraut. The main dish changes, but one thing remains the same: the bread. The bread is a soft, buttery, melt-in-your-mouth, baked creation of deliciousness. I think I could eat a four-course meal of just bread.

I don't know what manna tasted like, but I do know that it sustained the Israelites for 40 years as they wandered in the desert. The Lord said to Moses, "I will rain down bread from heaven for you" (Exod. 16:4). The people were given specific instructions on gathering the bread. Physically speaking, this bread from heaven sustained and saved them.

A little later, Moses referred back to that miracle and used the bread as an analogy for something much more important.

Be careful to follow every command I am giving you today, so that you may live and increase and may enter and possess the land the LORD promised on oath to your ancestors. Remember how the LORD your God led you all the way in the wilderness these forty years, to humble and test you in order to know what was in your heart, whether or not you would keep his commands. He humbled you, causing you to hunger and then feeding you with manna, which neither you nor your ancestors had known, to teach you that man does not live on bread alone but on every word that comes from the mouth of the LORD.

—Deut. 8:1–3

Physical bread only goes so far. We need spiritual bread—the words of the Lord.

This bread analogy shows up several times in the Bible. The prophet Jeremiah writes, "When your words came, I ate them; they were my joy and my heart's delight" (Jer. 15:16). In the New Testament, Paul tells Timothy that he is "nourished on the truths of the faith" (1 Tim. 4:6). When Jesus fasted for 40 days in the wilderness, the devil came to Him and tempted Him with bread. Jesus quoted the words of Moses from Deuteronomy, "Man shall not live on bread alone, but on every word that comes from the mouth of God" (Matt. 4:4).

Jesus makes it even more personal in John 6:35 when He said, "I am the bread of life. Whoever comes to me will never go hungry, and whoever believes in me will never be thirsty." Just as the Israelites were physically sustained and nourished by the manna from heaven, we are sustained and nourished by the words of the Lord.

The Bible is our primary source for learning and understanding the words of the Lord. It is like bread that is offered to a starving wanderer. It is our spiritual four-course meal.

Chapter 17

Bread Basics: What Is the Bible?

If we are going to eat this spiritual bread, it is good to have a basic understanding of the Bible. The Bible is not just one book. It is a library of 66 books. The Bible is written in three languages: Hebrew, Greek, and Aramaic. It was written on three continents. The Bible was written by about 40 authors over a 1,500-year period of time. That amazes me because the Bible reads like one continuous story even though it was written many times by authors who did not even know one another.

The Bible is not just a piece of literature. It recounts the real interaction between God and His creation. The events recorded in the Bible actually happened. How can a book written by so many people over so many generations that covers so many controversial topics and is based on actual events read like a novel? The only answer that makes sense to me is that God directed the writing and events recounted in His Word.

The Apostle Peter gives us insight into this:

Above all, you must understand that no prophecy of Scripture came about by the prophet's own interpretation of things. For prophecy never had its origin in the human will, but prophets, though human, spoke from God as they were carried along by the Holy Spirit.

—2 Pet. 1:20–21

The authors spoke from God as they were carried along.

I enjoy epic movies with kings, castles, and kingdoms. In those movies, there is often a messenger who travels many miles over rough terrain to deliver a message from the king. His job is to deliver that message just as the king would if the king himself were carrying the message. He is the king's agent. The king may choose to send along a group of knights to protect him. He might notify other kings of his passage. In the same way, the Holy Spirit of God oversaw and protected the writing of scripture.

The Bible is a history book. It records the relationship of God with humans throughout the course of history. The Bible is a book of promises from God. There are more than 3,000 promises that God makes for those who follow Him. The Bible is filled with both challenge and encouragement. It encourages the faithful and challenges the rebellious. The Bible is a story of redemption. It is a love story about God's love for His creation and His deepest desire to reunite with those He loves. The Bible is a personal invitation from God Himself. He invites us into another world so we can experience all He desires for us.

Bread Basics: What Is the Message of the Bible?

Jon Weece, Pastor of Southland Christian Church in Lexington, Kentucky, gave an outline in a sermon a while back. I don't know if the outline was original or not, but it was a beautiful, simple way to understand the message of the Bible. Here is the outline: the Bible is from God, about Jesus, and for our good.*

Paul gave instruction to Timothy that gives us insight into the author and purpose of the Bible.

> But as for you, continue in what you have learned and have become convinced of, because you know those from whom you learned it, and how from infancy you have known the Holy Scriptures, which are able to make you wise for salvation through faith in Christ Jesus. All Scripture is God-

---

*Jon Weece (used by permission).

breathed and is useful for teaching, rebuking, correcting and training in righteousness, so that the servant of God may be thoroughly equipped for every good work.

—2 Tim. 3:14–17

The Bible Is from God

All scripture is God-breathed—that's Paul's way to tell us that the Bible is from God. In His love, God chose to reveal Himself to us. That is the reason we know God. He revealed Himself through creation (Rom. 1:20), through the Holy Spirit (1 Cor. 2:10), and through the coming of Jesus to the world (Col. 1:15). He also revealed Himself through His Word. Paul writes in 1 Thessalonians 2:13, "We also thank God continually because, when you received the word of God, which you heard from us, you accepted it not as a human word, but as it actually is, the word of God, which is indeed at work in you who believe." The Bible is from God.

When I think about the term *God-breathed*, I think about my voice professor at Milligan College. I remember him saying something like this: "Stephen, when you sing, it is all about your breathing. If you want the instrument of your voice to work properly, then you must have proper breathing. As breath passes your vocal chords, a beautiful sound is created." God breathed, and He spoke the most beautiful and meaningful words ever created. God says, "I will raise up for them a prophet like you from among their fellow Israelites, and I will put my words in his mouth. He will tell them everything I command him" (Deut. 18:18). God composed the music. He inspired the song. He wrote the lyrics. He put the words into the mouths of the prophets and apostles.

The Bible Is about Jesus

Paul said that the scripture is "able to make you wise for salvation through faith in Christ Jesus" (2 Tim. 3:15). The Bible is about Jesus. There is an amazing encounter that Jesus had with a couple of His followers. His death had occurred a few days before, and now rumors of His resurrection were circulating. As the two disciples were discussing these events, the resurrected Jesus started to walk with them on the road to Emmaus. The men were kept from recognizing Him.

It is interesting that rather than just revealing Himself right then and there, Jesus decided to show them how the scripture is all about Him. Luke 24:27 records this encounter. "Beginning with Moses and all the Prophets, he explained to them what was said in all the Scriptures concerning himself." I have often wondered what that conversation was like. The walk probably took about two hours. Can you imagine having a two-hour Bible study with the resurrected Jesus? He walked these two men through every section of the Bible and told them how the Messiah can be found through the scriptures.

Dr. Norman Geisler wrote a classic book that was rereleased in 2002. It's called *To Understand the Bible Look for Jesus*. In a chapter called "Christ in Each Book of the Bible," Geisler describes how Jesus is evident through the pages of scripture. Start in Genesis and the books of the Law, and you will discover the foundation for Christ. Here you will see the reasons for a Messiah to come. Move to the books of history, the kings, and the judges, and you will discover the preparation for Christ. He will be a prophet, priest, and king. In the books of poetry—Psalms, Proverbs, Ecclesiastes—the people looked up in aspiration to Christ. The prophets are building the expectation for Christ. They tell the people that the promised Messiah is coming.

In the New Testament, Jesus comes to our world, and the Gospels describe the manifestation of Christ. The Messiah has come. The book of Acts is the evangelization or proclamation of Christ. Jesus has come, and now the world will forever be changed because of His gospel. The epistles are the application of Christ. The letters describe how Christians are to live like Jesus. Revelation is the consummation of Christ, who will return as a victorious and conquering King.[16]

The Bible is all about Jesus. Jesus opened the eyes of these two men who walked with Him on the road to Emmaus by reveal-

---

16. Norman Geisler, *To Understand the Bible Look for Jesus: The Bible Student's Guide to the Bible's Central Theme* (Eugene, OR: Wipf and Stock Publishers, 2002).

ing to them the true message of the entire Bible. In Luke 24:32, they asked each other, "Were not our hearts burning within us while he talked with us on the road and opened the Scriptures to us?" When they understood the central person of the Bible, their hearts burned inside of them. The Bible is not a religious book about rules and regulations. It is not a fictional book filled with once-upon-a-time stories. It is a book about the living Jesus. When you encounter Him in the pages of the Bible and then personally in your life today, everything changes.

The Bible Is for Our Good

Paul tells Timothy that the Bible is for our good. It is written "so that the servant of God may be thoroughly equipped for every good work" (2 Tim. 3:17). The Bible is not a self-help book. It is the actual message of God to the world. It contains very precious promises. It provides warnings on destructive habits to avoid. It convicts and challenges us to right thinking and behavior. The Bible gives direction and advice on hundreds of practical topics.

Even though the Bible was completed generations ago, it is still relevant today. The writer of Hebrews puts it this way: "For the word of God is alive and active. Sharper than any double-edged sword, it penetrates even to dividing soul and spirit, joints and marrow; it judges the thoughts and attitudes of the heart" (Heb. 4:12). The Bible is not an outdated, irrelevant book. It is living and active.

Have you ever been reading the Bible and suddenly feel convicted by something you need to change? Has the Word of God revealed something to you about your character? Have you learned something about God and His character that you did not know before? Have you been listening to a sermon, and as the speaker teaches on a verse in the Bible, your eyes fall on a completely different verse? That verse was not on the speaker's manuscript, but God used it to direct you or correct you. The verse just happened to be exactly what you needed. The Bible is for our good.

The primary purpose of the Bible is to introduce us to the living Word and to give us hope. It is through the Word of God that we learn about what Jesus did, how we can accept His payment on the cross for our sins, and how we can be adopted as children of God. Because of Jesus, we have forgiveness of sins, help in our day-to-day lives, and hope for the future. Paul writes, "For everything that was written in the past was written to teach us, so that through endurance taught in the Scriptures and the encouragement they provide we might have hope" (Rom. 15:4). The Bible encourages us in times of need and gives us hope always.

Art Merkel was a friend of my father and the long-time preacher at the Wilmington Church of Christ in Wilmington, Ohio. After he died, my dad and mom went to his visitation, and Art's wife told them a great story. It seems that Art's heart was giving out, and he went into the hospital. Nothing they could do helped much with his prognosis or with the pain. The doctors told him of a new laser procedure, and Art said, "Let's give it a try." When they started the procedure, Art's heart stopped. They did what they could to revive him, but they couldn't. The doctor came out to talk to the family and ask if they should continue life-saving procedures. Art's wife just asked, "How long has he been gone?" The doctor said, "A few minutes." Art's wife thought for a moment and said, "You know, he's been in heaven then for a few minutes. I sure wouldn't want to take him from there. Let's just leave him there." That is hope. That hope is available to those who hear the Word, receive the Word, and put it into practice. Jesus said, "Everyone who hears these words of mine and puts them into practice is like a wise man who built his house on the rock" (Matt. 7:24).

Bread Basics: Why Would God Choose the Medium of Written Communication?

Much of the Old Testament was delivered orally from generation to generation, but over time, there was a need for the words of God to be written down. The words *written* and *as it is written* occur more than 200 times in scripture. Jesus often used *as it is written* to point back to a prophecy and demonstrate its fulfillment. Luke, the author of Acts, begins his history with these words, "In my former book, Theophilus, I wrote about all that Jesus began to do and to teach" (Acts 1:1). Luke wanted to provide a detailed account of the life of Jesus and the early days of the Church, so he wrote it down. The Law was written for the people of God. The apostles wrote their messages as letters to churches. The angel in Revelation told John to write down what he saw. Why did God want His words recorded? In Romans 15:4, Paul explains why: "For everything that was written in the past was written to teach us, so that through the endurance taught in the Scriptures and the encouragement they provide we might have hope." The written words teach us and give us encouragement.

I think one of the reasons God chose the medium of written communication is because it is enduring. My grandparents—Papaw and Mamaw—both died in 1995. Our family still owns their home. The house looks much like it did more than 20 years ago. In fact, it even has the original green shag carpet from the 1970s. I guess you could call us nostalgic. The last time I visited their home, I found a shoebox of old letters. There were many interesting cards and letters from family and friends in the box, but one letter caught my attention. The letter was written from Papaw to Mamaw in 1942, in the middle of World War II. My mother, his daughter, was only four years old. Papaw was a preacher and had traveled many hours by train to conduct a revival meeting in Atlanta, Georgia. He began by telling about the revival meeting and the many people he had baptized. He ended the letter with travel arrangements and what time he would need to be picked up at the train station. The heart of the letter was filled with very loving and tender words from my grandfather. He said things like, "I miss you, my darling. I can't wait to hold you in my arms again. I miss my girl, Nancy." I felt like I was invading their privacy because his words were so tender.

After I closed the envelope and gently placed the letter back in the box, I thought to myself, "I am so glad that Papaw wrote those words, and I am so grateful that Mamaw saved them." Then I thought, "We sure are missing something these days with all the electronic communication. Messages are here one moment and gone the next." Those words were written more than 70 years ago, but they are just as clear and important as they were in 1942.

God wanted His words recorded so they would endure. The prophet Isaiah wrote, "The grass withers and the flowers fall, but the word of our God endures forever" (Isa. 40:8). The Bible was preserved so all future generations would be able to feast on it for their spiritual nourishment. The author of Psalms tells us that God's words are "more precious than gold...[and] sweeter than honey" (Ps. 19:10). The words in the Bible are sweet, rich, and precious.

Bread Basics: What Is the Difference between the Old Testament Books and the New Testament Books?

This is an important question because I often hear people attempt to disprove the Bible or criticize Christians because of some of the teachings in the Old Testament.

This is how the conversation usually goes:

A critic of the Bible asks, "Do you believe the Bible?"

Christian: "Yes."

Critic: "Do you believe the entire Bible?"

Christian: "Yes, of course."

Critic: "Do you follow the Bible?"

Christian: "Yes."

Critic: "Do you follow the entire Bible?"

Christian: "Yes."

At this point, the critic begins to list a series of teachings from the Old Testament that the Christian no longer follows. Some will even point out the violence of the Old Testament and ignorantly assume that these teachings still apply today.

My friend Steven Donnally helped me understand the difference between the Old and New Testament. He pointed out that in modern language, we are not accustomed to using the word *testament*.[17] One of the few places we use it is in referring to our last will and testament. It is really a legal term. It can be translated as "covenant" or "contract" as we see in Hebrews 9:14–17 (KJV). The Old Testament

---

17. Steven Donnally (used by permission).

is an old contract, and the New Testament is a new contract. With any contract, there are parties to the contract and also terms of the contract.

Who were the parties of the old contract? All the way back in the first book of the Bible, God gave Abraham an offer to enter into a covenant. God said He would provide a fertile land for Abraham and his descendants. We call this the Promised Land. God said that Abraham would have numerous descendants, "as numerous as the stars in the sky and as the sand on the seashore. Your descendants will take possession of the cities of their enemies" (Gen. 22:17). Most importantly, God promised that a Messiah or Savior would come from Abraham's descendants, and the world would be blessed through Him.

There were certain terms and provisions of this old contract. For his part, Abraham was asked to obey the Lord and keep His commandments, ordinances, and instructions (Gen. 26:5). Some of these ordinances and instructions had very specific applications for Abraham and the Israelites. There were instructions on food, relationships, religious feasts, parenting, and even sexuality. Not all these commandments and ordinances carried over into the new contract.

The Old Testament also provides a foundation for understanding the New Testament. It gives us insight into the nature of God. The Law reminds us of our own imperfection and the need for a Savior. The prophecies point us to the Messiah and God's solution to the problem of sin.

The New Testament is God's new contract. The parties of this contract are God and those who decide to accept God's gift of Jesus and His payment for sin on the cross and follow Him as Lord. The New Testament tells us about the life of Jesus and the beginning of the church. It gives us instructions on living as children of God and being part of His Kingdom. It tells us what will happen in the future when Christ returns for His bride. It describes the beauty of heaven and life everlasting.

There are some laws and principles from the old contract that still apply to us today as part of the new contract. How do we know if we are to follow an Old Testament scripture or if it only applied to the Israelites? There are two ways. First, did Jesus or the apostles affirm the teaching and therefore carry it into the new contract? In the Sermon on the Mount, Jesus reminded His followers about the command to not murder. He reaffirmed that command and even made it more specific by saying, "Do not be angry with your brother" (Matt. 5:22). Jesus reaffirmed the command so it carried over into the new contract. Second, is it a universal principle? There are simply some promises and principles that are universal. "Honor your father and mother" is not just a good idea, it is commanded by God and reaffirmed in the New Testament (Eph. 6:2).

Questions for Reflection

What is your favorite part of a good meal?

Why is bread a good analogy for our need for the Word?

Why is it good to eat the bread (the Bible) regularly?

Do you keep old letters? Do you have a letter that is especially important to you? Why?

Do we treasure the Bible as much as these personal letters? Why? Why not? How can you value it more?

How has the Bible been good for you personally?

Read the Bible verses about how God revealed Himself to us (Rom. 1:20, 1 Cor. 2:10, Col. 1:15). Where do you see God in creation, in the Holy Spirit, and in the life of Jesus?

Chapter 18

The Spiritual Wellness Tool:
A Balanced Diet

We are bombarded with information today on a proper diet. There are diets that focus on eating less carbohydrates but consuming as much protein and fats as desired. On the other hand, there are diets that encourage high carbohydrate intake. There are diets that look for nutritional balance among carbohydrates, proteins, and fats. Are you confused yet? There are diets that want you to limit your calories. There are other diets that encourage you to eat as much as you want from a list of nutrient-dense foods, including bacon. This is my personal favorite. Any diet that includes bacon is worth pursuing.

Honestly, I have tried all these approaches at one time or another. My own experience has led me to a personal belief that a balanced diet is the best. I am at my best when I find a healthy balance between appropriate levels of consumption and movement. What is true for the physical body is even more needed when it comes to our spiritual health.

Jesus addressed this balanced approach:

Therefore everyone who hears these words of mine and puts them into practice is like a wise man who built his house on the rock. The rain came down, the streams rose, and the winds blew and beat against that house; yet it did not fall, because it had its foundation on the rock. But everyone who hears these words of mine and does not put them into

practice is like a foolish man who built his house on sand. The rain came down, the streams rose, and the winds blew and beat against that house, and it fell with a great crash.
—Matt. 7:24–27

On the one hand, Jesus addresses those who hear the words but do not put them into practice. These are takers. They hear the words. They take them in, but they do not practice them. There is consumption but no movement. James said something similar in James 2:17. "Faith by itself, if it is not accompanied by action, is dead."

Just prior to these words, Jesus described another group of people.

Many will say to me on that day, "Lord, Lord, did we not prophesy in your name and in your name drive out demons and in your name perform many miracles?" Then I will tell them plainly, "I never knew you. Away from me, you evildoers!"
—Matt. 7:22–23

Here Jesus talks about those who did things for Him but did not actually have a relationship with Him. They did not know Him. There was movement but no desire to sit at the table with Jesus and consume knowledge and enjoy a relationship. We illustrate that in a tool we call the Spiritual Wellness Tool.

Two Ends of the Spectrum: Starvation and Stagnation

On one side of the spectrum, we see *starvation*. This is the extreme example of someone who receives no spiritual nourishment. They are not eating the words of God. They are not taking in worship. They are not filling themselves with spiritual truth. It includes both those who have no relationship with God and, at times, those who did have a relationship with God but moved away from the table. That can happen gradually. There is a lack of consistent consumption. It can even include men or women in ministry who find themselves serving but not eating the bread regularly. They are giving away, but they are not refilling. They are running on empty.

On the other side of the spectrum, we see *stagnation*. This is the other extreme where someone is filled to the brim. They have eaten so much that they are now immobile. They never leave the table. These are the men and women who eat often. They know their Bible. They can argue doctrine with the best of them. They might attend every event the church hosts. They are consumers. They can't get enough knowledge, but they are completely inactive. They consume, but they don't move. Paul addressed this when he wrote, "Knowledge puffs up while love builds up" (1 Cor. 8:1). Don't get me wrong. Knowledge is wonderful. Truth matters. But hearing the words is only part of what makes you spiritually healthy.

Both of these extremes are deadly. Spiritual starvation ends in a lack of spiritual nourishment. Spiritual stagnation ends in a lack of spiritual movement. They are both deadly spiritual conditions. When I work without nourishment, I become weak and ineffective. When I eat but never work, I become lethargic and needy. When I eat and work, I am balanced, fit, and ready to be deployed.

The Goal: Spiritual Health and Satisfaction

The pinnacle of spiritual health is when someone maintains a good balance of hearing and doing. That person hears the words of Jesus and puts them into practice. It is what we call *spiritual satisfaction.* The person who is spiritually satisfied is someone who enjoys the fellowship and nourishment from the table but also slides the chair back, gets up, and goes to work. Satisfaction comes when I am both learning from the Lord and working for the Lord. Health happens when I am filled, poured out, and refilled.

Pathways to the Peak: Habits

If you are on the stagnation end of the spectrum, then begin to move. Start to exercise your spiritual muscles. You have allowed atrophy for too long. Begin to develop the spiritual habits and disciplines that will reignite your spiritual wellness.

Believe me, I do not always enjoy going to the gym. Left to my own devices, I would rather sit on the sofa, eat sour punch straws, drink ginger ale, and watch *Family Feud*. I need a routine. I need a schedule. I need people to keep me accountable. Inevitably, when I leave the gym, I am exhausted, but I am also refreshed and stronger than when I entered.

Health comes from developing good habits. Do something for others. Join a church. Worship. Find a purpose. Say positive things. Refrain from being critical of yourself and others. Be a team player. Give an anonymous gift. Say yes to opportunities. Be the first to volunteer. Do something. Develop a routine that will help you run as far as you can from stagnation.

Pathways to the Peak: Hunger

If you find yourself on the starvation end of the spectrum, then begin to eat again. You don't need to be in a hurry. It doesn't need to be a big meal at first. Just start eating again. Sometimes just taking a bite will create a new hunger.

Consider the young child who proclaims, "I'm not hungry!" The wise parent does not force the child to eat but requires her to sit at the table. Watching others eat begins to create a hunger. Finally, the parent says, "Just try a bite." Suddenly, something is awakened in the child. One bite leads to the next. She rediscovers a hunger she did not know existed.

If you are spiritually starving, then simply take a bite again of spiritual bread. "Taste and see that the LORD is good" (Ps. 34:8). Download a Bible app and read the verse of the day. Open the Psalms and recite one of the heartfelt prayers of David. Jesus said that those who hunger and thirst for righteousness will be filled (Matt. 5:6). We have developed an acronym—EAT—that we hope will be a lifelong model for you as you hunger for spiritual bread.

Chapter 19

A Plan That Works: EAT

I heard a sermon some years ago that was very convicting. I don't remember the speaker, but I do remember the statements he made.

He told us to turn to our neighbor and tell them our favorite main course for a meal. The crowd responded with a lot of enthusiasm as they said things such as pizza, steak, and fried chicken. Then he told us to turn to our neighbor and tell them our favorite scripture—book, chapter, and verse—not including John 3:16 or "Jesus wept." The crowd was a bit quieter, but about half of us were able to come up with some response to his question. Then he said to turn to our neighbor and tell them our favorite dessert. Again, there was a great amount of chatter as people yelled out ice cream, cheesecake, chocolate cake, and apple pie. Now turn to your neighbor, he told us, and quote them your favorite scripture. And he reminded us that "God helps those who help themselves" and "Cleanliness is next to godliness" are not in the Bible. At that point, the crowd started to catch on. Maybe a quarter of the crowd was able to mumble out some response. The speaker continued and told us to turn to our neighbor and tell them our least favorite food. Almost everyone had an answer. There were many votes for liver and onions. A few people yelled out sushi and anything green. The speaker made one final request. He said to turn to our neighbor and tell them the scripture verse we read recently that we struggled with the most. The room was almost completely silent.

Why is it so much easier for us to focus on physical food than it is for us to think about spiritual food? What is more important? What has eternal benefits? Paul once wrote, "Physical training is good, but training for godliness is much better, promising benefits in this life and in the life to come" (1 Tim. 4:8 NLT). Job said, "I have not departed from the commandment of his lips; I have treasured the words of his mouth more than my portion of food" (Job 23:12 ESV). The question is this: Do we?

My guess is that most of us would say we do value the bread of the Word of God more than physical bread. Most of us believe Deuteronomy 8:3: "Man does not live on bread alone but on every word that comes from the mouth of the LORD." The challenge is that most of us do not consume the spiritual bread with the same consistency that we do physical bread. Why do you think that is?

I think most of us do not read the Bible regularly because we are busy. We find it difficult to carve out the time to read and study scripture. Our schedules are full, and the demands on our time are great. While that is true, most of us find time to eat more than once every day. We do not think twice about spending 30 minutes to an hour for lunch at work or sharing a family meal in the evening. The truth is that we make time for what we value. Consistency follows priority. If something is a priority, you do it consistently.

Some might say they do not read the Bible because it is too hard to understand. They have become convinced that the message of the Bible is just too difficult to understand, so they avoid it altogether. Whenever someone says that to me, I just randomly pick out a teaching like this from the Apostle Paul: "Serve wholeheartedly, as if you were serving the Lord, not people" (Eph. 6:7). I want the person to understand that many of the verses in the Bible are actually pretty straightforward. Other times, I read a story from the Gospels where Jesus healed someone or showed love in some way. The stories in the Gospels and many of the teachings of Jesus are surprisingly not difficult to understand, even for someone new to the Bible. Admittedly, there are difficult and confusing portions of the Bible, but too often, we allow our fear to keep us from consistently eating the Word.

EAT

EXAMINE - APPLY - TALK

E: Examine

When we examine the scriptures, we look at what the verses are actually saying. What is the context of the story?

Have you ever walked into a movie late? You mistimed how long the previews would run and showed up about 10 minutes after the movie started. The plot of the story has already been established. The characters have already been introduced. You find yourself trying to play catch-up. You are left with a decision: Do I break movie protocol and talk to the stranger seated near me? Do I google the movie and risk reading too much and having the movie spoiled for me? Do I just stay quiet and simply hope that I will figure it out?

Reading the Bible in context is similar to seeing the movie from the beginning. Rather than only seeing part of the picture, you are zooming out so you can more fully understand the story. Reading the Bible in context means that we ask questions about the verses we are reading.

- *Who* wrote it?
- *When* did they write it?
- *Why* were they writing?
- *Who* were they writing to?
- *What* were they trying to say?

The good news is that you do not have to do all the research on your own, and excellent resources are available to help you understand the context. Study Bibles provide additional commentary on each page of the Bible so you can better understand what it means. There are commentaries written by scholars who provide the context and meaning of the verses and thousands of online resources that do the same thing. I personally like biblegateway.com and biblestudytools.com. Once you examine the scriptures and ask the context questions, you then move to the next concept in the EAT tool—Apply.

A: Apply

When you apply the Bible, you are asking this: How can I apply it to my life? What action steps will I take? What is the Bible saying to me? Application is key.

I started doing CrossFit in 2013. The "box" (CrossFit terminology for the space you use for your gym) I go to is actually attached to the building we rent for Axis Church. Originally, I started going to simply build relationships with people who may not have a relationship with God. I was working out there with a few friends from Axis Church, including Josh and T. J. Within a few months, the owner came to us and said he was going to shut down his box and move farther south. Little did I realize the impact of that decision. Josh and T. J. came to me and said, "Let's start our own CrossFit gym. We don't want to lose our relationships with this community." We did. Within two months, we had our affiliate license and opened CrossFit Mason. It wasn't very long before I was immersed in the world of functional fitness.

One of the goals of CrossFit is to learn proper movement to make a positive impact on every facet of your life. Everyone needs to know how to properly lift objects or move in the strongest, most stable way possible. That applies to everyone. We have several clients who are in their 50s and others in their teens. We have a client who has MS and walks with a cane, and we have others who win competitions.

When we started the gym, I knew very little about functional fitness. I would work out occasionally, but I certainly was a novice when it came to movement. Years later, I can say my knowledge base has grown significantly. I recently went through CrossFit Level 2 certification. One of the principles I learned at that training was that your athletes are watching you. If your movement is bad, then their movement will be bad. You have to personally apply the principles you teach. It is one thing to know something, but it is better to know and apply. I can read every training manual and watch every online video about movement standards, but if I don't apply the principles, then what good do they do? I need to apply what I know.

When it comes to the Bible, there are training seminars, educational opportunities, online resources, and Bible classes aplenty. The question is this: Are you applying what you know? The Bible says:

Do not merely listen to the word, and so deceive yourselves. Do what it says. Anyone who listens to the word but does not do what it says is like someone who looks at his face in a mirror and, after looking at himself, goes away and immediately forgets what he looks like."

—James 1:22–24

It is not enough to examine the scriptures and forget to apply what you learn.

Read every verse with these questions in mind: What is God saying to me? What will I do about what I just read? Examine the Bible in context, and then apply what you read to your life. I do not know who originally wrote these questions, but they have been helpful to me as I study the scriptures.

- Is there a sin exposed that I need to repent of?
- Is there a command given I need to obey?
- Is there a promise made I need to hold on to?
- Is there a truth revealed that I need to believe instead of some lie I have been believing?

Use these questions or create your own. Then, after you apply the scriptures, talk about what you learned.

T: Talk

Talk to God, and talk to others. Talk to God. Pray about what you read. Ask God to help you understand the verses. Pray that you will have wisdom as you read. Pray that you will have the strength to actually follow the principles you learned.

Talk to other people. It is helpful when you state something out loud. There is commitment in words we speak to another person. It keeps me accountable when I read Ephesians 4:29 about unwholesome talk and I admit to a friend, "I was critical today. I need to season my words with love. Can you ask me about that next time I see you?" The essence of discipleship is helping one another become more like Jesus by applying His Word.

It is life-changing, for example, when I verbalize the principles of Ephesians 4:32 about being kind, compassionate, and forgiving. I read and examine the verse. I ask, "What is the verse saying to me?" I am convicted that I need to let go of an old grudge. This is application. Then I talk to God, admit my struggle, and ask for strength to take the next steps with the person who wounded me. I talk to a friend and seek their advice, counsel, and prayers. This is the EAT tool in action. I believe when you follow and embrace this little tool, you will discover what Paul told Timothy: "[You are] nourished on the truths of the faith and of the good teaching that you have followed" (1 Tim. 4:6).

Questions for Reflection

In your life, what is keeping you from reading the Word of God more?

Look at the spiritual wellness tool. Where are you now? What do you need to do today to move toward the peak of health?

What's your spiritual meal plan? What is your personal plan for EATing?

How will you feed your family? How will you provide food for those you lead?

Is there anything God is telling you right now?

The Stone

Josh

Let any one of you who is without sin

be the first to throw a stone at her.

—John 8:7

Chapter 20

Drop the Stones

One of our family's favorite pastimes is rock-throwing. With a house full of boys, there is nothing like a night at our favorite spot, the Little Miami River. Our kids could easily throw rocks for hours. I'm not exaggerating. My kids can't do much of anything longer than five minutes, but rock-throwing is the exception. Truth is, I'm just as entertained as they are skipping rocks and tossing rocks out into the water. Jess doesn't get it, but she has accepted this as part of being in a house of all boys. Every now and again, she will join in on the fun.

There is an acute danger involved in gathering on a crowded bank with a couple kids who have rocks in their hands. They don't have the best aim or the keenest awareness of who's around them. Needless to say, there have been a few casualties during our rock-throwing excursions. I have been on the wrong side of one of those rocks. Getting whipped in the side of the face with a side-armed rock is not my favorite thing. Whether I was the intended target was irrelevant. Nobody likes getting hit with rocks.

In Jesus's day, rocks were used as a form of punishment. There was this cruel practice known as "stoning." It was a fate that many who broke the laws of the day were forced to face. One day when Jesus was teaching in the Temple courts, the religious leaders brought a woman before Him who had been caught in the act of adultery. She was a notorious sinner. Adultery was a high crime, and according to the Old Testament Law, authorities had every right to stone her to death. They presented Jesus with her crime as a way to trap Him. If He ignored the Old Testament Law, they would say He has no regard for the Law. If He allowed them to stone her, it would seem to contradict His constant teaching on mercy for sinners. As the tension continued to build, Jesus knelt down and wrote something in the dirt. We don't know what He wrote. Maybe He was taking a breath, knowing their ill intentions. Then, in one line, Jesus once again reset the paradigm, leaving them no room for rebuttal: "You who is without sin be the first to throw a stone at her" (John 8:7).

His response must have absolutely stunned them. His point definitely landed because one by one, they dropped their stones and walked away.

I would be lying if I didn't acknowledge that every time I read that I do a little internal dance and chant in my head, "Go Jesus, go Jesus, go Jesus!" Then I remember. It applies to me, too. I have no right to throw stones, either. This message wasn't just for the religious leaders. It's a message for you and me. The only person who has the right to hold and throw stones is the person who has lived perfectly up to this point. Does that describe any of you? Then it's time to let go of the stones you are holding so you can follow the example of Jesus.

Relational stones come in lots of different shapes and sizes. I know I've been guilty of carrying some of them around from time to time, and the danger is that they keep us from truly grabbing hold of the way of love that Jesus lays out for us. Stones vary in weight and potential for damage, but here are a few of the most common stones we hold.

For each of these, we will look at the stone and then what it will require for us to drop that stone. Each of them could have a chapter of their own, but let's just take a quick look. This is not meant to oversimplify complex issues but to get us thinking about the process of living relationally, unencumbered.

Superiority and Self-Righteousness

The stone of superiority and self-righteousness can be the hardest one to detect. It is most potent in the lives of those who hold high expectations for themselves and, by extension, those around them. It is a stone that can be held with good intentions. If you find yourself looking down on others, it's possible you are holding stones of this sort. This is the parent who never sees what his or her kid does as good enough. It's the spouse who is never satisfied, no matter what efforts are made. Those who are difficult to please are apt to hold this stone. It's driven by a preoccupation with things being fair and the rules being followed. If you find that other people's behavior frequently gets under your skin, if you easily and frequently spot the faults in others yet rarely see your own, you might be holding on to the stones of superiority and self-righteousness.

How do I drop it?

The relational remedy here is humility. To drop this relational stone, we have to come to grips with our own imperfection. Rather than comparing ourselves to what we perceive as the unrighteousness of others, we should compare ourselves to the righteousness of Jesus. If you want to do a more accurate self-assessment, put your sin list up against the sinless Jesus.

He is the one who tells us in Matthew 23:12, "For those who exalt themselves will be humbled, and those who humble themselves will be exalted." Paul echoes Jesus's sentiment when he writes in Ephesians 4:2, "Be completely humble and gentle; be patient, bearing with one another in love."

The more aware we are of our own guilt and need for grace, the more likely we are to extend it to others. The more we realize we need forgiveness, the easier it is to let others experience the same gift. Healthy relationships among imperfect people require us to bear with one another out of mercy.

Bitterness and Blame

Another stone comes in the form of bitterness and blame. This is a stone we often carry when we have been or are being wounded by someone else. Some of us have some deep scars that have been inflicted on us due to no fault of our own. If you are reading this and have been wounded in some way, I'm genuinely sorry, and you should take heart in knowing God has not turned a blind eye. You need to know that God sees your pain and wants to bring healing to your hurt. I know that is something that is far easier for me to write than for you to fully experience. Healing is certainly a process that must be blanketed in prayer and God's provision.

The unfortunate side effect of being wounded is that we not only carry the initial wound but we carry the weight of our own bitterness and blame. Sometimes this forms a desire in us for revenge or payback. It may be the only thing you can think of to right a wrong that has been done to you. What you may have already realized is that the old saying "Time heals all wounds" isn't necessarily true. Time can help or hurt depending on how we deal with it. Time also has the power to intensify wounds if we let it. Forgiveness means refusing to keep carrying bitterness around and letting it control you. Forgiveness is handing your pain over to God who knows you and sees what you have been through. Forgiveness is entrusting Him to be the One who administers justice so we don't have to.

How do I drop it?

We do as the Lord commanded us to do, not just for the person who wounded us but out of obedience to Jesus. They may not deserve forgiveness, but forgiving as the Lord forgave us means that with God's help, we carry out the seemingly impossible task of letting go and moving on.

Maybe your objection to forgiveness rests in the belief that forgiving someone takes two people. Perhaps your fear in letting go is that the other person won't respond well. Forgiveness doesn't take two; forgiveness takes you. Romans 12:17–21 is very instructive on this:

> Do not repay anyone evil for evil. Be careful to do what is right in the eyes of everyone. If it is possible, as far as it depends on you, live at peace with everyone. Do not take revenge, my dear friends, but leave room for God's wrath, for it is written: "It is mine to avenge; I will repay," says the Lord. On the contrary: "If your enemy is hungry, feed him; if

*he is thirsty, give him something to drink. In doing this, you
will heap burning coals on his head." Do not be overcome by
evil, but overcome evil with good.*

Forgiveness is making a decision to break the cycle of wrongdoing
and living wounded, by doing good instead of evil. It may or may
not result in reconciliation. We can't control how someone else
responds, only how we respond. The best place for our bitterness
and blame is in God's hands.

Prejudice and Prejudgment

Most of us at some point or another pick up a few stones of prejudice and prejudgment, probably without even noticing. Our past,
upbringing, and unique experiences have a way of shaping our
perception of the world and the way we see others. Most of these
preconceived notions we hold are not rooted in evil but are simply
a product of our limited perspectives.

In Jesus's day, there were a lot of people groups, social classes,
and distinct backgrounds. There were a lot of preconceived notions
that, just like today, formed barriers. There were groups of people
who simply didn't associate with one another. There were people who
were viewed as sinful and unclean simply because of some affliction they had, like leprosy. Many were outcasts and forced to the
fringes of society. Jesus was viewed as radical in His day because He
kept taking a sledgehammer to every social barrier that had been
erected. He sat down and ate with sinners. He touched the unclean.
He didn't just tiptoe around class and cultural lines; He jumped right
over them. He showed us that the gospel builds bridges, not barriers.
The gospel doesn't presuppose or assume or make prejudgments.
The gospel, like Jesus, moves in closer to people every chance it gets.

How do I drop this stone?

Brené Brown, a leader in the area of human relationships, writes,
"People are hard to hate close-up. Move in."[18]

_____

18. Brené Brown, *Braving the Wilderness: The Quest for True Belonging and the
Courage to Stand Alone* (New York: Random House Books, 2017), 63.

This is the way forward in this category. If we want to drop our prejudices and prejudgments, we must do something uncomfortable: get to know people who are different than us. Misunderstanding one another will perpetuate cycles of hate and apathy toward one another. Instead, if we follow Jesus's lead and lean into the lives of others, we will have a clearer view of who they truly are.

If we do what we are told in James 1:19, *"Be quick to listen, slow to speak,"* we will be able to see others the way God sees them and love others the way God loves them. We will have more conversations. We started a coffeehouse in our city because we thought, "What brings people together for good conversation like a good cup of coffee?" I've started a little something personally called "open table Tuesday." I'll admit that many days it could be called empty table Tuesday. But the idea is that every Tuesday morning, the table is open. It's all in an effort to learn more about the people in our local context. If you are ever free on Tuesday, come and pull up a chair. I'm trying to widen my perspective little by little so I can make sure I'm not carrying around any unnecessary prejudices and prejudgments. Nothing builds your listening skills and breaks down barriers quite like hearing someone's story face-to-face. It may be a bit unnatural at first, but listening is the best place we can start.

Grudges and Grievances

Back in my day (okay, I'm only 33, probably too soon to use that phrase), we used to say we had "a beef" with someone. A beef could begin with someone trash-talking behind your back, trying to move in on your girlfriend, or doing something to disrespect you. A beef could also result from something you fundamentally disagreed on. I had a few friendships that ended because of one beef or another.

I want to think that I've matured since those days. Certainly the issues that cause concern are less petty, but the tendency to hold grudges seems to be a common struggle for many of us. Sometimes we don't even remember the root of said beef. Often, it is the result of two different opinions or views on who's right. Something I've learned about grudges is that unchecked, grudges grow. Something small has a way of getting larger and larger if we let it.

How do I drop it?

Paul once had a beef with Peter: "When Cephas came to Antioch, I opposed him to his face, because he stood condemned" (Gal. 2:11).

That may sound harsh, but it's actually a much healthier relational approach than what we tend to do. Rather than opposing others to their face, we tend to oppose them behind their backs or oppose them in our head. Sometimes, we oppose them in a passive-aggressive social media post. The biblical manner of response is to go to that person and have a face-to-face. We need to see confrontation as a natural part of biblical relationships. Matthew 19 lays out a great pattern to deal with conflict. It begins by going first to the person you have a beef with.

Paul summarizes our response well to the Colossians.

> *Bear with each other and forgive one another if any of you has a grievance against someone. Forgive as the Lord forgave you. And over all these virtues put on love, which binds them all together in perfect unity.*
>
> —Col. 3:13–14

Drop the Stones

It's time to part ways with the stones we carry. It's not just a suggestion if we want to live the way Jesus did. It's imperative.

When Jesus's disciples asked Him how many times they should forgive someone, His response was not just seven times but 70 times seven. In other words, never stop forgiving. Never stop dropping those stones.

The stones we hold on to will hold on to us. They will keep us from living free and unencumbered. And if our hands are holding stones, we won't be able to grab hold of what God actually wants us to hold and hand out—His love.

Questions for Reflection

What other relational stones might we be tempted to hold?
Which stone are you most likely to grip on to?
What will it take to release that stone?
Pray for God's help. Will you seek to release the stones you are holding?

Chapter 21

Take Up Love

Let's look some more at John 8. Jesus has just given a strong dose of self-realization to a crowd of self-righteous stone-throwers. Their desire was to condemn a woman in her sin and trap Jesus in the process. Jesus never disappoints, and with one line, He dismantles the crowd—he who is without sin "be the first to throw a stone at her" (John 8:7). His point couldn't be missed in that moment. Whoever is perfect gets the first throw. One by one they walked away until it was just Jesus and the woman. We can only imagine the shame and embarrassment the woman was shouldering at that moment. She was guilty. She stood condemned. She had been singled out and publically humiliated, and her fate was unsure. It was in that moment that she stared into the face of pure love, just when she needed it most. Instead of the condemnation she deserved and expected, she received something else: compassion.

Jesus, now down on her level, coming to her defense, asked the question He already knew the answer to. He asked where her accusers were. Maybe she hadn't yet realized the angry mob was gone. Then, with two more well-placed lines, He demonstrated the full measure of His love. Jesus, the one person in the crowd who could have thrown a stone, does not. Instead, He tells her, "Neither do I condemn you.... Go now and leave your life of sin" (John 8:11).

There are two essential components of God's immense love, and they represent what we call the Grace and Truth Tool.

GRACE + TRUTH = LOVE

Grace: "Neither do I condemn you."
Truth: "Now go and leave your life of sin."

Grace: There Is No Sweeter Sound

Can you imagine how sweet the words of mercy must have sounded to this guilty, disgraced woman?

What a refreshing sound grace is in a world that is full of the opposite. Shame and blame run rampant in our modern society. Our culture seems to delight in seeing people get what's coming to them. We eat up stories of scandal and corruption in our news feed. News sources constantly publish these stories. We willingly step right into the cycle, picking up stones of our own, becoming outraged when someone does something wrong. We shake our heads and talk about them to others. We stand armed with self-righteousness. What we forget is that we, too, were once deserving of condemnation. We, too, were that woman at one time or another.

Remembering this should trigger a different sentiment within us. Rather than being eager to condemn, we should be eager to extend the same compassion God has extended to us. Rather than giving people what they deserve, we should be eager to dispense grace.

First Corinthians 13 is often known as the love chapter. Maybe you've heard it read at a wedding. It's actually more descriptive of God's love, not our love. Our love usually has strings attached; God's doesn't. When God lives in us, we possess a different kind of love. It's called *agape* love, which means unconditional love. It's love that is soaked in grace.

First Corinthians 13 tells us that truth that lacks love and grace is just a whole lot of noise:

> If I speak in the tongues of men or of angels, but do not
> have love, I am only a resounding gong or a clanging

cymbal. If I have the gift of prophecy and can fathom all mysteries and all knowledge, and if I have a faith that can move mountains, but do not have love, I am nothing. If I give all I possess to the poor and give over my body to hardship that I may boast, but do not have love, I gain nothing.

—1 Cor. 13:1–3

There is no shortage of noise in my house. Most of it is completely unnecessary. One of my least favorite things is toys that make noise. If you have young kids, the last thing you need help doing is creating additional noise. My friends and family who don't have kids think it's funny to buy the most obnoxious toys they can find. Little do they know that their kids are getting drum sets and air horns for Christmas one day. As someone who gets very easily overstimulated, I have developed selective hearing to cope with the noise. That has created a problem for me because now I don't hear things I need to hear. I just slip off into my happy place until my wife has said my name for about the fifth time.

That is the unfortunate effect of all truth and no grace. Paul says we can have all the wisdom in the world, but if we don't lead with love, we might as well be the teacher on Charlie Brown, because nobody is listening. One of the ways I challenge those on our team and in our church is by saying that we need to be careful how we use our voice or we will eventually lose our voice.

God has given us a voice in our generation and with the people in our lives, but if we fail to approach them with a posture of grace and mercy, we will lose their attention over time. They will inevitably develop selective hearing, and who can blame them with all that noise?

So rather than being a resounding gong, may we be a sweet sound in the ears of a generation desperate for God's love. May we follow the example of Jesus who says, "Neither do I condemn you" (John 8:11).

When we express His love in the form of grace, it is like music to God's ears, and there is no sweeter sound. There is nothing quite like compassion where condemnation once stood. Like the old hymn says, "Amazing Grace! How sweet the sound that saved a wretch like me!"[19]

When we have been on the receiving end of the sweet sound of grace, it is our job to keep the song going as we encounter others, especially those who stand condemned.

Truth: There Is No Greater Freedom

If we are following Jesus's example, we also have to remember that He doesn't sidestep the truth. While He withholds condemnation by getting down on the same level as a sinful woman, He also speaks truth into her life, which leads to greater freedom.

There is a common misunderstanding today that truth is somehow oppressive. I think the truth can often be presented in an oppressive way that lacks grace. Truth, in the way Jesus gives it, is anything but oppressive. In fact, it's quite the opposite. It's a route to greater freedom and fullness of life. There is an all-too-familiar line of thinking today that teaches us to reject truth. We believe nobody else should be able to tell us what to do with our lives.

However, if we truly love someone, we want what's best for them. Withholding information that is going to help people we love live healthier and become all that God created them to be is cruel and unloving.

If you have children, you understand that there are certain limits and boundaries you set, not simply for the sake of restricting them but because you want to protect them. I don't want my kid playing in the middle of a busy street. I don't want them to eat only candy. I don't let them play with my power saw. Why? Because I love them, and I don't want anything bad to happen to them.

---

19. John Newton, "Amazing Grace," *Amazing Grace*, http://www.hymntime.com/tch/htm/a/m/a/amazing_grace.htm.

One of the most misused scriptures is when Jesus said, "Do not judge, and you will not be judged. Do not condemn, and you will not be condemned. Forgive, and you will be forgiven" (Luke 6:37).

Jesus uses an illustration about pulling specks out of other people's eyes when we have a giant two-by-four in our own eye. Of course, this is ridiculous, and that is Jesus's point. His point is not that we should never help one another or challenge one another or speak truth to one another. The part we forget to quote is the part where He says to first take the plank out of your own eye, and then you will be able to see clearly to help your brother or sister with their speck issue.

Not judging doesn't mean we refuse to help one another or withhold truth. It means we are tending to ourselves as well. We are acknowledging we have things that need addressing in our own lives and are taking care of those things so we can speak from a place of wisdom, clarity, and credibility.

When I'm coaching people at the gym and I see someone lifting in a way that could be harmful or inefficient, my role is to help them move in a better, safer way. I might tell someone, "Don't round out your back when you're lifting from the floor" because I don't want them to hurt themselves. I might give someone a tip that helps them improve a movement. It's all in an effort to help them be the best athlete they can be. I have never once had somebody say, "Don't judge me!" when I've corrected their form or offered advice. The reason is because they know I'm there to make them better. It's because I love that I speak truth.

Truth is freedom. We should welcome it, especially when it comes from someone who loves us. We should also speak truth into one another's lives out of love because we don't want people getting trapped in sin or destructive patterns. We don't want to see any harm come to those we love. We want the best for those around us. The Bible tells us to "consider how we may spur one another on toward love and good deeds" (Heb. 10:24).

Truth helps people progress. Where there is no truth, there is no love. If we truly love people, may we gracefully and truthfully guide people into greater freedom.

Grace + Truth = True Love

I believe there are two kinds of people when it comes to cooking. There are those who follow the recipe and those who freestyle. This is not official culinary theory, just my own observation. I fall in the freestyle category, and my wife is more of a recipe follower. The downside to my approach is that sometimes things come out tasting wonderful, and sometimes they are barely palatable. Jess's recipes, on the other hand, have been perfected and have just the right amount of everything.

God has given us the perfect recipe for love—a love that was perfected in the person of Jesus. It's our responsibility to follow His recipe so others might delight in His love. God's recipe for love has two essential ingredients: grace and truth. Anything less is not love at all.

That is why Jesus responds to the woman in John 8 in two ways:

I don't condemn you – grace

Now go and leave your life of sin – truth

Grace and truth are the substance of true love. It's not either/ or It's both/and.

Jesus doesn't condemn the woman, even though He is the one person who has the right to do so. He waives this right, giving her the opposite of what she deserves. He loves her in spite of her sin, yet He also doesn't ignore her sin. He challenges her to leave it behind. He loves her enough to show her who she could be. He doesn't leave her in bondage. He illuminates the path to freedom through repentance.

It is this recipe of true love that people are craving, whether they recognize it or not. We live in a world desperate for true love, a perfect blend of grace and truth—the love perfectly balanced in the person of Jesus. And Jesus wasn't part grace and part truth. He was overflowing with both.

I know I've missed my fair share of opportunities to represent God's love. My humanity has a way of taking over sometimes. I remember one day I ended up randomly working on my sermon at a coffee shop in a different part of town. I'd never been there and haven't been there since, but I believe I was supposed to be there that day. Typical Josh would have walked in, put on his headphones, and drowned out everything around me. For some reason, I had forgotten my headphones on that particular day. Behind me was a group of local students meeting with a teacher for a study group. I'm not sure what the class was, but it wasn't long before I detected a certain hostility in the group toward faith.

They were discussing Karl Marx and other opponents of faith. Typical Josh would have informed them on areas in which they were misinformed. I had to reach underneath and grab my chair multiple times to keep myself from spinning around. I was fully armed with a heavy dose of truth, but something kept me from serving it up. As the conversation continued, I started to learn more about their individual stories. The teacher had been in a relationship with a Christian who had become controlling and even abusive. Some of the students had been in families where narrow-minded and overprotective parents had used the Bible as a weapon to beat them over the head. Had I spun around in my chair, I would have simply reinforced everything they already believed about God. Instead, I felt God prompting me to do something different. Buy them baked goods. It felt strange to me, but I got up, bought a hefty portion of baked goods from the counter, walked over, and started handing them out. Then the words I wasn't even sure I said came out of my mouth: "Sounds like you've had some bad experiences with Christians. I wanted to make sure you had at least one good one."

It's taken me a while to figure it out, but a little love goes a long way.

It may feel unnatural to you at first, but love is worth living out, not just in our words but in our actions. Maybe it's actually harder than we make it. Perhaps it could be as easy as pie (or any other baked goods for that matter), as long as the ingredients are grace and truth.

Questions for Reflection

What would a world, a church, a family, a friendship with all grace and no truth look like?

What would a world, a church, a family, a friendship with all truth and no grace look like?

Which do you tend to favor in your relationships?

How are you at receiving grace?

How are you at receiving truth?

How are you at extending grace?

How are you at speaking truth?

Chapter 22

Join Together

I remember a segment on the *Planet Earth* channel that sent shivers down my spine. The last creature I would want to encounter in the wilderness is a snake. It's not easy for me to admit it, but if I see a snake in the wild, my natural instinct is to run, regardless of the actual level of danger. My reactions to a king cobra and a garter snake are roughly the same. That's why this segment on *Planet Earth* was guaranteed to replay itself in my nightmares.

The camera zooms in on a lone baby iguana in the middle of a rocky desert region. At first you see one snake slowly making its way near the iguana, and then as the camera zooms out, you realize that thousands of snakes are making their way out of the rock crevices and chasing after the poor innocent iguana with fangs wide open. The faster the iguana runs, the more snakes are alerted to him, and that's when you want to cover your eyes. But you can't help but watch. Needless to say, many of the other baby iguanas never make it out alive. They are simply outnumbered and outmatched.

It can be easy to feel a bit like that when we try to live a life of faith in Christ. The odds may sometimes seem like they are against us. We feel outmatched against the enemy who first appears in scripture as a serpent. Maybe that is why I've always hated snakes. If we attempt to tackle life alone and live out our faith alone, it's only a matter of time before we are outmatched.

But God never intended for us to do life alone.

We were made *from relationship*.

We see this in Genesis 1:26 when God says, "Let *us* make mankind in our image" (emphasis added). The use of the word *us* shows that there is more than one person who pre-thought and carried out creation.

This is the first of many indications that God is a communal being. We call it the Trinity, which comes from the root *tri* meaning three and the word *unity,* three in one. We know these distinct persons to be the Father, the Son, and the Holy Spirit.

We were made *for relationship*.

God made us in His own image. If He lives in community, we are also meant for community. He indicated that again after He made Adam and said, "It is not good for the man to be alone. I will make a helper suitable for him" (Gen. 2:18).

The bottom line is that we are relational beings. We need one another not only to survive and thrive but to fully embody the way of love.

We were made to experience life in loving relationships just as God has modeled for us. This is life at its best.

Jesus tells us this is how they will know we are His disciples: If we *love one another.*

How we live in community with one another speaks volumes about who we are and the God we serve. That is why it is crucial for us to find and foster a healthy, loving community. We need one another.

There are a lot of places where some sense of community can be found, but what is it that truly separates the people of God who are living in community together? The answer is love. What does it mean to be the community of love?

It means we have a shared identity, shared unity, and shared fidelity.

It's God's love that marks us, His love that unites us, and His love that propels us. God's community is referenced in the scripture as the bloodline, the body, and the bride of Christ. Here is how each distinguishes us as his people.

Identity (Bloodline of Christ)

God's love is what gives us our identity as a group of people. It's what sets us apart. One of the words used in the New Testament to describe the people of the God is *ekklesia*. It means the called-out ones.

God has called us to Himself and called us to represent Him as members of His holy family.

> *But now in Christ Jesus you who once were far off have been brought near by the blood of Christ. For he himself is our peace, who has made us both one and has broken down in his flesh the dividing wall of hostility by abolishing the law of commandments expressed in ordinances, that he might create in himself one new man in place of the two, so making peace, and might reconcile us both to God in one body through the cross, thereby killing the hostility. And he came and preached peace to you who were far off and peace to those who were near. For through him we both have access in one Spirit to the Father. So then you are no longer strangers and aliens, but you are fellow citizens with the saints and members of the household of God, built on the foundation of the apostles and prophets, Christ Jesus himself being the cornerstone, in whom the whole structure, being joined together, grows into a holy temple in the Lord. In him you also are being built together into a dwelling place for God by the Spirit.*
>
> —Eph. 2:13–22 ESV

There is this old saying, "Blood is thicker than water." It's used to elevate the significance of family. According to this saying, there is nothing stronger than the bond of a family. In Christ we are a family. We were once strangers, but now we are part of the household of God. We are the bloodline of Christ.

No matter what else we think is true of ourselves, the most important truth is that we are children of God. This is our true identity. We are God's own.

As members of His household, we carry on the family name. We bear the family resemblance. We show the world what love looks like as it is lived out in the context of healthy community.

> *This is love: not that we loved God, but that he loved us and sent his Son as an atoning sacrifice for our sins. Dear friends, since God so loved us, we also ought to love one another. No one has ever seen God; but if we love one another, God lives in us and his love is made complete in us.*
>
> —1 John 4:10–12

The more closely we follow Him, the more we think like He thinks and act like He acts. That's how it works in my family. People comment all the time how my oldest especially looks just like me. He doesn't look just like me, though. He has similar expressions. He acts like me. When people tell me he acts just like me, I joke, "Take that as a compliment, buddy."

The Christians were paid a great compliment when they were first called Christians. The name *Christian* wasn't a name that followers of Jesus first gave themselves. It was actually meant more as an insult. They were called Christians first at Antioch. They were called Christians because they were like little Christs.

What was intended as an insult was really a badge of honor because, as the bloodline of Jesus, there was nothing they wanted more than to carry the family resemblance. That, too, should be our aim, to resemble Jesus and lean into our true identity as His people.

Unity (Body of Christ)

This unique identity gives way to a greater unity. Another analogy that is used in the New Testament to define the community of love is a body. Paul uses this visual representation to capture the importance of everyone's contribution to the community. He also emphasizes that the effort of each individual helps advance the collective mission of the church. The result is that the body is both edified and further unified. He writes these words to the church at Corinth:

The human body has many parts, but the many parts make up one whole body. So it is with the body of Christ. Some of us are Jews, some are Gentiles, some are slaves, and some are free. But we have all been baptized into one body by one Spirit, and we all share the same Spirit.

—1 Cor. 12:12–13 NLT

There was a song we used to sing in elementary school when we were first learning about some of the parts of the body. Like any good kids' song, there was a dance to go along with it. It was one of those songs that embeds itself in your head for the entire day so you unknowingly burst into song. It was about the toe bone being connected to the foot bone and the foot bone being connected to the ankle bone, then to the leg bone, and so on...now shake dem skeleton bones!

The best part was the line "Now shake dem skeleton bones" because that was the cue for my elementary self to completely lose control and jump around, crashing into my friends along the way. The very basic principle is that in a healthy body, everything is connected. The community of love has many individual parts, and each one is intimately connected to another.

We are most effective when we are most connected. A healthy body is one that is connected. A healthy body is one in which every part is fulfilling its unique and valuable function. Our diverse backgrounds, experiences, and giftings contribute to a stronger, more vibrant expression of love, both inside and outside the walls of the church.

Yes, the body has many different parts, not just one part. If the foot says, "I am not a part of the body because I am not a hand," that does not make it any less a part of the body. And if the ear says, "I am not part of the body because I am not an eye," would that make it any less a part of the body? If the whole body were an eye, how would you hear? Or if your whole body were an ear, how would you smell anything? But our bodies have many parts, and God has put each part just where he wants it.

—1 Cor. 12:14–18 NLT

When I was in high school, I took a class called human anatomy. We had verbal tests where we had to stand in front of the class and the teacher would test us by pointing to one of those life-sized skeletons and asking what each part was and what each part did. I would have preferred to fail my test while sitting down at my desk rather than have an added layer of public humiliation. The good news is that I always knew what would be asked of me. Identify the part. Describe its unique function. I actually ended up doing pretty well in that class, and I retained a lot. It turns out that the threat of looking like a fool in front of my friends provided some added incentive to study.

We are most effective when we are most connected. We are most effective when each part is activated. One of the most fascinating things about the body is that each body part was designed with a very specific and unique function. It has a negative impact when one or multiple parts are not fulfilling their functions. All of us have been designed with unique characteristics, abilities, backgrounds, and experiences that equip us in distinct ways to edify the body. It's our job to seek God and identify the part we were meant to play within the body.

Paul goes on to list a variety of important functions. Some are visionaries, others are teachers, some have the ability to bring healing, some are great listeners, others can help others see the heart and revelations of God. This is not an exhaustive list. Whether you thrive in areas of creativity, financial support, relating well to others, or some other craft, the church of the future needs each of us to discover our unique places within the body.

A healthy community of love understands that each person is valuable and brings something unique to the overall body. The job of church leaders is to help people identify their functions to serve the greater good of the body. Sometimes it's seeing something in someone they may not see in themselves. A healthy church is a church in motion. It takes everyone discovering the part they have to play. Apathy and inaction hurt both the individual component as well as the body. They keep us from being fully utilized as God's agents to bring His love to the world.

I broke my arm when I was a kid. Unfortunately, that wouldn't be my last break. They had to reset my elbow, and thankfully, I was heavily sedated. To stabilize my elbow, I had a cast that went up past my elbow. Not only did it make me have to do everything with my right arm for six weeks, but my left arm came out of that cast stinky, shriveled, and stuck at a 90-degree angle, the position it had remained in for weeks. The bone had healed, but atrophy had taken over.

The only way to reverse the effects of atrophy is with action. We were made to move. The same is true for us spiritually. If we don't move it, we eventually lose it. As the community of love, God's church, we were meant to move. If we don't move, everybody loses.

I've seen this trend play out for people in the church. Those who are growing the most are the ones who are saying yes to opportunities to contribute to the body. The bystanders, critics, and seat warmers get stuck due to atrophy. One of the things we remind people at Axis Church is that church is not just somewhere to go; it's something you are part of. We know it is vital for the health of the body and the individual member for all of us to fulfill our unique functions, utilize our unique giftings, and contribute in our own unique ways. We are most effective when we are most connected. We are most effective when everyone is activated according to God's purpose.

We are one body with many parts, each fulfilling an important function.

Fidelity (Bride of Christ)

Your wedding day is one of those days you don't forget. That is especially true if you have a bride as beautiful and wonderful as I do. I hope she's reading this. It didn't take me long to determine that this was the girl I wanted to spend my whole life with. We fell more and more in love, and on June 13, 2009, I got to watch my bride walk down the aisle. I remember that morning—the excitement, anticipation, and nerves.

Just as I was about to take my walk down the aisle, my grandpa stopped me and said, "This is a really big decision, Josh." He wasn't trying to talk me out of anything, but I did find his timing rather ironic. It probably was not the best time to be pointing out the enormity of my decision. Could we have maybe talked about it, I don't know, any other time? He wasn't wrong, though. My grandpa has been married to my grandma for more than 50 years, so if anyone had a right to drop this truth bomb on me, it was him. I didn't take it lightly, either.

Marriage was the biggest commitment I had ever made. When Jess walked down the aisle, I was overwhelmed. I remember thinking I would do absolutely anything for her. As we exchanged vows, I meant every word and intended to keep every promise. "I, Josh, take you, Jessica, to be my wife, to have and to hold from this day forward. For better, for worse; for richer, for poorer; in sickness and in health; to love and to cherish as long as we both shall live. I give you my promise." That was the moment I declared my fidelity to Jessica. Grandpa was right. This was a really big decision, but I've had zero regrets.

That was the biggest commitment I have ever made, except for one—my commitment to Christ. It was when I said I believe that Jesus is the Christ, the Son of the living God and I accept Him as my Lord and Savior. That is our highest duty and biggest commitment.

When Paul compares Jesus to our role as Christ's community, he uses an analogy of a bride and a groom. He paints a picture of a marriage:

Husbands, love your wives, as Christ loved the church and gave himself up for her, that he might sanctify her, having cleansed her by the washing of water with the word, so that he might present the church to himself in splendor, without spot or wrinkle or any such thing, that she might be holy and without blemish. In the same way husbands should love their wives as their own bodies. He who loves his wife loves himself. For no one ever hated his own flesh, but nourishes and cherishes it, just as Christ does the church, because we are members of his body. "Therefore a man shall leave his father and mother and hold fast to his wife, and the two shall become one flesh." This mystery is profound, and I am saying that it refers to Christ and the church.

—Eph. 5:25–32 ESV

What we have learned is that marriage takes mutual sacrifice and commitment. This is what fidelity is all about, making a decision and staying true to that commitment. It is a commitment birthed out of God's love for us. Christ loved the church (you and me) and gave Himself up for her. Our lives should be marked by love and sacrifice.

We have a shared fidelity. God is devoted to us, and we are devoted to Him.

It All Hangs on This

When Jesus is asked what the greatest commandment is, He responds:

"Love the Lord your God with all your heart and with all your soul and with all your mind." This is the first and greatest commandment. And the second is like it: "Love your neighbor as yourself." All the Law and the Prophets hang on these two commandments.

—Matt. 22:36–40

Love God with all your heart and soul and mind, and love your neighbor as yourself. It all hangs on those two commandments. If you retain nothing else from this chapter, read that verse a second time and a third time, and ask God to embed this mantra into your heart and life. Love holds the power to change everything, starting with us, overflowing into our families and friends and spreading from one person to the next. I believe what the scripture says in 1 Corinthians 13:8: "Love never fails."

It has been proved true over and over. It starts with you and me. Jesus went first. Let's follow His lead into a life of love.

Drop the stones. Let love in. Live love out. Spread love around because love never fails.

Questions for Reflection

Are you living out the identity of Christ? Do you carry the family resemblance? What do you believe should separate the people of God?

Are you contributing to the unity of God's community?

Are you playing your part? What talents, gifts, and passions could you be utilizing better?

How are you doing in the area of fidelity to God and His people? What sacrifices are you making or should you be making for God and His church?

The Voice

Josh

*When he has brought out all his own, he goes
on ahead of them, and his sheep follow him
because they know his voice.*
—John 10:4

Chapter 23

Knowing the Voice

My personal assistant has issues delivering on my requests. It's not so much that's she's subordinate or unwilling to help. It has more to do with her ability to actually understand what I'm saying. Of course, it doesn't help that she's automated and I'm human. No, I don't have the luxury of a real-life personal assistant, so I rely on my iPhone companion, Siri, to help me throughout the day. Don't tell her I told you, but most of what I'm asking is pretty basic. "Siri, call Steve Sams." Siri: "I'm sorry, Josh, there is no Eve in your contacts." Or "Siri, remind me that I have a lunch meeting tomorrow." Siri: "I'm sorry, Josh, I didn't get that." I just shake my head and try again.

I'm sure if I actually upgraded my phone once in a while, the voice-recognition software would be bound to catch up to my demands. To think I can tell something inanimate what to do is pretty amazing. But when you think about it, artificial intelligence will always operate on a different level than human intelligence.

Sometimes I picture God shaking His head at the impossibility of trying to communicate things to me. There are times I miss the message altogether because I'm not paying attention. There are other times when I'm just standing there looking confused. "I'm sorry, God, I didn't get that. Can you say it again?" I'm grateful that He is patient with me.

The analogy Jesus uses in John 10 about us being like sheep makes a lot of sense. Sheep wander. Sheep have a limited perspective. Most sheep, if left to their own direction, would end up lost at best or, at worst, probably dinner for a wolf. Sheep need a shepherd. And so do we.

I could insert plenty of stories here where I've followed my own distorted sense of direction and ended up somewhere I never intended to end up. I've ignored God's voice. Every time I do, I come to regret it.

Jesus tells His disciples in John 10:11, "I am the good shepherd. The good shepherd lays down his life for the sheep." I love this description of Jesus as the good shepherd because a good shepherd is exactly what we all need.

Good shepherds protect and preserve the sheep.

Good shepherds guide the sheep.

Good shepherds lead the sheep to greener pasture.

Good shepherds would give up everything for their sheep.

Jesus wants to be our shepherd if we will allow Him to. Jesus tells us that He has come to lead us into life at its best, but that only happens as we learn to live in intimate communion with Him. In John 10, Jesus makes some important distinctions about those who are His sheep.

My Sheep Know My Voice

I am the good shepherd; I know my sheep and my sheep know me.

—John 10:14

The personal nature of God can't be missed here. Jesus declares that He knows us and that we can and should know Him. The Greek word for *know* in John 10:14 portrays this idea of recognition.

I never thought I would be the guy who talked to my wife's pregnant belly, but when I learned of the parental bonding that can take place, even in the womb, I was willing to go the extra mile. I imagined my voice would be a bit muffled, but the doctors assured us, "Baby can hear you." Sure enough, sometimes I would speak, and baby would kick. I would sing, and baby would squirm uncomfortably. I did whatever I could to ensure that my baby knew me even before I would ever hold him.

That's one of the most remarkable things I remember about the day each of my boys were born. When I laid eyes on them and held them, I felt an instant connection to them, but it wasn't until I spoke that I could see the initial recognition from them. It was a breathtaking kind of moment to see their eyes lock onto mine as if to communicate. Their faces said it all. "I know you! Please don't sing anymore."

It really is true that repetition builds recognition.

There is something powerful in being able to detect God's voice in our lives. It may sound a bit muffled at first or even incoherent, but God is speaking to us. Our ability to know His voice will grow through readiness and repetition. One of our first tasks as His sheep is to learn to recognize His voice.

My Sheep Follow My Voice

When he has brought out all his own, he goes on ahead of them, and his sheep follow him because they know his voice.
—John 10:4

Jesus shows that His sheep don't just know Him; they trust Him enough to follow after Him. It takes more than just voice recognition. It takes voice reliance. We have to trust the Shepherd enough to lead us along the best path and walk in obedience to His voice.

Even before Jesus walked the earth, David, who was also a shepherd and understood the charge of a shepherd, wrote these words about the Lord.

The Lord is my shepherd, I lack nothing. He makes me lie down in green pastures, he leads me beside quiet waters, he refreshes my soul. He guides me along the right paths for his name's sake. Even though I walk through the darkest valley, I will fear no evil, for you are with me; your rod and your staff, they comfort me.
—Ps. 23:1–4

As we read through the Psalms, we discover that there were times when David did walk through dark valleys. It wasn't just quiet waters. What's striking is that although the valleys were dark, he took comfort in knowing that the Shepherd was with him, guiding him on.

Do we trust the Shepherd to lead us into what's right and best?

When Stephen went to Israel on a spiritual retreat, he brought me back a small figurine that I keep in my office. It is hand-carved out of wood, and the attention to detail is quite stunning. It depicts a shepherd carrying a sheep on his back. In ancient times, shepherds would sometimes break the leg of sheep that wandered. They would then carry the sheep on their back so they would learn to be reliant on the shepherd. That may seem cruel to us, but when you understand the heart of a good shepherd, you realize the reason they would do that is not to punish the sheep but to prevent the sheep from a more devastating fate. I don't think God deliberately inflicts pain on us, but I do believe He uses and allows us to face challenges, adversity, and heartbreak to draw us nearer to Him. He does that to prevent the devastation that results from our drifting. He knows that the closer we are to Him, the better off we are.

Sheep don't just know the shepherd; they learn to depend on the shepherd. They follow in close proximity to the shepherd. They take one step of obedience at a time. They don't just blindly follow. They know the shepherd can be trusted because, as we see in this verse, the shepherd goes before them.

Not everywhere Jesus leads us will be easy, painless, comfortable, or desirable, but we can be confident in following Him because He never leads us where He has not first been willing to go.

Jesus has earned the title Good Shepherd because His words are backed up by His actions. He lays His life down for His sheep.

For this reason the Father loves me, because I lay down my life that I may take it up again. No one takes it from me, but I lay it down of my own accord. I have authority to lay it down, and I have authority to take it up again. This charge I have received from my Father.

—John 10:17–18 ESV

My Sheep Resist Other Voices

But they will never follow a stranger; in fact they will run away from him because they do not recognize a stranger's voice.

—John 10:5

I have an older truck. I tell my wife I'll keep driving it until it's undrivable. It does just fine for me, but one thing I wish it had was the ability to stream and play music off my phone. My only real option is the radio. I love some of our local radio stations, but because we live halfway between Cincinnati and Dayton, there is constant interference with radio stations. I'll be listening and worshipping my heart out, and all of a sudden, a mariachi band breaks into the worship as the local Latin station takes over. Sometimes it's more subtle. Sometimes I just hear another voice in the background talking through the song. It's too much for me, so I often sit in silence, which probably isn't a bad idea considering how noisy life can be.

Jesus is definitely not the only voice in our lives. We often find ourselves halfway between two powerful signals. Some of the noise in our lives is neutral. It's not necessarily harmful, but it's also not helpful. The pure volume of it just makes it harder for us to hear God and His still, small voice. But it's not small in magnitude. The voice of God could level mountains. It's just that He isn't going to talk over the noise. It's our responsibility to tune Him in and tune other voices out.

Some of the noise in our lives is negative noise. It has adverse effects on our heart and mindset. It draws us away from the voice of the Good Shepherd. Jesus was keenly aware of the fact that there would always be other voices competing for our attention. There was a phrase He used that I like. "He who has ears to hear, let him hear" (Matt. 11:15 ESV). I love this phrase because it's a creative way to say, "Listen up! What I'm about to say is important."

It's like in grade school when the teacher would flash the light on and off or make us do some random clap pattern to get everybody back on pace with what was happening in the room. I like Jesus's tactic better. If you have ears, use them. Jesus isn't going to talk over all the other noise in your life, so we need to tune in or miss out.

We need to keep turning up the volume on Jesus and turning down the volume on the voices and influences that lead us astray. The more we tune in to that station and tune out other stations, the more the signal strength will improve. There is no more vital voice than the voice of the Good Shepherd. If we want to know Him and live in relationship with Him, we must seek to hear His voice.

Questions for Reflection

What do you think makes a good shepherd? In what ways does the analogy of sheep and shepherd speak to our relationship with God?

What do you find most difficult: knowing His voice, following His voice, or resisting other voices?

How might we turn up the volume and tune in to our Good Shepherd?

How might we turn down the volume on other voices?

Chapter 24

The Two-Way Interaction: Hearing

Even as technology advances, there will never be a replacement for the simple two-way radio, or Walkie Talkie. When I was a kid, I even had my own Walkie Talkie handle just so my identity could never be revealed over the airwaves. Since I believe I can trust you to keep a secret, I'll tell you what it was. It was J/R—that's pronounced J slash R.

My friend Rob Carpenter also had a handle. It was R/C. His brother went by TJ, and we would call him T/J. I'm sure you are amazed with our level of creativity. Our Walkie Talkies were the best, especially because we got to use all the trucker talk like "Roger that, good buddy." Whenever we were finished talking, we would say, "over," which to me was pretty straightforward. It meant my part was over and the other person was free to respond.

When I got older and started working at a hotel, I got a Walkie Talkie. It's a little less fun when it comes with responsibility, but I felt pretty cool having it. Regardless of where I was in the massive hotel, the line of communication was always open. I didn't have to dial a number or anything like that. As long as I was on the same frequency, the line was open.

The one thing you need to understand about two-way radios is that if your thumb is on the talk button, nobody else can be talking. That is probably the aspect of communicating with God I have found most difficult over the years. I'll be the first to admit (if my wife doesn't beat me to it) that I have no problem talking.

I like to keep my thumb on the talk button. Yet when I'm talking, that means I'm not listening. Something I've gotten better at but truthfully takes work is saying "over," stop talking, and let God get a word or two in.

I'm grateful to know that the line is always open, and no matter where I am, God makes Himself accessible to me through the vehicle of prayer. That's the ability to both talk and listen, which is why we developed the following tool to help us be better at both.

Let's look first at letting go of the talk button and letting God speak. God speaks into our lives in a variety of ways if we allow Him to. Here are a few prominent channels through which God speaks.

Let's use the acronym HEAR to help us remember to tune in to these channels.

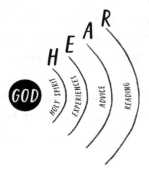

H (Holy Spirit)

But the Helper, the Holy Spirit, whom the Father will send in My name, He will teach you all things, and bring to your remembrance all that I have said to you.

—John 14:26 NASB

The Greek word for *counselor* in John 14 means the one who is called alongside. When Jesus left earth, He promised that the third person of the Trinity would be coming and that He would not just live among them but would take up residence within them. I wonder how confusing that must have sounded. The Spirit of God is going to live where? Inside of me.

It's a remarkable truth that God, in the form of His Spirit, takes up residence inside His followers.

Here are the key functions of the Holy Spirit:

Convicts us of sin (John 16:7–9)

Guides us into all truth (John 16:13)

Magnifies Christ (John 15:26, 1 Cor. 12:3)

Equips us for good works (1 Cor. 12)

Produces fruit in us (Gal. 5:22–23)

Empowers the church (Acts 1)

The Holy Spirit is the often overlooked and sometimes abused and misused person of the Trinity. Though we may underappreciate and undervalue His work, we would be lost without Him. We must be careful to not smother or stifle His work. Paul writes, "Do not quench the Spirit. Do not treat prophecies with contempt but test them all; hold on to what is good, reject every kind of evil" (1 Thess. 5:19–22).

The Spirit works as a guide for us as we invite Him to lead us day by day. He is our counselor, our true helper. He is not a mere emotion but a physical presence, impressing mysteries of God on our hearts.

E (Experiences)

The heart of man plans his way, but the Lord establishes his steps.

—Prov. 16:9 ESV

Experience can be a powerful teacher. Seeing God's providence at work teaches us. Everyday moments are saturated with God's presence if we know what we are looking for.

The Poet Elizabeth Barrett Browning wrote:

Earth's crammed with heaven,

And every common bush afire with God;

But only he who sees takes off his shoes,

The rest sit round it and pluck blackberries,
And daub their natural faces unaware.[20]

Stephen has often referred to these moments as "thin moments." These are moments when the distance between heaven and earth is so thin we can't mistake the fact that God is near. It's often in these thin moments that God reveals something about Himself to us. He uses these moments to also help us discover something about ourselves.

An experience can be a closed door or an open door. There have been times when God has slammed a door in my face, and it wasn't until much later that I understood why.

Not every experience or open door is a sign from God, but with God's help, we can learn something from every experience. I try to ask myself what God is teaching me through this. Where is He leading me with this? Failures, mistakes, successes, and everyday moments all can be revealing as we seek God through them.

A (Advice)

It is true that advice is only as good as the person giving it. We should be careful to choose our sources wisely. However, one of God's greatest mouthpieces is His people. Trusted advisors are an invaluable resource in the life of a disciple. But be careful who you allow to influence your life. We should be seeking Christ-centered, Spirit-led advisors, not just those who tell us what we want to hear.

Beloved, do not believe every spirit, but test the spirits to see whether they are from God, for many false prophets have gone out into the world.

—1 John 4:1 ESV

---

20. Elizabeth Barrett Browning, "Aurora Leigh," in *Poetical Works of Elizabeth Barrett Browning* (New York: Thomas Y. Crowell & Co., 1882), 134.

One indicator for me is when several of God's people seem to be communicating the same thing to me. It's like things have a harder time penetrating my thick skull, so God sends multiple messengers until I finally get the message. I've seen this time and time again.

Writing this book has been one such time when more than one person has said, in one way or another, that we need to put pen to paper on this stuff. The main reason we are writing this book is because we simply feel it is something God wants us to do, and many trusted voices in our lives affirmed it.

If we are humble enough to receive it, a trusted advisor can reorient our lives, inspire us to live out some aspect of God's calling, or challenge us with something we otherwise wouldn't have seen. I try to leave room for people to speak truth into my life. Sometimes that means correction. Sometimes that means encouragement. Sometimes it means a new perspective altogether. God speaks through His people.

R (Reading His Word)

There is no replacement for God's Word when it comes to hearing from God. God has already spoken through His Word, and even better than that, God still speaks to us through His Word. The author of Hebrews tells us this:

> *The word of God is living and active, sharper than any two-edged sword, piercing to the division of soul and of spirit, of joints and of marrow, and discerning the thoughts and intentions of the heart. And no creature is hidden from his sight, but all are naked and exposed to the eyes of him to whom we must give account.*
>
> —Heb. 4:12–13 ESV

We have already discussed this in greater detail in our bread element, but God's written Word should be our primary channel for hearing God. It gives us solid and unchanging footing for God, His character, His intentions, and His expectations.

If something we hear contradicts God's Word, we can disregard it because God never contradicts Himself. If the advice we are given, the experience we believe we have had, or the desire in our heart is not aligned with God's Word, we should always give God's Word the final say.

God *has* spoken through His Word.

God *is* speaking through His Word.

The question is, are we consistently tuning in to this channel?

We should all be students of His Word. The Apostle James refers to God's Word as the implanted word of God.

> *Therefore put away all filthiness and rampant wickedness and receive with meekness the implanted word, which is able to save your souls.*
>
> —James 1:21 ESV

Are you receiving with meekness the implanted Word of God?

Planting God's Word in our hearts means we read it, we study it, we memorize it, we revisit it, and then we *live it out*.

We should follow the model of David in his delight in God's voice.

> *I seek you with all my heart; do not let me stray from your commands. I have hidden your word in my heart that I might not sin against you.*
>
> —Ps. 119:10–11

Questions for Reflection

Holy Spirit: What has God been impressing on your heart and mind through His Spirit?

Experiences: What is God teaching you through life experiences and His work in your life right now?

Advice: What spiritual challenge or wisdom have you recently gained through other Spirit-led people?

Reading His Word: What has God been teaching you through His Word?

Chapter 25

The Two-Way Interaction: Praying

One of my best friends asked me a few years back if I would perform his wedding. That sounds like kind of a no-brainer. How could I miss out on an opportunity like that? There was a minor detail to consider. The wedding would be in Colombia. No not Columbia, South Carolina. Colombia, South America! I wasn't going to miss it, but I had a few reservations. The biggest one was that I don't speak Spanish. His fiancée's family was mostly Spanish-speaking, which would mean I would have my work cut out for me since my vocabulary was limited to *si*, *no*, and *no comprende*.

I was intimidated because I was going to a different country and had no ability to communicate. It is a pretty helpless feeling. Going through customs, getting a taxi, and explaining where to take me were just a few things that are much harder when people have zero idea what you are saying. My first objective was simply to not get kidnapped, to get in touch with my friend through some text messaging app because my phone didn't work, and to go from there.

That's when I heard someone call my name. "Josh!" It was a stranger, but at least he was speaking my language. "I'm a friend of Kyle's. He told me you would be on our flight and to look out for you. Don't worry. I speak fluent Spanish. I got you covered." I can't even describe the relief.

From then on, I could breathe easier. Once I arrived, I realized there were many people in our group who were bilingual, so I followed their lead. When I got stuck, I just signaled one of them to order for me or get me a taxi or explain something for me. I had a translator at the wedding who repeated everything I said in Spanish, or at least I trusted she was repeating what I was saying. I even started to pick up some of the language in my short time down there and got better at communicating despite the language barrier.

When I got back to the airport to fly home, the gate agent was helping me with tickets and baggage. She was trying to tell me something, but I just couldn't understand. She must have said it 10 times, and I just looked back blankly. I said, "No comprende!" Then she mimicked holding something in her hand and said, "Your license." She had been speaking English the whole time. I guess it turns out that I don't speak English very well, either.

Learning to pray can be like learning a new language. What do we say? How do we say it? How can we know we are heard? Like any language, the best way to start as we venture into new territory is to find someone who knows the language and speaks it fluently.

The disciples identified this person. They would often watch Jesus as He prayed, and one day they made this request: Lord, teach us how to pray! You speak God's language so fluently. Teach us to communicate with Him the way You do. We want to speak the language of prayer as fluently as You do.

You have to love the heart behind their request. This is how Jesus responded:

> This, then, is how you should pray:
> "Our Father in heaven, hallowed be your name, your kingdom come, your will be done, on earth as it is in heaven. Give us today our daily bread. And forgive us our debts, as we also have forgiven our debtors. And lead us not into temptation, but deliver us from the evil one."
>
> —Matt. 6:9–13

Jesus lays out a pattern for prayer. He isn't saying to them that this is your script, but rather that these are the key components when speaking the language of prayer. We should balance them as we converse with God.

Not only do we need to learn to HEAR God. We must learn to PRAY more effectively in order to fully reap all the relational benefits and blessings of prayer. Visually, we picture it like this:

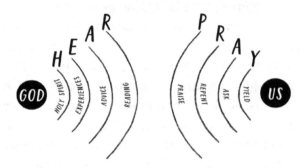

We learned this well-known acronym at some point and found it helpful as we taught people how to pray. It has four actions words that describe four key aspects of prayer found in the Lord's Prayer.

P (Praise)

Our Father in heaven, hallowed be your name.

—Matt. 6:9

A friend of mine who admittedly has some reservations about God was telling me recently that one of his challenges with church is all the singing to God stuff. He said he would rather just come in for the message, if that's cool. It makes him uncomfortable to sing to someone like God. After all, he claims, wouldn't God be more humble than that, having people singing to Him all the time? I can see where his confusion is coming from. If we think about it in human terms, no human would be worthy of our singing about how great they are all the time. The difference is that God actually is infinitely great. The fact that He even associates with humans is incomprehensible. He is God in heaven. His name is holy. He is the only one who is worthy to be praised. Yet Jesus teaches us that He is also approachable. Jesus tells us to pray, "Our Father in heaven, hallowed be your name" (Matt. 6:9). Great and holy is Your name O God our Father!

Praise and thanksgiving should overflow from our hearts as we approach God in prayer. He is holy. He is righteous. All His ways are good. He is the epitome of perfection. In every way, He deserves for us to place Him on the highest pedestal.

If you doubt this is something that is useful in relating to God, just look at King David. Nobody on earth had more authority than King David during his time, yet David wrote countless songs and prayers devoted to magnifying the greatness of God and acknowledging his own frailty. Psalms is filled with people like David who understood the value in declaring God's praise.

One psalmist wrote:

Shout for joy to the LORD, all the earth. Worship the LORD with gladness; come before him with joyful songs. Know that the LORD is God. It is he who made us, and we are his; we are his people, the sheep of his pasture. Enter his gates with thanksgiving and his courts with praise; give thanks to him and praise his name. For the LORD is good and his love endures forever; his faithfulness continues through all generations.
—Ps. 100

R (Repent)

And forgive us our debts, as we also have forgiven our debtors.
—Matt. 6:12

A second part of the language of prayer is seeking and extending forgiveness. Confessing where we have fallen short is a healthy part of walking in an ongoing relationship with the Good Shepherd. We all wander, we all fall short, and acknowledging this taps into His power of forgiveness.

This can be both things we have done and things we have left undone. Both are forms of rebellion against our holy Father. Handing these things over to God through prayer allows us to walk away, free of the burden of guilt and shame, knowing that nothing has the power to cleanse us like the blood of Jesus.

When I was in college, I rarely did laundry. The laundry room was in the basement, and I lived on the 22nd floor. That meant that piles of disgusting laundry would grow on my dorm room floor. I was active, and some of the dirtiest clothes were after a game of flag football, a game of soccer, or a workout. I don't know if I thought that eventually this pile would simply disappear, but it never did. I'm a bit embarrassed to share this, but during my freshman year, I would throw that pile into my car, drive home to Cincinnati, and drop it in the laundry room. Miraculously, it would end up clean and folded. Almost like magic, the stains would be gone, and my clothes would smell like a field of wildflowers. We all know that wasn't a miracle. My mother was a saint, and no, she doesn't still do my laundry. But the clothes at my house keep getting cleaned and folded, too. My wife is a beautiful soul and should get an award for the mounds of laundry she has to put up with. I do quite a bit of sweating, too, so there are bonus points for getting it smelling so fresh and clean. Hope that wasn't too much information.

The point is that we all have piles of spiritual dirty laundry we need to deal with. Maybe you are like me and wait until it piles up high, but God gives us this invitation through prayer to bring whatever pile we have amassed and drop it at the foot of the cross. James charges his readers to hand over their dirt to God. "Therefore, confess your sins to each other and pray for each other so that you may be healed" (James 5:16). Isaiah forecasts the work of Christ and the cleansing of His blood. "Come now, let us reason together, says the LORD: though your sins are like scarlet, they shall be as white as snow; though they are red like crimson, they shall become like wool" (Isa. 1:18 ESV).

A (Ask)

Give us this day our daily bread.

—Matt. 6:11

We should not be afraid to ask our loving Father for His provision. I consistently pray for God's provision, protection, and providence. We can be assured that He always hears us, even if He doesn't respond the way we hope. God will always bring about what's best, even if what's best doesn't make sense.

Notice that the prayer here is for our daily bread. It's a prayer that is rooted in what we need today. That highlights a couple of things.

1. Daily bread means praying for what we need the most, which may or may not be the thing we want the most.

2. Daily bread means that sometimes we get just enough for the day, and sometimes it's way more than we could have dreamt up on our own.

God is able to do immeasurably more than we could *ask* or imagine.

But it takes us humbling ourselves and asking our God and loving Father. God wants us to ask Him.

Mark Batterson writes in his work on prayer, *The Circle Maker*, "100 percent of the prayers I don't pray won't get answered," and "The script of your prayers becomes the transcript of your life."[21]

James tells his readers that they don't receive because they don't ask. And when they do ask, they don't receive because they ask with wrong motives (James 4:2–3).

Jesus instructs us to be persistent in our asking.

Ask and it will be given to you; seek and you will find; knock and the door will be opened to you. For everyone who asks receives; the one who seeks finds; and to the one who knocks, the door will be opened. Which of you, if your son asks for bread, will give him a stone? Or if he asks for a fish, will give him a snake? If you, then, though you are evil, know how to give good gifts to your children, how much more will your Father in heaven give good gifts to those who ask him!

—Matt. 7:7–11

---

21. Mark Batterson, *The Circle Maker: Praying Circles around Your Biggest Dreams and Greatest Fears* (Grand Rapids, MI: Zondervan, 2011), 91, 16.

Jesus isn't guaranteeing God will always do what we want. Jesus is promising that when we ask, when we seek, and when we knock, He will go beyond what we think is best and bring about what He, in His infinite wisdom and unfailing love, knows is best. Those who ask will receive what is best. Those who seek will find what is best. Those who knock will see God swing open the door to what is best.

Y (Yield)

Your kingdom come, your will be done, on earth as it is in heaven. And lead us not into temptation, but deliver us from the evil one.

—Matt. 6:13

Yielding to God is one final aspect of prayer that cannot be overlooked. Jesus showed the disciples that when speaking the language of prayer, the objective was to align our hearts with God's, to want what God wants, and to see God's purposes fulfilled in our midst. That means we have to slow down and allow God to move out ahead of us. That is what yielding is all about.

When I taught high school students about this, I asked them what it means to yield. I figured that many of them would know since most had recently passed their driver's tests. The level of confusion about the word *yield* scared me a little bit, if I'm being honest, especially since I had to share the road with them. Yielding and merging are actually very different things. A lot of people in Mason, where we live, also don't know the difference. We have one of those roundabouts, and people often merge, meaning they just jump in whenever, or they stop when nobody is around. Yielding is not merging or stopping completely. It's giving someone else the right-of-way. When two cars merge, it creates problems to say the least. At the least, somebody gets cut off, or at the worst, there is a collision.

Yielding to God means we let Him go, and we follow behind Him. Sometimes the lane is clear, and He gives us the freedom to go.

I always end up regretting the times when I move out ahead of God or cut Him off to carry out my own agenda. There are other times when I stop altogether, and God ends up waiting on me. I hear people say they are waiting on God when really they are just stalling.

Yielding is praying, "God, I want your will to be done. Let me move in conjunction with Your will." It's inviting God to bring more of His Kingdom and desires into our lives, homes, and communities.

Prayer Is Powerful

There is nothing like the power we possess when we become fluent in the language of prayer. We have the full force of heaven behind us because the maker of heaven of earth resides within us.

In 2010, 33 Chilean miners became trapped 2,300 feet below the ground after a coal mine collapsed around them. Hours became days, which turned into months. With supplies lacking, limited oxygen, and low morale, hope diminished by the day. Rescue crews worked tirelessly around the clock to find a way down to the trapped miners. While many felt this mine might become the miners' final resting place, others called out to God in prayer night and day. To this day, they share many stories of how God showed up during their 69 days underground. From healing men who were sick to making their rations last, to comforting others and helping them hang on to hope, God's presence was unmistakable. Their shift leader, Luis Urzua, when asked how lucky they were to have survived, said he doesn't believe in luck, but he does believe in faith, even when it seems like there is no hope. "The devil couldn't do anything because God was present," he said.[22] After 69 days, all 33 miners were rescued. Many gave credit to the one they called the 34th miner. They said He—the Lord Himself—was with them all along.

Prayer is powerful. Prayer is effective. Keep learning the language of prayer, and watch God move among you and within you. God's presence is just a prayer away.

---

22. Sarah Butler, "The Chilean Miners' Miracles: How Faith Helped Them Survive," *CNN*, https://www.cnn.com/2015/08/02/world/chilean-miners-miracles/index.html.

Questions for Reflection

Praise: What are you praising God for?
Our Father in heaven, hallowed be your name.

Repent: What are you repenting of?
Forgive us our debts, as we have forgiven our debtors.

Ask: What provision are you asking God for? What deliverance or protection are you asking God for?
Give us today our daily bread. Lead us not into temptation. Deliver us from the evil one.

Yield: What are you yielding to God on? Responding to God on? What aspect of God's Kingdom are you inviting into your life, your family, or your ministry?
Your kingdom come, your will be done, on earth as it is in heaven.

The Towel

Stephen

Now that I, your Lord and Teacher, have washed your feet,
you also should wash one another's feet.
I have set you an example that
you should do as I have done for you.

—John 13:14–15

Chapter 26

Serving Changes the Atmosphere

Many years ago, before 9/11 and the security upgrades at airports, I flew from Newport News, Virginia, to Columbus, Ohio, with a layover in Atlanta. When I arrived at the airport at Newport News, I saw several people standing in line who were aggravated with the people at the front desk. It was a small airport, and I was surprised to see the number of people lined up behind the desk.

My plane was to leave at 7:05 in the evening. When I finally got to the desk, I asked Larry, the airline employee, what was happening. He said, "Your flight is delayed an hour and a half. It is not going to leave until 8:30." I thought, "I need to check my layover time in Atlanta because I might miss my connecting flight." Admittedly, I can be impatient at times, but on this particular night, I actually felt bad for Larry. Everyone in the line was aggravated and upset and yelling at the poor guy, so I said, "That's all right. Thanks for being the bearer of bad news. I know it's not your fault."

I walked down the terminal and found my gate. The same scene repeated itself. There were people standing in a long line, all waiting for their turn to tell the gate employees what they thought about this delay. At 8:30, almost 90 minutes after our flight was scheduled to leave, we got more bad news over the intercom. "Ladies and gentlemen, because of weather in Atlanta, your flight will now be delayed until 10:00."

Certainly everyone was now going to miss their connecting flights. People were furious. It was not the fault of the poor employees, but they were surely taking the heat for the delay. I started thinking, "What can I do to make this situation just a little bit better?" I remembered there was a Burger King just down the aisle. A kind-looking, middle-aged woman was there to take my order. "What can I get you?" she asked. I said, "My flight is delayed." She said, "I know. People are very upset." I said, "Wanda, I want to buy drinks for everyone on my flight." Wanda said, "You are kidding, right? Lennie, come here, this guy wants to buy drinks for everyone on that delayed flight." Lennie was the manager of that franchise. I said, "Lennie, I was just sitting there seeing everyone get upset, and I was thinking, 'What can I do to help this situation?' Could you give me a discount on some drinks or something?" Lennie said, "Why sure! Wanda, start filling drinks up for this guy!"

Wanda said, "Do you want to make them large? Let's give them large drinks!" I didn't even have time to answer. Then she said, "Do you want just Coke? How about some Diet Coke? Sprite? How about orange drinks?" I said, "Sounds good! Let's get a variety." By that time, other employees started to help. They were putting the drinks on trays and getting lids on the cups. When it was all done, we had four trays filled with large drinks. I looked down and said, "Wanda, I think I need help." Wanda looked at another employee and said, "Come here and help me carry these trays." She looked over at Lennie for permission. Lennie nodded in approval.

As we walked to the gate, I told Wanda, "Let's make this a party." Wanda nodded in enthusiastic approval. When I got to the gate with the four trays of drinks and two Burger King employees, I yelled out, "I want the grumpiest people on this delayed flight to come get yourself a Coke!" People looked up in surprise. We started to pass out the drinks. One guy said, "Hey, got a Sprite?" A girl named Julie jumped up and said, "Let me help you pass them out!"

Just then, an announcement came over the intercom, "Ladies and gentlemen, your flight has left Atlanta and is on its way here!" Everybody started clapping! They had a Coke in one hand, so they had to clap with one hand on their leg. The mood completely changed. For about half an hour, people kept coming up and saying, "Thank you so much for that Coke!"

We finally got on the plane at about 10:00 p.m. Somehow, I had the last boarding pass. The gate employees caught me as I was boarding. "That was a lifesaver. Thank you so much. We were getting destroyed. People were so mad." As I got on the plane, I stopped one of the flight attendants. I started to tell him what happened in the terminal. He already knew. The story had already been shared. I said, "Hey, would you let me talk to my people?" He laughed and said, "Sure, when the captain finishes his announcement, you can talk."

I got on the intercom and said, "Ladies and gentlemen, I'm glad you've made it here with us on Value Jet! I just want to let you know that if you want a drink or anything, just let me or one of the flight attendants know. We'll be sure to get it for you." People started to laugh and applaud. I sat down, and a gentleman next to me said, "Are you the president of Value Jet?"

I learned a lesson that day. Simple acts of service change the atmosphere.

The atmosphere in the Upper Room was tense. Jesus was hours away from His death. The apostles were selfishly arguing about which one of them was going to be the greatest in the Kingdom of God. The devil had already prompted Judas Iscariot to betray Jesus for 30 pieces of silver. During the meal, Jesus looked around the room and said that one of them was going to betray Him. Judas swallowed hard and realized he was caught red-handed. Jesus wasn't finished. Apparently, there were others who would abandon Him. To say that the atmosphere was tense is an understatement. But a simple act of service changed the atmosphere.

Jesus, the creator of the universe, got on a knee and humbly washed the disciples' feet. That seems like a time for hand-slapping, not feet-washing. Jesus would be justified for being angry or reprimanding His friends, but instead, He knelt down and did the menial task of a common servant. All the Gospels record this beautiful and unexpected moment. John describes the scene like this:

Jesus knew that the Father had put all things under his power, and that he had come from God and was returning to God; so he got up from the meal, took off his outer clothing,

and wrapped a towel around his waist. After that, he poured
water into a basin and began to wash his disciples' feet,
drying them with the towel that was wrapped around him.

—John 13:3–5

There is power in the towel. Jesus had every right and reason
to demand that He be served. He was God in the flesh. He was the
one who should have been served, but instead, He was going to be
abandoned, betrayed, and even killed. He was witness to a petty
argument over who was going to be greatest, but He was greatness
personified. He did the unexpected. He hushed the room. He picked
up the towel. He grabbed the tool of the servant.

We are far more likely to pick up a stone than a towel. Too often,
we seek revenge rather than restoration. We hold grudges rather
than release tension. We focus on our agenda rather than see from
another's perspective. We demand our own way rather than bow
a knee in a simple act of service. If we are going to be disciples of
Jesus, then we follow the example of Jesus.

Serving Follows the Example of Jesus

I want to be very clear about something. Those who are saved,
serve. This is not optional for followers of Jesus. Selfishness is the
opposite of sacrifice. Jesus said it this way: "Now that I, your Lord and
Teacher, have washed your feet, you also should wash one another's
feet. I have set you an example that you should do as I have done for
you" (John 13:14–15). The very essence of Jesus's followers is found
in the act of picking up the towel of service. We serve because Jesus,
our Lord and teacher, said so and modeled it for us.

Jesus left His throne to serve us.

In your relationships with one another, have the same mindset as Christ Jesus: Who, being in very nature God, did not
consider equality with God something to be used to his own
advantage; rather, he made himself nothing by taking the
very nature of a servant, being made in human likeness.

—Phil. 2:5–7

The example of Jesus compels us to do the same. How much better would our world be if we followed the example of Jesus? How much would our relationships change if we simply followed these few verses? What would happen if we looked to the interests of others and humbly picked up the towel?

We would have better marriages if each of us threw down the stones and picked up towels. We would be better employees if we sought to serve. We would be better citizens if we looked for opportunities to bring good to the community without regard to self-promotion. We would hold fewer grudges if we took on the nature of a servant and forgave someone who offended us.

Serving Puts Others First

The life of Jesus is always our example. You can't be a servant if you put yourself first. In Matthew 23:11–12, Jesus said, "The greatest among you will be your servant. For those who exalt themselves will be humbled, and those who humble themselves will be exalted."

Years ago, I had an employee who oversaw the building and grounds. He was highly educated and desired to be in full-time ministry. Honestly, he was overqualified for this job, but it was the only job we had open at the time. Even he admitted that he was a bit rough around the edges and sarcastic sometimes. One day, our children's minister politely asked him, "Can you put up some shelves in the classroom downstairs?" He responded, "You have two hands; you can put it up yourself," and I knew I needed to address the issue. I asked him to come into the office and sit down with me. I pulled out his job description and said, "These are the tasks that have been assigned to you. These are the areas for which you are responsible. But I want to remind you today what your real job is." I turned the paper over and wrote just one word: *Serve*. I handed the paper back to him and said, "That is your new job. Just serve." To his credit, he has continued to grow in both his leadership capacity and his personal humility.

Just serve. That is the job description for every follower of Jesus. It does not matter what tasks are assigned to you. You may be the top of your company or at an entry level. Our job description is the same. Just serve. Put others above yourself.

Serving Is a Lifestyle, Not an Event

Too often, serving in the church has been relegated to a ministry task or role. We want people to "serve" in a certain ministry. Rock a baby. Teach a class. Greet newcomers at the door. Play an instrument. The problem with this approach is that once the task is completed, many consider their service completed for the week. But for Jesus, serving was never an event; it was a lifestyle.

Serving marked His everyday living. No matter where He went or who He encountered or what was on His agenda, He looked for opportunities to serve. One time He said, "Whoever wants to become great among you must be your servant, and whoever wants to be first must be your slave—just as the Son of Man did not come to be served, but to serve, and to give his life as a ransom for many" (Matt. 20:26-28). This statement defines the entirety of Christ's ministry on earth. He came to serve. Every moment, every interaction, every relationship was marked by service to others. In His sacrificial death on the cross, He ascended to the pinnacle of servanthood.

When we serve like Jesus, we follow the example of Jesus. We put others first, and we embrace a lifestyle of serving others. Do not worry so much about status or achievement. God has a history of using the humble. He tends to pick the ones who are least likely to succeed. Dwight L. Moody once said, "We may easily be too big for God to use, but never too small."[23]

---

23. Dwight L. Moody, *AZ Quotes*, https://www.azquotes.com/quote/876618.

Questions for Reflection

In what area or relationship do you need to pick up the towel and
   serve? Why?

Are you better at picking up stones or picking up the towel?

How does the life of Jesus inspire you to serve?

What are the barriers to service in your life?

Chapter 27

The How of the Towel

I was speaking to a large group of high school seniors. It was a baccalaureate service, and I stood before the crowd of students, teachers, parents, and family. It seemed like an occasion when some decorum should be observed. My speech did not start that way. After the customary greeting and thanking the principal for the opportunity, I pulled a Bop It Extreme out of my bag. I said, "How many of you have ever played this game?" Bop It Extreme is a game that requires listening, timing, and reaction. The voice inside the game instructs you to bop it, pull it, twist it, or flick it, and you hurry to follow the commands of the voice before you get buzzed. The game can be played individually or as a competition in which you are instructed to pass it to the other players. All of this happens as the speed of the commands and the music continue to intensify.

I challenged one of the high school seniors to a Bop It Extreme duel. This event, which generally requires decorum, suddenly became a rowdy competition as the crowd applauded wildly for the student. Each round became more intense. The voice commanded, "Bop it, flick it, bop it, twist it, twist it, twist it, pull it. The commands came faster. The music intensified. The voice said, "Pass it." This went on for several rounds. The student was at an unfair disadvantage. I had been practicing at home for this moment for a week. The competition ended, and the crowd cheered.

The truth is that I have been practicing this game for years. You have, too. It is pretty normal these days to feel bopped by life, twisted inside, and pulled in every direction. Everywhere I go

195

I meet people who feel beaten down by the circumstances of life, people who just need someone to care.

In Luke, chapter 10, we find the story of a man who was bopped and beaten. We call this the story of the Good Samaritan. An expert in the Law came to Jesus and asked Him how to inherit eternal life. Jesus responded with what is known as the Great Commandment. "'Love the Lord your God with all your heart and with all your soul and with all your strength and with all your mind'; and, 'Love your neighbor as yourself'" (Luke 10:27). The expert pressed Jesus further and asked, "Who is my neighbor?" (Luke 10:29). Jesus answered the question by telling a story of a man who was beaten, robbed, and left for dead. In this story, we find principles about how to serve.

Overcome Barriers

When we serve, we do so without prejudice. In the story, Jesus said that a priest and a Levite passed the wounded man and ignored him. "But a Samaritan, as he traveled, came where the man was; and when he saw him, he took pity on him" (Luke 10:33). It was well known that the Jews hated the Samaritans. To them, the Samaritans were second-class citizens.

Are you indiscriminate in your service? Or are you more likely to serve someone who is like you?

Years ago, I was preaching through a series on the book of James. When we got to the verses in chapter 2 that talk about not showing favoritism, I decided to model the verses rather than just teach them. James tells his readers to not show favoritism to a rich, well-dressed man who comes into church and to treat a man who is poor and filthy the same.

Our worship pastor, Tom, was very well known in our city as an outstanding theatrical performer. He was also a makeup artist. I went to a local thrift store and picked out the outfit I would wear. On Saturday night, I met Tom at his apartment so we could prepare for the next day. Tom had a long wig he had used in local productions. He practiced putting on my makeup. He made my eyes look dark, like smoker's eyes. He gave me a scraggly beard. We decided that it wasn't good enough for me to just look the part; I also needed to smell the part. Tom went to a local convenience store and bought a package of cigarettes. We put my thrift store clothes in a plastic bag. We lit a cigarette, blew the smoke into the bag, and quickly closed it up tightly. We laughed about how funny it was that the pastor and worship pastor were out smoking on the balcony and blowing the smoke into a bag. It would be just our luck that a church member would walk by and think, "Oh my. I am never going to that church again!"

The next day, I arrived early at the apartment. Tom applied my makeup, and I put on the smelly, smoke-filled clothes. No one at the church was aware of our plan. A few minutes before the first worship service started, I came around the corner and walked in the front door. I could see the nervousness in the greeter's eyes, but to his credit, he stuck out his hand and said, "He-hello, welcome to church. Is this your first time here?" I grunted out an answer. He said, "I would love to get you some coffee. Do you want some coffee?" I quietly grunted, "Yeah." The greeter got me a cup of coffee and continued to try to engage me in small talk. He walked me into the worship room and seated me. He introduced me to a couple who were actually good friends of mine. They did not recognize me. Mike sat down first. He introduced himself and then sat down two seats from me. He left the seat next to me for his wife, Christy. We laughed about this later. Christy sat down next to me. She was very kind. My hands were shaking. I really embodied the persona of this homeless, filthy man. In our suburban church, I was very out of place. Just then, something happened I will never forget. As everyone else was singing, Christy leaned over to me and whispered, "That coffee sure smells good. I wish I had some." Here I was, this foul-smelling, dirty man, and she focused on the aroma of my coffee.

The time came for the sermon. No one came to the stage. People started to nervously shift in their seats. "Where is Stephen? Did he sleep in today?" I got out of my chair and very slowly began to limp toward the platform. I was a little surprised that the security team didn't tackle me. I walked up to the microphone. In a very low, unrecognizable tone, I grunted, "This is my grandma's Bible. She taught me that you love everyone and don't pick no favorites. She told me that Jesus said, 'If someone is hungry, you feed 'em. If someone is lonely, you visit 'em. If someone is a stranger, you invite 'em in.'" I said a few other things and then walked off the stage. Most people still did not fully understand what just happened, but they got the message, and I felt loved.

The second worship service was a completely different experience. I came to the front door. I walked right past the greeters. No one stuck out their hand. I walked around in the lobby, waiting for an invitation for coffee. No one offered. I finally sat down in the lobby. One man tried to start a conversation but eventually walked off uncomfortably. Children saw me and literally pointed at me, laughed, and then ran off. Some parents told me later that they got up from their seats and went to check on their children to make sure I was not harming them. The music started. I will never forget the feeling when the ushers closed the doors to the worship center. We had four sets of doors, and they closed each set. They were all inside, and I was outside, alone, in the lobby. I finally got up and limped slowly into the room. No one sat near me. When the music stopped, I began to walk to the platform. Again, I walked up to the microphone. In a very low, unrecognizable tone, I grunted, "This is my grandma's Bible. She taught me that you love everyone and don't pick no favorites. She told me that Jesus said, 'If someone is hungry, you feed 'em. If someone is lonely, you visit 'em. If someone is a stranger, you invite 'em in.' But you, you did not invite me." You could hear a pin drop. It became a defining moment for our church. I later told our church that we would never again miss an opportunity to reach out in love. We would always be a place where everyone is welcome. We would overcome any barrier and remove any fear to reach out with love.

The Samaritan didn't allow the man's beaten body, torn clothes, or racial difference to become a barrier to love. If you are going to serve like Jesus, then look past all social, economic, racial, political, and even religious divides.

Make Yourself Available

Acts of kindness require us to be on the lookout as we go. Jesus said that the Samaritan "came where the man was" (Luke 10:33). He certainly had his own agenda. He was walking on this road for a reason. The religious leaders were content to walk from one town to the next without paying attention to the people they passed. I imagine they were walking from home to worship or from worship to home. Think of the irony. Imagine leaving your church after worship, and there on the side of the road is someone beaten up and left for dead. Imagine just driving by the person in need. It is not unusual. In our busy and overstressed culture, it is easy to be distracted.

The Samaritan did what was best. He made himself available to serve. Regardless of his schedule or commitments, he saw a need and filled it. I am intrigued by the phrase "as he traveled" (Luke 10:33). He stopped to help the beaten man as he traveled. So many of the miracles of Jesus happened as He traveled from town to town. Matthew 9:35 says, "Jesus went through all the towns and villages, teaching in their synagogues, proclaiming the good news of the kingdom and healing every disease and sickness." I love that Jesus was just available.

If you are going to serve like Jesus, then never allow your own agenda to rob your availability. Leave room in your busy schedule to attend to the hurting.

Take Time to Notice

Luke 10:33 tells us that the Samaritan "saw him." The priest and Levite also saw the man, but they didn't take time to truly see him. The Samaritan took extra time to actually notice.

Do you ever get so busy that you miss the obvious? I saw a video of a guy who was driving a dump truck. Somehow the bed of the truck raised up while the guy was driving, and he didn't notice. The driver behind him obviously noticed because he pulled out his phone and started taking a video of the moment. Just then, the truck driver went under an overpass. The raised bed slammed into the road signs that hung overhead. When I saw that, I thought, "What was that truck driver doing? Why didn't he notice? How could he miss something so obvious?"

The man who was beaten was so obvious to everyone, but only the Samaritan took time to actually notice him. The truth is that everywhere you go, there are people in need. In every grocery store, playground, Saturday soccer game, workplace, and school there are people who are hurting. Maybe their wounds aren't as obvious as the ones on the body of the beaten man, but they are just as real.

You and I don't need to change the paths that we walk; we just need to pay better attention as we walk. We need to lift our eyes and, as my son's lacrosse coach says, "Keep your head on a swivel." Many of the people we run into may not have as obvious a need, but it is there.

I once got on a flight from Chicago to Cincinnati. I was flying back from a Christian leader's conference with a pastor friend. We got on the airplane, tracked our seat number, and sat down in our row. There was a businesswoman in the window seat, and I joked as I sat down, "I bet you were hoping to have a row by yourself. Sorry about that." Somehow that greeting broke the ice. We started a bit of small talk. The conversation was genuine and comfortable. Soon after takeoff, I asked what seemed to be a mundane question: "Do you have family?" She began to quietly tear up. After she gathered herself, she said, "My divorce papers are in my briefcase now." She went on to describe the relationship with her husband and what led to this decision. She talked. I mostly listened. Over the next two hours, we talked about relationships, isolation, frustrations, and faith. I soon discovered that she literally lived within a mile of the church. I told her that we had a group of other people who were navigating through similar life stories. In that moment, I followed the example of Jesus. I took time to notice.

I would love to tell you that I always get it right. I don't. I have missed many opportunities in my life. For every time that I have noticed a need, I have probably ignored a hundred. Julie's marriage did end, but this was not the end of her story. She began to come to church. She started to meet other wounded people. She ultimately met the one who notices every need. Her newfound faith led her to a person, a new love. He was a loving and devoted man. She asked me to perform their ceremony. As I watched her walk down the aisle, I tearfully reflected on her story. What would have happened if I hadn't noticed?

Allow Your Heart to Feel

"He took pity on him" (Luke 10:33). Not only did the Samaritan notice, he actually cared about the man. It's easy for us to get calloused. We hear stories of tragedy. We move on in a few days. It impacts us for the moment. We are conditioned to become apathetic. If it doesn't affect our house or those we love, we move on.

Matthew 9:36 says about Jesus, "When he saw the crowds, he had compassion on them." Be honest. Are you calloused or compassionate? Are you cynical or caring? Do you genuinely empathize with those you meet?

In my experience, people who go through tragedy or hardship generally end up going in one of two directions. They either become more compassionate or they become bitter. I mentioned earlier that our family has endured unexpected tragedy with the passing of both my father and my sister. They were both warriors. They fought with faith and joy. My mother was a warrior, too. She cared for both of them. Imagine being the caregiver for your husband and then your daughter. When you go through so much pain in such a short time, it gives you an acute awareness of the pain that others are facing. When you sit by the bedside of a dying loved one, it gives you a compassionate heart toward others who face a similar fate. When you see the pain that a caregiver suffers, it makes you more attentive to their needs.

When you see people in need, allow your heart to feel. Listen to their stories. Put yourself in their shoes. Don't just write the cursory social media message of "thoughts and prayers." Take time to be face-to-face. Listen with your heart and not just your ears.

Respond in Love

When you truly care, you can't help but respond in love. Jesus said that the Samaritan "bandaged his wounds...and took care of him" (Luke 10:34). He went the extra mile. He moved beyond words and took action.

Feeling for someone and caring for someone are two different things. You can feel but not respond. You can do good things for someone but not care. You need both. You need right actions based on right motivations. First John 3:18 says, "Let us not love with words or speech but with actions." Do something that will make a difference in someone's life.

Jeff Stone is a friend who preaches outside Cincinnati, Ohio. He shared a story of something that happened in his family's life several years ago. It is a moving example of loving with more than words.

My godly grandmother had died a few months earlier of a heart attack. Throughout her fifty years plus of marriage my grandparents had lived on a farm that her father had given her. Her father had made a provision in his will that the ownership would pass on to her five children upon his daughter's death. My grandfather became angered at being bypassed, although my mother and her four adult brothers insisted that nothing need change. They invited my grandfather to live the rest of his life on the family farm just as he always had, but in a burst of pride he announced that he was leaving the farm and moving to town to buy a house of his own. Farm equipment and my grandmother's personal belongings would be sold at a public auction to liquidate her estate and provide him the cash that he would require. Again, his loving children tried to point out that they wanted him to remain living there rent-free for the rest of his life on the family farm, but his mind was made up.

The day of the auction was very emotional, as you can imagine. Furniture, personal items, farm implements were displayed in a large barn on that cold winter Saturday. My brother, my uncles, and I had an unspoken understanding that we would not bid against one another if any of us wanted the same item. An old children's wagon was wheeled out to be sold. I thought that would make a nice buy for my son, Jason, who was approaching his third birthday. I prepared to bid but noticed my uncle Phil raised his hand. I stopped. He probably played with that wagon as a little boy, I thought. Phil bought the wagon for four dollars. As the wagon was wheeled over to my uncle, I saw the other side of the wagon for the first time and I noticed the crude hand-painted lettering where forty years earlier he had painted, "Philip," on his wagon. I later learned that before the sale he had asked his dad if he could have his wagon. He had been told sharply, "No, you'll have a chance to bid on it like everybody else."

One of the items that my mother was most interested in bore great sentimental value. It was a beautiful, handmade wedding-ring-design quilt that my great-grandmother had made for my grandmother as a wedding gift. My mom wanted this quilt that had held such special meaning to her mother, but a determined antique dealer wanted it to resell. As the bidding reached a point beyond my mom's self-imposed, preset spending limit, she turned with tears in her eyes and briskly exited the auction barn while her cherished memory was being sold to the highest bidder.

That's when I decided I wanted to buy the quilt. I resolved that no antique dealer was going to have what rightfully should be my mom's. I spent more than I really had and I paid more than I probably should, but I never regretted buying that quilt that day. The auctioneer said, "Sold!" They folded up my purchase. I went outside the auction barn to find my mom. I handed her the quilt and I said, "I love you, Mom." She started crying as I hugged her. I cannot recall giving any gift that brought me more pleasure than to give that gift at that moment. That day those circumstances called me to express love through listening and lifting and by living and giving.[24]

---

24. Jeff Stone (used with permission).

Who is around you right now who needs the gift of love? Who do you know that needs to be served? Who do you know that is lonely or abandoned or in pain or fighting temptation? They might be in your own house. Don't walk by on the other side. Don't ignore the obvious. Look, listen, and respond in love.

Questions for Reflection

Rate yourself on the five things mentioned in this chapter (overcome barriers, make yourself available, take time to notice, allow your heart to feel, respond in love). Which one do you do best, and which one needs attention? Why?

Why do you think people struggle to notice those in need?

What is the Lord telling you to change right now?

Chapter 28

The Anatomy of a Servant

What does a servant look like? What are the qualities that mark the life of a servant? In every area of discipleship, Jesus is our leader and example. He is the model for our discipleship. When He picked up the towel and washed the disciples' feet, He set an example for us. In John 13:14, Jesus said, "Now that I, your Lord and Teacher, have washed your feet, you also should wash one another's feet." He was reminding the disciples that if He, the Lord and Teacher, serves others, then we should, too.

The head, heart, and hands concept has been widely used in various arenas to describe a leader, a change process, or a model for learning, but it is also a very powerful and easy way to check ourselves and coach others when it comes to this element of discipleship. When we serve like Jesus, we have the mind of Christ. We have His truth and perspective to guide us. When we serve like Jesus, we have the heart of Christ. We embody His compassion and care. When we serve like Jesus, we have the hands of Christ. We respond and act in the way that He responds and acts. We picture it like a circle because the life of a servant involves these three aspects working together in harmony.

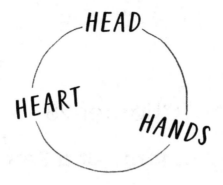

Head

We live in a culture with a me-first mindset. We think about image management. We carefully create our perfect Instagram theme. We take 20 selfies just so we get one with the right angle and lighting. We are motivated by more. We often buy things we want without considering the long-term implications of debt. Our mindset too often centers on ourselves and our desires.

If you want to serve like Jesus, then it begins in your mind. First Corinthians 2:16 says that because we have the Spirit of God, "we have the mind of Christ." Jesus was motivated by an others-first mentality. Serving like Jesus means that we have a Christlike mindset that flows from our relationship with Him. Being a disciple is not an obligation; it is an invitation.

When most of us think about serving others, we think about it as an obligation or a duty to serve. The mindset is a "have to" rather than a "get to." In Philippians 2:5, Paul writes, "In your relationships with one another, have the same mindset as Christ Jesus." What was Jesus's mindset? He willingly and humbly came to serve. He was not coerced to serve. It was His choice to serve.

When Jesus first encountered His would-be disciples, He extended to them an invitation. He captured the essence of discipleship when He said, "Come, follow me...and I will send you out to fish for people" (Mark 1:17). The invitation was a relationship with Jesus first. The outflow of the relationship was the desire to then "fish for people." When you have a relationship with Jesus, your mindset begins to change. You begin to see service through His perspective. You begin to serve willingly.

If you see service as an obligation, then you will begin to find excuses. On the other hand, if you accept the Lord's invitation to serve, then you see every relationship as an opportunity to love the way He loves. If you view service as a job, then you will feel that you have finished serving when you complete a task. When you serve with joy and in partnership with Christ, you find fulfillment. If you think serving others is a duty, you will begin to begrudge the very people you are trying to help. If your service flows out of your relationship with Christ, then you will begin to see every person as a unique creation of God. If you see service as an obligation, you will be burned out and discouraged. When you love God and others, then serving others brings refreshment and renewal to your spirit.

Do you need a change of mind? Is your first instinct to think about yourself or to think about others? Do you make conscious choices every day to say no to self and yes to service? Do you look for opportunities help?

Heart

If we want to serve like Jesus, we have to have the same heart as Jesus. Not only do we have a change of mind, we also have a change of motive. Our compassion for people is genuine. We serve out of pure motive. We don't do it to be recognized or rewarded. We serve for the benefit of those we serve.

When I was a young boy, I bought a shoeshine kit from a yard sale. It was not your typical shoeshine kit with just brushes and polish. It was a deluxe shoeshine kit that included an electric shoe buffer. It literally looked like the buffer a car detailer would use to shine a BMW. After I bought that buffer, I looked for ways to use it. I remember sneaking into my parents' closet on Saturdays to polish my dad's shoes. He was a pastor, and I wanted to help him look good for Sunday church. I waited for him to go outside to work and then ran to get my shoeshine kit. I polished, buffed, and removed every scuff mark. I sat anxiously in the family room and awaited the reaction when my dad opened the closet door. "Well, look at that! My shoes look brand-new! How did that happen?" Looking back, I appreciate his overreaction to my imperfect efforts to serve.

One thing that was so impressive about Jesus was that He served not because of the reaction He received. He served despite the reaction He received. He served from completely pure motives. He did not serve for the "atta-boy" or the public reaction. In fact, He was far more likely to receive threats and speculation than praise and adulation.

Paul writes in Philippians 2:3–4, "Do nothing out of selfish ambition or vain conceit. Rather, in humility value others above yourselves, not looking to your own interests but each of you to the interests of the others." Do *nothing* out of selfish ambition. When you serve, do it because you are following the example of Jesus, not because you want attention. Do it because other people need you to serve, not because you want to impress someone. Do it because, through your service, you are actually working for the Lord. "Whatever you do, work at it with all your heart, as working for the Lord, not for human masters, since you know that you will receive an inheritance from the Lord as a reward. It is the Lord Christ you are serving" (Col. 3:23–24).

A heart of compassion leads us to serve others. It allows us to see beyond the surface to the deeper needs within the people we encounter. Jesus was motivated by genuine love. He came, served, and died because of love. The Apostle Paul describes it well:

Love must be sincere. Hate what is evil; cling to what is good. Be devoted to one another in love. Honor one another above yourselves. Never be lacking in zeal, but keep your spiritual fervor, serving the Lord. Be joyful in hope, patient in affliction, faithful in prayer. Share with the Lord's people who are in need. Practice hospitality.

—Rom. 12:9–13

Paul describes tangible acts of service. Honor others above yourself. Share with those who are in need. Be hospitable. Each of these acts of service follows the command to love sincerely. That is our motivation.

Hands

If we serve like Jesus, then we have the hands or movement of Jesus. That is where we actually serve. We have the right mindset. We have the right motive. We now put them into motion. Many times, we have good intentions but don't follow through with action. We have the desire, but we do not respond by doing.

When you have time, do a simple word search in your Bible concordance for how many times the New Testament talks about the hands of Jesus. His hands were used to touch the leper and make him clean. His hands put mud on the eyes of the blind man and made him see. He held out His hand to keep Peter from sinking into the sea. He reached out His hand to children to pray for them. He touched the dead woman by the hand and gave her new life. He stretched out His hands and received the cross. He showed Thomas His hands to prove He was alive. Jesus did not come to just sit idly by and pontificate about loving others. He came to demonstrate what it means to give of yourself.

I wonder why people are reluctant to serve. One of the challenges of leading any volunteer organization, especially the church, is trying to get people to serve. Have a spring-cleaning day, and at best, 10 percent come. Take a regular Sunday off to go serve the neighborhoods around the church or the needy in the community, and attendance plummets. Why? Is it lack of promotion? Is it busy schedules? Is it a problem with mindset or motive? It is probably some or all those things. Why is serving so difficult?

I am certain it was not convenient for Jesus to leave heaven and come to earth as a baby. I am confident that a deity living within the confines of a human body was not comfortable. I know that giving up His life on the cross was excruciating. But Jesus did all these things and more. Hebrews 12 tells us that He did it with joy. He entered our world, took on our flesh, endured the rejection of people, and suffered a criminal's death with joy. That is the power of love. How can we as His children and the recipients of His grace do anything less than serve sacrificially as well?

Questions for Reflection

What is your mindset when it comes to serving others? Do you see it as a duty or an obligation? What is your attitude when you serve? Is it the same attitude as Christ?

What is the motive behind your serving? Are you serving for reward or recognition? What does it mean to serve with pure motives?

What are some of the barriers to service? In your own life, what do you let get in the way of serving others? How can you overcome that? In what areas is God calling you, right now, to step out of your comfort zone and serve?

The Fruit

Josh

If you remain in me and I in you, you will bear much fruit;

apart from me you can do nothing.

—John 15:5

Chapter 29

Rooted

I love plants. I'm not so sure they love me, though. I have roughly a 50 percent success rate when it comes to plants. I think, "How hard can it be? Plant it, and watch it grow." It turns out that it isn't quite that easy. Not everything that's planted grows.

My wife's family owns a garden center in central Kentucky, so I can feel them shaking their heads as they read this. They have given us so many beautiful plants over the years. They came to us with a vibrant future only to meet a slow death. Jess does have a better track record than I do with plants. She was raised better than that. She has challenged my plant-it-and-forget-it approach over the years, and I will say I've learned a thing or two. It turns out that things like the right amount of sunlight, consistent watering, and the right soil really do go a long way when it comes to growth.

A few years ago, we built a raised garden bed and planted all kinds of veggies. We picked the right spot with plenty of light and bought specific organic soil loaded with nutrients. We planted tomatoes, peppers, cucumbers, and squash. Then we consistently watered the garden each day. That was much harder than my previous approach to planting, but I was invested this time. I couldn't wait to eat from my very own garden. I would go out every day for the slightest signs of something sprouting. Days went by, but nothing was growing. I guess it takes longer than a few days. It was going to test my feeble patience in the plant department, especially when I could go to the grocery store and get a tomato in less than 10 minutes, but it would be worth the wait.

Finally, after many weeks, the first green tomatoes started to appear. Slowly but surely, tomatoes started popping up left and right. There were tomatoes for days. I even forgot that I don't like tomatoes. I was eating them like candy. Eventually, we couldn't keep up. We were canning them, making salsa, and eating tomato soup. Eventually, more vegetables started to grow. There is nothing like the harvest.

Growth takes time. Growth takes intentionality. Growth takes the right conditions. Every seed contains the potential for a fruitful harvest, but not every seed produces a fruitful harvest.

The same is true of the seed of the gospel in the life of a disciple. There is no seed that is riper with potential than the seed of Jesus, but it takes the right soil, the right setting, and the right amount of cultivation to see the fullest potential come to life.

We can't just plant it and forget it. We must learn to cultivate it and even be patient with it. The right conditions and right placement make all the difference.

Jesus tells His disciples, "If you remain in me and I in you, you will bear much fruit; apart from me you can do nothing" (John 15:5).

If we want to see greater fruit in our lives, we must learn to deeply root ourselves in Jesus. There is power in proximity to His presence. That is where the nutrients flow most freely.

The truth found in John 15 reminds us that today's roots become tomorrow's fruit. So our first focus should be on developing a deepening network of roots so we can see God's fruit come to bear.

Matthew recounts a story Jesus once told about some different kinds of seeds and the conditions that spur growth and those that don't. There are four different seeds in Jesus's story in Matthew 13. Each represents a different spiritual scenario. There is a seed that falls along the path, and the birds devour it. There is a seed that springs up quickly and dries out in time because it lacks mature roots. There is a seed that gets choked out by weeds. What gets in the way of your growth?

Lack of Understanding

In Matthew 13:19, Jesus said, "When anyone hears the message about the kingdom and does not understand it, the evil one comes and snatches away what was sown in their heart. This is the seed sown along the path."

For some, the seed never even gets planted. Like a seed that falls along a path, no roots begin to form. The missing component in this scenario is understanding. Jesus always made the message of God accessible, but not everyone truly desired or absorbed the things He said. Jesus could detect the ones who were most curious and most hungry for the things of God. That is why He taught so frequently in parables. They were a relatable way to draw out the truth seekers. As the greatest teacher, He taught in a way that propelled the student to keep digging.

This is one of my favorite parts about parenting young kids. My oldest has way more questions than I have answers. Some days we field a full week's quota of questions before 10:00 a.m. My son wants to know everything about everything. How is this person related to that person? How does that work? How did I get in Mommy's belly and now I'm here? Why do people hurt other people? Are you sure this is the right way to get home? He's not only asking, he is listening, and often he still isn't content with my answer. That's something I love about him. He is so inquisitive. Often he stumps me, to which I reply, "Ask your mom!"

A drive to know more is something that separates the fruitful from the dormant. As we've said, one of the most basic definitions of a disciple is a learner. That is the person who is never content with where they are in their understanding or development. They know there is constant room for growth and depth. They have a habit of digging deeper every chance they get.

Disciples are learners. Disciples are always digging deeper. They are always seeking greater understanding.

One condition that stunts growth is a lack of understanding. Another condition is a lack of maturity.

Lack of Maturity

The seed falling on rocky ground refers to someone who hears the word and at once receives it with joy. But since they have no root, they last only a short time. When trouble or persecution comes because of the word, they quickly fall away.

—Matt. 13:20–21

Some people start strong but, like a plant without roots, dry out and die rather quickly. There is an instant surge of growth only to be followed by a shriveling over time.

This dynamic plays out time and time again in our gym setting. You can usually tell who the first-timers are because they don't pace themselves. Our workouts are timed or scored in one way or another, which makes things fun and competitive. There is usually one in every group who sprints hard, only to find themselves bent over, hands on their knees, and gasping for air a few minutes later. Contrast that with our trainer Steph. She beats most people, most days. That's because she is deliberate, purposeful, and, most importantly, steady.

It doesn't matter how strong you are at the start if you stall out before you finish. One of the most disappointing scores you can get in CrossFit is a DNF. That stands for "did not finish."

DNF is the last score any of us want to submit when it comes to our spiritual race. It will inevitably happen, as Jesus points out in the Parable of the Sower. There will always be those who begin to embrace Jesus and the fruitful life with enthusiasm and even show early progress, but then neglect the necessary work of development and spiritual training.

Paul uses the sport comparison as he challenged the believers in Corinth:

Do you not know that in a race all the runners run, but only one gets the prize? Run in such a way as to get the prize. Everyone who competes in the games goes into strict training. They do it to get a crown that will not last, but we do it to get a crown that will last forever. Therefore I do not run like someone running aimlessly; I do not fight like a boxer beating the air. No, I strike a blow to my body and make it my slave so that after I have preached to others, I myself will not be disqualified for the prize.

—1 Cor. 9:24–27

Paul's message is that we won't hit a target we aren't aiming for. We won't reach a goal we aren't training for. Maturity requires making purposeful progress over time. It's not about perfection; it's about spiritual preparation that gives way to fruitful progress.

We have to keep moving forward, staying steady, and making spiritual progress so we might receive the prize.

Lack of Maintenance

The seed falling among the thorns refers to someone who hears the word, but the worries of this life and the deceitfulness of wealth choke the word, making it unfruitful.

—Matt. 13:22

For others, fruitfulness gets choked out over time by worldly concerns, stress, and lesser passions that take over a life once fruitful. Little by little, weeds and thorns overtake a once-lush landscape.

There is a playground area in my backyard that has been my constant nemesis. Every weed you could imagine has decided at one time or another to take up residence there. They mock me daily. I've tried everything to permanently evict them from my property, but they just keep moving back in with more of their little spiny friends. I've taken a shovel to the area, chopping off every one of their little green heads, only to have them pop up a week later laughing harder at me than before. "Fine. I didn't want to play it this way, but Roundup it is." A few sprays of that stuff and they shriveled away until a new generation was born. One day I looked out, and there were more weeds than there was mulch. "I'll stay out here all day and pull every one of you and your dirty little roots out of the ground." So I did. Then I put down a plastic weed barrier to double down my efforts. Despite all odds, they still rose from the ashes, breaking through the plastic barrier. They are pesky and persistent. I thought weeds were just inevitable.

Then we visited a place on vacation called Fred Meyer Gardens. The place was immaculately kept. There were beautiful plantings and lush gardens everywhere I looked. I started searching for weeds on the property. If I can't even keep a small area free of weeds, this place has to have them. Nope. I could not find a single weed. There were just acres upon acres of beautiful gardens. What was the secret? That's when I saw teams of volunteers walking around with one job: pull weeds. All they do every day is pull weeds.

The secret wasn't some formula or kill-all method. It was consistency. It was maintenance. So I now try to employ this method of consistency. I've even recruited my own team of weed pullers: my children. The more weeds you pull, the more money you earn. It's not a one-time effort. It's a constant vigilance. There is good news! We are winning now! The match is far from over, but if we just pick a few weeds each day, they will not overtake us!

This is the only approach I've found to work with sin, stress, and other obstacles to faith in my life. If I let time go by and I'm not watching closely enough, sin will pop back up in my life, worry will start to take root, and the cultural current will begin tugging at my heart. If I look the other way for too long, those things have a way of taking root and taking over. The good news is that God has given us victory over sin. We hold power over it, but we must guard our heart because it is the wellspring of life. Consistent heart maintenance keeps us healthy and growing.

Sin is one of the greatest threats to our growth. It may appear harmless in some of its forms, but it is far from harmless. It is an invasive species that will take over our hearts if we let it and undermine the word of God. Worry will dissolve our peace. Fear will rob our joy. Complacency will hinder our progress. Selfishness will make our purpose shallow. Sin is the enemy and opposition of fruit in our life. It has to go. It must be pulled out of our lives repeatedly and consistently. We must practice constant heart and life maintenance if we want to bear the fruit of Jesus.

We don't just take the trash out monthly. We don't just cut the grass yearly. We don't just pull weeds once a decade. It takes maintenance.

So does the fruitful life. Today's roots become tomorrow's fruit.

So keep cultivating the roots. Keep building habits and making the effort to draw nearer to Jesus. It's the only way to see your fullest spiritual potential unleashed.

If you lack understanding, keep seeking.

If you lack maturity, keep training and developing.

If you lack maintenance, keep clearing out the old and making room for the new.

Do it because you want to see the kind of harvest that Jesus talks about in Matthew 13:23: "But the seed falling on good soil refers to someone who hears the word and understands it. This is the one who produces a crop, yielding a hundred, sixty or thirty times what was sown."

Draw near to God with the belief that today's roots become tomorrow's fruit.

Questions for Reflection

How would you describe the soil condition of your heart? Is there anything lacking?

What patterns do you have in place to strengthen your roots in Christ?

What do you do daily? What do you do weekly? What do you do monthly? What do you do yearly?

What habits might be helpful for you to develop a deepening connection to Christ?

Chapter 30

Pruned

I can think of lots of excuses why, but I'm bad at waiting. I just don't have time for it. See what I did there? Everything I do in life is on the clock, even if only in my own mind. How fast can I get this job done? How fast can I complete this workout? How fast can I get in and out of this grocery store? I don't have time to grab a cart. I'll just get as much as I can hold and bobble it all the way to the checkout line. What's the fastest route to my given destination? I will often drive way out of my way to avoid waiting in traffic. I know it's a flaw. It's one I'm working on.

I'm clearly not the only one who doesn't like to wait. Companies everywhere are finding ways to meet our needs faster. Things like On-Demand allow us to watch what we want when we want to watch it. Amazon is one of the best at putting a product in our hands within days or hours of our realizing we want it. Amazon Prime gets packages on my door within two days. If that isn't fast enough for me, Amazon Prime Now can get certain things to me within hours of ordering. Even grocery stores have been finding ways to eliminate or reduce our wait time. You can order your groceries online and go pick them up. Some stores are even delivering groceries.

The problem with this on-demand philosophy is that most good things in our lives, especially when it comes to our inner lives, take time. Those of us who desire to bear the fruit of Jesus, thinking the way He thinks, living the way He lives, have come to recognize that it takes time.

Developing roots takes time. Part of our healthy development is a process called pruning. We can't become the person we desire to become without the work of God through His discipline, His work through good times and hard times, and His constant redirection. He uses difficult experiences to bring the best out of us.

James says it this way:

Consider it pure joy, my brothers and sisters, whenever you face trials of many kinds, because you know that the testing of your faith produces perseverance. Let perseverance finish its work so that you may be mature and complete, not lacking anything.

—James 1:2–4

Does that strike anyone else as strange? James is telling us to consider it pure joy when we face trials and pruning. I consider trials and pruning a lot of things, but pure joy is the last thing I consider them to be. I don't say, "Well isn't this lovely and joyful?" But that's the point. We have to think about trials differently than just pointless irritations and hardships.

James says we should see life's difficulties and challenges as blessings because they will ultimately yield greater fruit for our future. Fruitful living requires ongoing pruning.

Bearing fruit begins with strong roots and requires constant pruning.

If we want to see the fruits of Jesus and become more like Him in every way, we must be pruned. Pruning is hard because it means we have to do several different things that may come unnaturally to us. There are three key tasks we must take seriously if we want to allow God to prune us.

Depend on the Pruner

If there is ever a value that has been lost in modern culture, it is the value of dependence. We live in an age that is all about independence and self-sufficiency. A term such as *self-made* is used to describe those who are successful. It means they did it all on their own power.

That is not meant to undermine a positive work ethic, but what if relying on our own power, talent, and strength actually is working in opposition to what God is trying to achieve in us? What if we are actually standing in His way while we are trying to operate on our own? What if God wants to help us, but we are inadvertently refusing Him? Perhaps the most effective thing we can do to aid our growth in Jesus is to get out of His way and stop trying to do everything on our own.

We have this little tricycle outside our house that we used with each of our boys when they were biking for the first time. It is set up like a normal three-wheel tricycle with a little steering wheel and pedals, but it has a long handle that lets me aid them by pushing and steering. Aiden, my oldest, let me do most of the driving for a while, but over time, he wanted to do more of it. "I do it, Daddy!" he would say. I could feel him fighting against me as I would steer one way and he would try to steer a different direction. He was actually very strong for a toddler. The problem was that he would grab the handles and steer hard left and hard right, which would usually lead him right off the sidewalk and, at times, even flip him off the bike. Every time he fell, I would pick him back up and help reset his course. What he didn't realize is that if he would have just pedaled and worked in tandem with me, he would have had a smoother ride, and we would have gotten to the park a whole lot sooner.

Dependence doesn't mean God strips us of all autonomy. It doesn't mean we do nothing. It means we learn to work in tandem with Him. We trust that even if we don't like the direction He is taking us, ultimately He is leading us along toward what is best.

The wise King Solomon captured this truth about dependence on God: "Trust in the LORD with all your heart and lean not on your own understanding; in all your ways submit to him, and he will make your paths straight" (Prov. 3:5–6).

We must trust the pruner. His hand is steady. His intentions are good. His way is better than our way.

Trust the Process

Progress is an up-and-down process. As much as we would like growth to happen in a straight, upward ascent, it rarely does.

We use a tracking software at the gym that helps us see progress in things like how much weight you lift on a specific movement or how fast you completed a specific timed workout. It measures various components of performance over time. As I look back on where I've been and where I am today, in almost every category I see a wavy line, not a straight one. One day I might hit a new PR, while another day I may fail to hit even 75 percent of that. There are also seasons of time when I've dropped off because of injury or something else. Overall, the trend is upward, but progress is an up-and-down process.

Life has low points, we make mistakes, and we have good and bad days, but overall, the hope is that we are progressing. When God is at work in our life, we should become more like Jesus over time. We may have moments that we miss the mark or seasons where things feel drier, but the trend should be an upward trend as we measure Christlikeness. The word we were taught in seminary for this is *sanctification*. It's the process of being made holy. In one sense, this is something that happens instantaneously as God imparts His own holiness on us, but there is an aspect of it that continues until the day we die. That aspect is growing to be more like Jesus.

Pruning is what is happening beneath the surface of our lives to produce things above the surface of our lives. It's sometimes an invisible process that gives way to visible outgrowth.

Paul speaks to this process as he urges the Thessalonians:

Now may the God of peace himself sanctify you completely, and may your whole spirit and soul and body be kept blameless at the coming of our Lord Jesus Christ. He who calls you is faithful; he will surely do it.

—1 Thess. 5:23–24 ESV

God carries out the work of sanctification in us through the power of His Spirit. We must learn to trust this process.

One of my hobbies is grilling. I'm in the kitchen sometimes, but the grill is my true domain. I'm the grill master; at least that's what

I keep telling myself. At my house, we cook with real fire like the cavemen did. Okay, maybe I'm overselling a bit. I have a ceramic grill that doesn't use fuel of any kind, just natural lump wood and charcoal. Real fire takes more time than propane. Let's just say there are much faster routes to get food into your belly. In fact, it takes a good half an hour before the grill even gets up to temperature. The preparation of the meat sometimes takes all night. For some cuts, you cook low and slow rather than grilling. When we first started cooking this way, Jess would wonder what was taking so long. I would have to tell her, "Babe, you can't rush the process." The results would usually be worth it, unless I accidently did something wrong or overcooked something, but mostly things are juicy and delectable, to which I humbly state, "See? It was worth the wait!"

You may be in a season when things are moving slowly. Maybe you can't quantify the progress at all, or maybe you feel like there must be a faster way to see results. There are no shortcuts when it comes to sanctification. We can't rush the process. We have to trust even when we can't see the result. God is faithful. He will see us through, and the fruit on the other side will be worth it.

Seize the Promise

One of the most encouraging promises of scripture is from Paul's letter to the Philippians. Paul wrote this letter from a jail cell as he served a sentence for proclaiming the name of Jesus. He never questioned the pruner. He trusted the process. He encourages his readers to do the same so they might seize God's promise. "And I am sure of this, that he who began a good work in you will bring it to completion at the day of Jesus Christ" (Phil. 1:6 ESV).

Paul confirms with complete certainty that God will complete what He has started. God always finishes what He starts. He will finish what He has started in us. If we remain in Him, we will bear much fruit. If we stay rooted in Him and allow ourselves to be pruned by Him, there is a harvest coming.

After our son Aiden was born, we faced a trial that nobody could have prepared us for. We found out that we were pregnant again, and as you can imagine, we were ecstatic. We began to plan for the day when baby number two would arrive. Something wasn't quite right, though, and I'll never forget the moment my wife walked down the stairs with tears in her eyes. We lost our baby. It didn't make sense to us. We had questions we couldn't get answers for. We asked God anyway. We rode the emotional roller coaster. We confided in people around us to pray for us and strengthen us. As a memorial for our baby who lives with Jesus, we planted a tree in our backyard. For the longest time, it just felt like a reminder of something we lost. While I will never understand it all, we have watched God do what only God can do with situations like that.

He brings beauty out of the ashes. He finishes what He started. Every year that tree blooms, I remember the truth that God is faithful. He is a God who keeps His promises.

Time doesn't necessarily heal all wounds, but it does showcase God's goodness. We became pregnant again, and on September 3, 2016, our second little boy, Elias, was born. Elias means "my God is Yahweh."

I remember that first morning I held him in my arms, my eyes bloodshot from lack of sleep, body and soul worn out from a season of waiting and anticipation. I remember as I held "my God is Yahweh" in my arms and realized the truth in his name. We witnessed firsthand how God can bring promise though pain. He never fails us. I can't imagine not ever getting to experience life with this little boy. He brings so much joy into our family. God's goodness prevails for those who wait on His promises.

We now remind ourselves of a truth that has served us well and proved true over and over again: *God* things come to those who wait.

Some might be content with *good* things, but we are constantly amazed by *God* things. He is a God who can and continues to do more than we could ask or imagine. So while I'm still not the best at waiting, I'm strengthened to know that our waiting is never wasted if we are waiting on God.

God things come to those who wait. So keep waiting, knowing that your waiting is not wasted.

Keep depending on the pruner, and keep trusting the process so you might see His promises fulfilled. The pruner is faithful. The process is worth it, both in what it develops in us now and what we await in the life to come.

Questions for Reflection

Where do you sense that there is some pruning taking place in your life? (challenges, new experiences, learning opportunities, failures, etc.)

What lessons are you learning through current challenges, experiences, failures, and so on?

Are you resisting or submitting to the things God is trying to do in you and through you?

Chapter 31

Fruitful

I didn't mention this earlier, but I'm actually a seasoned actor. It's true. I had two brief seasons of acting classes and got to play a big part in a few high school productions. So maybe I'm more of a lightly seasoned actor. I was even in a musical that involved tap dancing. For everyone's safety, I was asked to not sing or dance. I got to stick to the acting and leave the dancing to the dancers and singing to the singers. It was a fun experience. The musical was called *Anything Goes*, and it was set in the 1930s on a cruise ship. My character was a wealthy investor who spent a little too much time with the liquor bottle. I carried a flask in my pocket and stumbled about the ship getting into arguments with people. We spent months in preparation for the show. We memorized our lines, worked on getting in character, and practiced each scene until it felt just right.

On the day of the show, we showed up early and spent hours getting dressed in our costumes. My costume involved gray hair, glasses, a suit, and some extra padding on my little teenage body to fill me out a bit. Makeup artists painted me so my baby face didn't give me away. It was time to shine. Tonight, I was not Josh Romano; I was Elisha Whitney. I had the very first line in the play, so you could say the show would not go on without me. I put on my best old, belligerent man accent, and the rest is history. I retired after that show, but I will never forget the experience.

The truth is that this wasn't the only acting I was doing in my high school and early college years. I had become pretty good at acting in a completely different arena. My life was an act. My faith was an act. I'm not going to say there wasn't anything genuine about my relationship with Jesus, but it also wasn't what I led others to believe. I was blessed to grow up in a home where faith was the norm. We rarely missed a Sunday at church. From Sunday school to VBS to youth group, I logged some serious church time.

I knew the Christian script pretty well. After all, I had heard the Bible stories and sermons for well over a decade. I knew what was expected. I knew how to play the part pretty well. I could go into and out of character as needed, depending on who was around. I'm not proud to admit any of this because that is the definition of a hypocrite. It's a word that is used often today to describe someone who misrepresents themselves.

The word was used in scripture as well. Jesus used it to expose those He identified as fakes. The Greek word is *hypokrités.* It was used in Jesus's day to describe an actor on a stage.

True disciples aren't mere actors. They are those who have rooted their lives in Jesus and, because of that, are outwardly bearing out the fruit of Jesus. It's more than just a part they play; it is who they are.

Jesus emphasizes this when He says, "You will recognize them by their fruits" (Matt. 7:16). True disciples will show themselves to be so because of the outward evidence in their lives. It's more than mere words; it's a lifestyle they embody.

Over the last couple of chapters, we've looked at what Jesus meant when He said that if we want to bear fruit, we will remain connected to Him.

Being rooted involves developing a deepening connection to Jesus.

Pruning is the required process of becoming more like Jesus.

Being fruitful is the visible outgrowth of a life connected to Jesus.

A fruitful life reflects Jesus both inside and outside. There are two other scenarios that often lead to hypocrisy and hollow faith.

Fruit without Roots Is Mere Imitation

My wife has a knack for making a house a home. If it were up to me, everything would be very plain, resembling my college dorm room. She can take a bland space and turn it into something cozy. I've learned a few things from her, and one is the placement of a plant. What I didn't realize is that she kept slipping these fake plants in on me. They had all the outward features of a real plant, but they weren't. Short of taking a bite out of one of the leaves (not that I tried), you wouldn't know the difference. The nice thing is that you don't have to water them. No matter how real they look, they are just an imitation of the real thing.

Appearance Isn't Everything

The substance of a person is just as important as the surface of a person. One scenario that Jesus was keenly aware of is when the outward appearance doesn't match the inward reality. That was the trend He aimed to expose with many of the religious elite. The Pharisees and Sadducees were notorious for appearing more spiritual than they actually were. Jesus confronted them often and one time said:

> Woe to you, scribes and Pharisees, hypocrites! For you clean the outside of the cup and the plate, but inside they are full of greed and self-indulgence. You blind Pharisee! First clean the inside of the cup and plate, that the outside also may be clean. Woe to you, scribes and Pharisees, hypocrites! For you are like whitewashed tombs, which appear beautiful, but within are full of dead people's bones and all uncleanness. So you also outwardly appear righteous to others, but within you are full of hypocrisy and lawlessness.
>
> —Matt. 23:25–28 ESV

Their lives were detached from God. Their inner realities were disgusting and darkened by evil, yet they dressed up the outside to appear righteous. Jesus charges them with being unclean on the inside. There was nothing but fake fruit hanging from those trees. My grandmother used to have a bowl of fake fruit on her kitchen table. Have you ever tasted a plastic apple? It doesn't take long to figure out that it isn't what you bargained for.

We can staple fake apples on a pine tree all we want, but that doesn't make it an apple tree. Likewise, we can quote all the scripture we want, we can stream all the worship music we want, we can pray all the flowery prayers we want, but if our heart is not rooted in Christ, we shouldn't expect to see real fruit any more than we should expect AstroTurf to start growing.

Instead, Jesus says to first clean the inside of the cup or dish.

I help with the dishes at my house. For a while, we had a dishwasher that would leave things with a nasty milky white residue on the inside of the glasses. Occasionally, residual food would accumulate inside a glass rather than draining off. Imagine if you came over to my house and I poured you a glass of milk in that glass. Not many of us would go bottoms up on a cup of milk with an assortment of floaties in it. In fact, many of us are disgusted at even the thought of it.

We should be just as disgusted at the effects of living a life that ignores the inside while dressing up the outside. If we took an inventory of our hearts, what would we find? Would remnants of jealousy, anger, or bitterness float to the surface? Would lust and selfishness reveal themselves? What's on the inside will eventually come to the surface. We may fool others and even ourselves, but what grows underneath the surface of our lives eventually produces outward effects.

When Jesus resides inside us, a powerful exchange takes place. "I will give you a new heart and put a new spirit in you; I will remove from you your heart of stone and give you a heart of flesh" (Ezek. 36:26).

God wants to exchange our heart for His. He changes us from the inside out. We no longer have to fake it. We simply allow His presence to infiltrate every area of our life so we produce authentic fruit. The new inward reality manifests itself into a new outward reality.

Roots without Fruit Is Dead

Some may say, "My life is rooted in Jesus," yet there is very little visible evidence. James challenges this kind of thinking:

> But someone will say, "You have faith and I have works." Show me your faith apart from your works, and I will show you my faith by my works. You believe that God is one; you do well. Even the demons believe—and shudder!
> —James 2:18–19 ESV

James calls out this common inconsistency between what we say and what we actually do. The things we believe will alter how we behave. The things we believe will shape who we are and the decisions we make. James was a close relative of Jesus, so he knew better than anyone that Jesus did this. Jesus didn't just talk about the things of God, he put God on display through the things he did and the life he lived.

The question for us is this: Does it show? Do the things you say match who you are and what you do? There is no such thing as invisible fruit.

It reminds me of my days playing sports. There would always be those who liked to talk while they played. Maybe it was part of their game to try to get in their opponent's head, maybe they were compensating, or maybe they were just having fun. I never really had a whole lot of respect for it, regardless. I've always thought that what spoke the loudest was what they did on the field or court. I've always respected the guys who didn't have to say much; you just knew they had the right stuff. Talk is cheap, as they say.

James agrees. He says to say whatever you want. But as for him, he won't just say it; he'll show it.

I remember somebody asking this question once: If you were on trial to determine if you were a Christian, would the jury convict you beyond a reasonable doubt? Does your life bear it out?

That has always challenged me to check myself, to take an honest inventory of where I'm at. I don't want people to come to the conclusion that I'm a Christian just because of an online bio or because I just say so or because I stand up on a stage and preach. I want it to be because of what I practice, not just what I preach.

Faith and works—they're not an either/or. They're a both/and. Our faith translates into works. The invisible becomes visible. A faith that is alive is vibrant and unmistakable.

Real Fruit Begins with Strong Roots

When someone has truly and deeply rooted his or her life in Jesus, the result is undeniable. Who we are, inside and out, becomes the evidence of Christ in us.

One of the greatest inventions of fashion history, in my humble opinion, is flex fit jeans. I don't have the body type for skinny jeans. If I attempted to get in a pair, I may never get back out. Flex fit jeans, on the other hand, shape to my likeness. They are flexible and moldable. Made of some magic, stretchy, yet stylish material, they take on the form of the person they belong to. When I discovered them, I never went back to regular jeans again.

We really have two options when it comes down to it. We can be stretched into the likeness of Jesus, or we can conform to the pattern of the world.

Here's a great way to capture this idea:

Don't become so well-adjusted to your culture that you fit into it without even thinking. Instead, fix your attention on God. You'll be changed from the inside out. Readily recognize what he wants from you, and quickly respond to it. Unlike the culture around you, always dragging you down to its level of immaturity, God brings the best out of you, develops well-formed maturity in you.

—Rom. 12:2 MSG

One of the great things about Axis Church, the community God allows us to lead, is that it's a group of everyday people aiming to live the kind of lives that represent Jesus well. We believe the best way to impact the present and reshape the future is rooting our lives in Jesus, allowing Him to produce His fruit in us, and reproducing His fruit in the lives of others. This is our very basic understanding of discipleship.

As we do this, we hope to fulfill Paul's desire:

Do everything without grumbling or arguing, so that you may become blameless and pure, "children of God without fault in a warped and crooked generation." Then you will shine among them like stars in the sky as you hold firmly to the word of life. And then I will be able to boast on the day of Christ that I did not run or labor in vain.

—Phil. 2:14–16

I believe that what our generation needs more than anything else is more people who will take seriously this charge to shine brightly in their generation by rooting themselves in Christ, producing the fruit of Christ, and reproducing the fruit of Christ in those around them.

The Fruit Wheel Tool

We developed the fruit wheel as a way of taking an inventory of our hearts and lives. Galatians 5:22–24 (ESV) captures some of the outward fruit that comes to the surface in the life that is truly rooted in Jesus. "But the fruit of the Spirit is love, joy, peace, patience, kindness, goodness, faithfulness, gentleness, self-control; against such things there is no law. Those who belong to Christ Jesus have crucified the flesh with its passions and desires."

This is not an exhaustive list of the things that emerge as we root our life in Jesus. Yet when we belong to Christ, He plants His spirit within us and reproduces Himself through us. The fruit of Jesus is the outward expression of a life that is devoted to Christ. Things like love, joy, peace, patience, and kindness rise to the surface.

When we remain in Jesus, we take on more of His character, qualities, and actions. We have a new life in Him. "Therefore, if anyone is in Christ, he is a new creation. The old has passed away; behold, the new has come" (2 Cor. 5:17 ESV).

Belonging to Jesus and living the life of a disciple means taking on this new life and all that comes with it.

Dallas Willard, one of the greatest visionaries for discipleship, writes that discipleship involves "learning from him how to live my life as he would lead my life if he were I."[25]

The best evidence of a life that is rooted in Jesus is the outward fruit of Jesus. If we notice less fruit in our lives, it's time to evaluate our inner reality, the depth of our roots. Only God can produce real fruit in us.

---

25. Dallas Willard, *The Divine Conspiracy: Rediscovering Our Hidden Life in God* (New York: Harper Collins, 1998), 285.

The fruit of those who know Jesus is unmistakable. The more we bear the fruit of Jesus, the more we are able to do what we were made to do: shine brightly.

You are the light of the world. A town built on a hill cannot be hidden. Neither do people light a lamp and put it under a bowl. Instead they put it on its stand, and it gives light to everyone in the house. In the same way, let your light shine before others, that they may see your good deeds and glorify your Father in heaven.

—Matt. 5:14–16

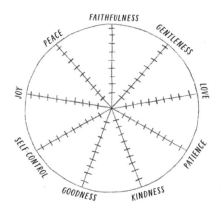

Questions for Reflection

As you look at the fruit wheel, assign numbers 1–10 to the marks by each fruit of the Spirit. The number 10 should be closest to the center, like a bull's-eye on a target. Is the number 10 where you hope to be? Now mark where you think you are for each fruit of the Spirit.

What does this reveal to you about your relationship with Jesus as it stands today?

Where have you seen the most growth in your life?

What fruits of the Spirit do you hope to produce more of? Since this isn't an exhaustive list, what other fruits do you pray to see more of in your life?

The Mission

Stephen

Peace be with you! As the Father has sent me,

I am sending you.

—John 20:21

Chapter 32

Mission

When my son graduated from the eighth grade, we decided to celebrate by going on a fishing trip on Lake Erie. Two other fathers brought their sons, and the six of us chartered a fishing boat. We were fishing for walleye, but we caught mostly smallmouth bass. The captain of our ship, Captain D, and his first mate did a really good job helping us find fish and advise us along the way. He told us that anytime we had a fish to yell, "Fish on!" and he would come and help us if we needed a hand.

In the afternoon, the boys were starting to fade, but the fathers were still fishing. Things seemed to have slowed down until one exciting moment when a good-sized smallmouth bass grabbed my line and jumped high out of the water. I yelled, "Fish on!" and Captain D came over to assess the situation. He said, "Oh, it's a good-sized one!" Just then, the fish swam under the boat, and Captain D yelled, "Keep it out of the prop. He might already be tied up under there!"

From behind me, I heard Jamie yell, "Fish on!" Captain D hurried over to help the other side of the boat. I heard the commotion behind me, but I was focused. This was the biggest fish I had hooked all day. I am pulling. My rod is bent. "This is a monster," I think to myself. "Be careful, don't break your rod!" Captain D yelled. This has not happened all day. I cannot get this fish in the boat. The commotion behind me was still going on. Guys were cheering on Jamie. "Come on, Jamie! Pull it in!" Apparently, Jamie was having the same trouble that I was getting his fish in the boat.

For the next five minutes, there was a titanic struggle that occurred on both sides of the boat. Both Jamie and I were pulling with all our strength. Finally, Captain D was able to reach down into the water and trace my line. He pulled up my hook. It was no longer attached to a large smallmouth bass. It was connected perfectly to Jamie's hook. There was no bait. There were no fish. There were just two hooks connected together. I don't know how that bass accomplished it, but somehow while under the boat, he got the hook out of his mouth, found Jamie's line, and hooked us together. It was a strange feeling. One minute I was catching fish, and the next minute I was catching Jamie.

That must have been strange for the disciples as well. In one moment, these fishermen went from fishing to following, from casting a net to catching people. Matthew retells the story:

As Jesus was walking beside the Sea of Galilee, he saw two brothers, Simon called Peter and his brother Andrew. They were casting a net into the lake, for they were fishermen. "Come, follow me," Jesus said, "and I will send you out to fish for people." At once they left their nets and followed him.

—Matt. 4:18–20

In an instant, their lives changed. Their life mission changed. Their purpose changed. Their identity changed. They had a new calling.

Those disciples could have never imagined what was in front of them or how different life would be when they accepted that invitation and left their nets and followed Jesus. They would go from being fishermen to having front row seats to watch the Creator and sustainer of the universe perform undeniable miracles through His power. They personally would go two-by-two to represent Christ to the communities. They would see His love and compassion firsthand. They would watch Him serve the hurting and hopeless. They would watch Him suffer and die. They would witness Him after He defeated the grave. Jesus was preparing them for a new mission. They were going to be fishing for people.

Once when I was in high school, we were on a family vacation in Myrtle Beach, South Carolina. Normally, our beach trips included camping in a pop-up camper, surfing the waves, playing in the sand, and eating at the cafeteria. We did not rent beach cabanas, sleep in a condo, or pay for excursions. So it surprised me a bit one day when Dad said, "We are chartering a boat to go deep-sea fishing." We loaded up with several other people. The captain of the boat made sure we had everything we needed. He gave us clear instructions. He took us to the exact places we needed to be to catch large numbers of fish. His crew literally did everything for us. They prepared the poles. They miraculously untangled the lines when three or four of us got them caught together. They used their fish finder to locate the perfect spots. If we wanted them to, they would even bait the hook and take the fish off for us. It truly was fishing for dummies. We had a blast and caught a lot of fish that day.

I realize something looking back. The captain of the boat knew a whole lot more about fishing than I did, but he still used me to cast the line. With those words, "Come, follow me...and I will send you out to fish for people," Jesus not only changed the lives of the disciples but also started a worldwide movement. His mission was not just for them. This mission was for us. Our Lord and leader entrusts us to carry out His mission.

Just after His resurrection, Jesus showed Himself to the disciples and reminded them that the mission is not over. In fact, the mission was just beginning.

> On the evening of that first day of the week, when the disciples were together, with the doors locked for fear of the Jewish leaders, Jesus came and stood among them and said, "Peace be with you!" After he said this, he showed them his hands and side. The disciples were overjoyed when they saw the Lord. Again Jesus said, "Peace be with you! As the Father has sent me, I am sending you."
> —John 20:19–21

With these words, Jesus took these men right back to the Sea of Galilee where many of them had been called. In the moments just after the resurrection, Jesus told His disciples that His mission was complete, but their mission was just beginning.

In 2011, I was invited to take a trip to Israel with other church planters and leaders from Ohio. A couple of pastors were so moved by what they saw and experienced on the trip that they wanted to mark this moment in time. They decided to go to a local tattoo artist and get a tattoo on their wrist. The tattoo was a Latin phrase *Missio Dei*, which means "mission of God." You may or may not get it written on your wrist, but it does need to be written on your heart and carried out in your life.

God's mission has always been to reunite people with Himself. His desire is for people to be rescued and restored. That mission has been in place from the very beginning of time. God planned a rescue mission for humanity. The mission is bigger than any one church, bigger than any one leader, bigger than any one philosophy, bigger than any one time or any one place. We get to be one small part of something God has been orchestrating since the beginning of time. Our calling is that we are being sent on a mission. If that is our calling, then why are we so reluctant to carry it out?

Why Are We Scared to Share?

If it is good news, then why don't we share this good news more? Why are we so hesitant to invite other people?

Here are what I believe to be the most common reasons Christians are hesitant to share the good news:

I'm unsure. I don't know what to say.

I'm scared. I don't want to be rejected.

I'm imperfect. I don't want to be called a hypocrite.

I'm busy. I don't have time to talk about it.

I'm indifferent. I don't think it matters.

There is a well-known story that Jesus tells in Luke 15 that gets beyond the excuses. In this story, we see answers to these objections. We learn how to get past the excuses and get on mission with Christ.

Priority

Here is a fundamental truth in life: we make time for what we feel is important. Isn't that true? We all feel, "I don't have any more time to give." You and I make time for what is important.

> *Now all the tax collectors and sinners were all gathering around to hear Jesus. But the Pharisees and the teachers of the law muttered, "This man welcomes sinners and eats with them." Then Jesus told them this parable: "Suppose one of you has a hundred sheep and loses one of them. Doesn't he leave the ninety-nine in the open country and go after the lost sheep until he finds it?"*
>
> —Luke 15:1–4

The owner left the 99 and went after the lost sheep. That is priority. He knew that the 99 were already safely in the sheep pen. He understood that time was of the essence. This sheep was helpless. It could easily be attacked and killed. He made his priority to find what was missing so he could bring it home safely.

Aren't you glad that Jesus made people His priority? In Mark 10:45, Jesus said, "For even the Son of Man did not come to be served, but to serve, and to give His life as a ransom for many." Jesus made coming to our world, serving us, and rescuing us His first priority. He also sends us as His messengers of that news.

> *I have appeared to you to appoint you as a servant and as a witness of what you have seen and will see of me. I will rescue you from your own people and from the Gentiles. I am sending you to them to open their eyes and turn them from darkness to light, and from the power of Satan to God, so that they may receive forgiveness of sins and a place among those who are sanctified by faith in me.*
>
> —Acts 26:16–18

That's the heart of Jesus. He wants to turn people from darkness to light, from the dominion of Satan to God so they can be forgiven and given an inheritance. He gave us this priority. It is a crystal-clear mission.

Are you beginning to understand the heart of Jesus and the priority He has to see lost people found? The question is this: Is it a priority for you?

My grandfather was an evangelist. He was a farmer. He only had an eighth grade education. He could hardly hear a word you said, but he loved the Lord and understood what the Lord wanted him to do with his life. He very sincerely wanted to be in heaven when he died and to take as many people with him as possible. At his funeral, story after story was told about people with whom he had shared his faith. I don't know that I have ever met anyone with a bigger heart for lost people.

The last time I saw him, the day before he died, he was in and out of sleep. When he would wake up, he kept asking me, "How is your church? How many additions have you had since you've been there? Last year? Last month?" He understood that the only things you take to heaven when you die are yourself, your character, your faith, and the people you bring with you.

A few years before he died, Grandpa was selling a woods mower. A couple in their 60s stopped by to look at the mower. During the conversation, Grandpa asked the man if he knew the Lord. The man said no. Grandpa said, "I can't really hear very well, so would it be all right if I brought my Sunday school teacher over to share Jesus with you and your wife?" The man said, "Sure."

The Sunday school teacher and one of the elders went to visit this couple. It turns out that the wife was a Christian, but she had turned away from the Lord some years ago. She was ill, and this encounter convinced her to recommit her life to the Lord. She died within a few months. After about six months of meetings, the man decided he needed to become a Christian, and he was baptized. He became an active member of the local church.

When my grandpa told me that story, he said very passionately, "Stephen, maybe others wouldn't, but I made it my business to tell that couple about the Lord." That couple came to buy a woods mower, and they left with much more. They'll be in heaven because a man in his 80s, a man who could hardly hear a word they said but loved the Lord and lost people, made it his business to tell them about Jesus.

To reflect the Father's heart, we need to care about people. We need to look for opportunities. We need to rethink our priorities. We need to make it our business.

Urgency

I really believe that one of the reasons we aren't sharing our faith is because we don't see the urgency of it. One part of our story about the 99 sheep and the one lost sheep really convicts me. "Doesn't he leave the ninety-nine in the open country and go after the lost sheep until he finds it?" (Luke 15:4). He goes until he finds it. That is urgency. He didn't wait to see if the sheep happened to wander back home. He left and searched until he found it.

I almost lost my daughter once. One day, our family went to the Strawberry Festival in Troy, Ohio. It was a great day. I love strawberries, and I love festivals. It was a perfect combination. The only thing I don't like about festivals is the crowds. Thousands of people go to the Strawberry Festival every year. At the end of the day, we finally gave in to our cravings and bought strawberry shortcake for everyone. We were there with two of our friends and our two children who were ages four and two.

I walked up, saw everyone standing there, including Hannah, and said, "Here are shortcakes for everyone." I started to hand them out, and within seconds I said, "Where's Hannah?" She was gone.

I quickly scanned around us. Hannah was nowhere to be seen. I went one direction. Our friends split up to look. My wife, Lisa, who was pregnant, stayed with our son. At first, I was doing okay. "We'll find her, no big deal," I kept saying. But as the minutes passed, I got more and more anxious. One friend came back and told Lisa, "No Hannah." The other friend came back and said, "No Hannah." I came back and said, "I can't find her." Lisa started to cry. There were thousands and thousands of people. There was row after row of crafts and food booths. Two minutes went by. Five minutes went by. Seven minutes passed. I started to think, "What if someone picked her up? These kinds of events draw predators."

I can tell you that as I ran up and down those aisles, the only thing that ran through my mind was the recovery of my daughter. My net worth, my reputation in the community, and the size of my house did not matter a bit. The only thing that mattered was her recovery. Nine minutes passed. Finally, after 10 minutes, someone said over the loudspeaker the words I won't soon forget: "We have found a lost two-year-old little girl with blue jeans and a red shirt. She is at the police tent." I saw a police officer and said, "That is my little girl! Take me to the tent." Lisa got there first. There was Hannah, seated on the lap of a police officer. She did not have a care in the world. She didn't know she was lost. It seems that she had gone straight across all the rows of crafts, down a steep hill, and into the middle of the parking lot.

When I got there, I picked her up and wrapped my arms around her. Then I pulled her back, looked at her, and hugged her again. I said, "Don't you ever do that again. We were so worried about you." I can still remember the emotions in that moment. I remember the urgency and desperation to find our lost Hannah. I remember the relief and joy when we finally found her. Why do we not feel that same sense of urgency when it comes to people we love who are lost for eternity?

Recently, I came across a message that I gave to our launch team one month before we started Axis Church.

I have heard so many of your stories about why you decided to help launch Axis Church. They are inspiring stories.

You know why I love them? I love them because God stirred something in you. And He is stirring something in me. And I believe He is already stirring something in this community. A new wind is about to blow!

I have heard from many of you that you are here because you can see that this world is taking a nosedive morally and spiritually speaking.

We can sense that we are losing our bearings.

You know the church in America is largely failing. Eighty-five percent of churches are plateaued or dying. In Warren County, about 17 percent of the population is active in a church. That's exactly what the national average is. I read a report a few months ago that if the trend continues, they project that number to be 10.5 percent by 2050.

That means that our kids and grandkids will grow up in a vastly different world. The moral compromises that we have already seen in our generation will continue.

God will become less of a focus. Humanism will rule the day. Right and wrong will become more gray rather than black and white.

I just can't sit idly by and let that happen. While the church sits back and "waits" for someone else to turn the tide, I want to stand and say, "Enough is enough." I do not want my grandkids to look at me and say, "What did you do?" "Why didn't you do anything?"

I want to say to you all today, "Not on our watch!"

For me personally, I was serving in a very comfortable place, but I realized that God had so much more that He needed from me.

I have no interest in just starting another church. I am interested in being the church.

I have no interest in being a gathering place for the already convinced. I am interested in leading a dynamic, impacting group of people who love people far from God.

I have no interest in sitting idly by while our country flushes right values and morals down the cultural toilet. I am interested in joining a revolution.

I have no interest in the masks or pretending. I am interested in an authentic, grace-filled place.

I have no interest in just providing ministry. I am interested in joining the greatest movement that has ever swept over the face of the world.

How many of you are with me?

I got a bit tearful when I found that and read it. I remember the feelings of anxiousness that happen when you step out of the comfort zone. I remember the confidence I had in the Lord and the insecurities I had about myself. With all of my heart, I wanted to see people who were far from God revolve their lives around Jesus and His mission. I wanted to see people in relationships with one another. I wanted to see people change. I wanted to see the trajectory of people's lives change. I wanted to see their family legacies change. Those words pulse with urgency. Do you feel that kind of urgency for your friends and family?

Party

This sheep owner made it his priority to find his lost sheep. He urgently looked until he found it. Then, after he found his beloved sheep, he celebrated.

> And when he finds it, he joyfully puts it on his shoulders and goes home. Then he calls his friends and neighbors together and says, "Rejoice with me; I have found my lost sheep." I tell you that in the same way there will be more rejoicing in heaven over one sinner who repents than over ninety-nine righteous persons who do not need to repent.
> —Luke 15:5–7

It may seem strange to you, but one of the reasons we invite other people is because there is a party in heaven when lost people are invited. I don't know about you, but I like a good party. I don't always like the preparation, but I do enjoy the celebration. I enjoy seeing the people and celebrating the occasion. When it comes to the mission, I think it is important to remember the target. The end goal is the forgiveness of sins and the reward in heaven. When I think about my friends and family who do not know the Lord, I think about both the reality of hell and the promise of heaven. I believe in the promises of God, and I understand that the road to heaven is narrow, and only a few find it. How can I say I love people but ignore the reality of eternity? I am motivated by the party in heaven, but I am also motivated by the tragedy of hell.

The Reality of Hell

Some authors and teachers today are attempting to explain away the scriptures on hell. They describe hell as a figurative idea or a temporary reality. The problem with this more progressive view of hell is that it does not align with the Bible.

The Bible teaches that hell is a real place that was prepared for the devil and the angels that followed him. Second Peter 2:4 says, "God did not spare the angels when they sinned, but sent them to hell, putting them in chains of darkness to be held for judgment." Jesus warns people, "Do not be afraid of those who kill the body but cannot kill the soul. Rather, be afraid of the One who can destroy both body and soul in hell" (Matt. 10:28).

These verses talk about the reality of hell.

The Bible also addresses the suffering experienced in hell. Paul reminds us that the tragedy of hell is everlasting.

> *He will punish those who do not know God and do not obey the gospel of our Lord Jesus. They will be punished with everlasting destruction and shut out from the presence of the Lord and from the glory of his might.*
> —2 Thess. 1:8–9

Nothing would be worse than being shut out of the presence of the Lord forever.

The idea of isolation is also seen several times in the book of Matthew. Matthew 25:30 says that people who reject Christ will be thrown outside. Have you ever been rejected? Have you ever been pushed aside? Have you ever experienced the feeling of being locked out?

When I was a kid, I shared a room with my brother. We had a bathroom that was connected to our room. One day, my brother and his friend Andrew were in the bedroom when I came out of the bathroom. As soon as I came out of the bathroom, Andrew yelled, "You stink! You stink!" He began pushing me toward the door. I was almost four years younger and no match for him. He finally pushed me out the door. I tried to get back in by pushing the door open just a crack and sticking part of my head into the door. I since have realized that making your head a doorstop is not the best idea. The door slammed onto my left eye and opened a deep cut. It hurts to be shut out. Can you imagine the reality of being shut out from the presence of God and isolated for eternity?

The Bible indicates that not only is hell a place of isolation, it is also a place of suffering. Matthew 13:41–42 says, "The Son of Man will send out his angels, and they will weed out of his kingdom everything that causes sin and all who do evil. They will throw them into the blazing furnace, where there will be weeping and gnashing of teeth." Hell is described as a blazing furnace. Revelation goes on to describe hell as a "lake of burning sulfur" (Rev. 20:10). It is difficult for me to ignore the vivid descriptions of hell in the Bible. The reality of hell underscores the urgency for sharing the good news.

The Beauty of Heaven

In contrast to the graphic and tragic descriptions of hell, the Bible gives us a picture of the beauty and companionship in heaven. Paul tells us that "'What no eye has seen, what no ear has heard, and what no human mind has conceived'—the things God has prepared for those who love him" (1 Cor. 2:9). Heaven is beyond your wildest imagination. You cannot even conceive all of what God has in store for you. John writes about heaven, "It shone with the glory of God, and its brilliance was like that of a very precious jewel, like a jasper, clear as crystal" (Rev. 21:11). He does his very best to describe the beauty of heaven by comparing it to a very precious jewel, but his description falls short of truly capturing all he sees.

Instead of the isolation of hell, we see the companionship in heaven. In Revelation 21:3, a voice in heaven declares, "God's dwelling place is now among the people, and he will dwell with them. They will be his people, and God himself will be with them and be their God." God will be with us. Have you ever experienced a glimpse of the presence of God on earth? Can you remember a time of desperation or sadness or loneliness when you prayed or worshipped and just felt the presence of God? You felt comforted, appreciated, and loved. The Bible tells us that in heaven, we will have all eternity to experience that presence.

Instead of the suffering of hell, we will experience the joy and reward of heaven. Matthew 16:27 says, "For the Son of Man is going to come in his Father's glory with his angels, and then he will reward each person according to what they have done." I do not know what all those rewards will be, but I do know that since God is the giver, it is going to be good! I know that God wants to give good gifts to His children. First Peter 1:4 says that in heaven, God has prepared for us "an inheritance that can never perish, spoil or fade." This inheritance is kept for us. It is kept safe, secure, and prepared. Again, I do not know all that will be in this inheritance, but I can't wait to find out.

I really look forward to worship in heaven. Revelation 4:10 says, "The twenty-four elders fall down before him who sits on the throne and worship him who lives forever and ever." Some of my favorite memories are times of worship.

The most incredible worship service I've ever participated in happened in February 1993. Before I tell you about the worship, let me tell you about the events leading up to the service. The summer before, I worked as an intern at the Southern Acres Christian Church in Lexington with Wally Rendel, the preacher. I got to know him, his wife, Barbara, his son, Bart, and his twin daughters, Jody and Jill. They are a great, godly family.

The February after that summer at about 5:30 one morning, I got a call from my mother. She was soft-spoken, and her words were brief: "Jill Rendel was killed this morning in a van accident." My heart sank.

Jill was on the Cincinnati Bible College girls' basketball team, and they were traveling home from a game in Michigan. The streets were icy. The van hit a patch of ice and went off the road. Jill was on the passenger side, asleep. The van flipped over. Jill was tossed from the van and killed. No one else was injured.

Only a week before the accident, Jill was selected as homecoming queen at the Bible College. One reporter in Lexington picked up on that story and wrote the headline, "The Queen Has Gone to Meet the King."

The visitation for Jill was held at Southern Acres Church. The line of people went all the way up the aisle, through the foyer, through the education wing, and out the back door. It took more than two hours to get to the front of the line.

At her funeral the next day, the church was totally packed. The service was inspirational and life-changing. One gentleman played "Amazing Grace" on a soprano sax. Wayne Smith, a preacher from Lexington, spoke about what a delightful girl Jill was and what an awesome God we have. But what really stuck out to me the most was when John Barfield sang the song "I Bowed on My Knees and Cried Holy."

It is a great song about heaven and what Jill was experiencing. John got to the part of the song that says, "I saw Abraham, Jacob and Isaac, talked with Mark, and Timothy but I said 'I want to see Jesus, 'cause He's the One who died for me,'"[26] and Wally, Barbara, Bart, and Jody leaped to their feet, applauded, shouted, and sang. When they did that, the whole place erupted in worship. Everyone was on their feet, hands raised, tears streaming, voices shouting because heaven was more real to us at that moment than it had ever been before. The only thing we could do was worship.

One of my friends calls this a "thin moment." It is a moment when heaven and earth touch. It is a moment in time when all the troubles of this world seem to fade in light of the glory of God and the promise of heaven.

Since heaven is real, shouldn't we do everything we can to make sure that as many people as possible are in heaven?

My dad told a story at my grandfather's funeral that I had never heard before that day. He said, "Years ago you got your car greased every 1,000 miles instead of every 3,000 miles. So Dad would go down to the local mechanic in Buford, Ohio, Paul Thompson. Every time he would go in, as he paid his bill, he told Mr. Thompson that God loved him and that he needed to become a Christian and go to heaven." Dad continued, "Mr. Thompson was the kind of man that had absolutely no interest in the church. He could care less about

---

26. Michael English, "I Bowed on My Knees and Cried Holy," *Lyrics*, https://www.lyrics.com/lyric/2334667/Michael+English/I+Bowed+on+My+Knees+and+Cried+Holy.

the Lord or church. But every time he'd go in, Grandpa told him about the Lord."

One day, Paul Thompson walked into the back of the Buford Church. He had become a Christian. And he became a leader in the church. He even taught Bible classes. Our family got word that Mr. Thompson passed away the same day that Grandpa died. They even had their funerals on the same day. My dad finished his story with these words. "I can just imagine, just as Paul Sams was about to walk into heaven he got a tap on his shoulder. He turned around. It was Paul Thompson saying, 'I'm here because you invited me.' And they went into heaven together."

Who's going to be in heaven because you invited them there?

Questions for Reflection

In your own words, what is the mission of Jesus?

Read through the list of reasons people give to not share the story of Jesus. Which reasons restrict you the most? How can you overcome that barrier?

What will motivate you to make the mission of Jesus a priority in your own life? What will make it more urgent for you right now? What about heaven do you look forward to the most?

Chapter 33

Message

We have been sent on mission with a message. The biblical word for inviting others to know Jesus is *evangelism*. In the original language of the New Testament, the Greek word for evangelism is *euaggelion*. It is the same root word for our English word *gospel*. It literally means good news.

It was simply sharing the good news of Jesus with people. You share good news by telling your story, preaching, sharing what good things God is doing in your life, or studying the good news story in the Bible with someone. You do all of this with the hope that someday they, too, will become a follower of Jesus and go to heaven when they die. God wants you to live your best life possible on this earth, and He wants you to experience eternal life with Him in heaven.

Paul describes our mission and message very clearly:

God was reconciling the world to himself in Christ, not counting people's sins against them. And he has committed to us the message of reconciliation. We are therefore Christ's ambassadors, as though God were making his appeal through us. We implore you on Christ's behalf: Be reconciled to God. God made him who had no sin to be sin for us, so that in him we might become the righteousness of God.

—2 Cor. 5:19–21

Our mission is to serve as Christ's ambassadors. We are delivering His message of hope and reconciliation to the world.

An ambassador is someone who represents a king or a leader. As the leader's representative, an ambassador can only deliver the messages the leader wants delivered. They do not have the authority to change or alter the message unless the leader gives them permission to do so. We are Christ's ambassadors. He has entrusted us to deliver a message to the world. The message is the message of salvation. The message is that God wants peace with the world. He wants to reconcile the world to Himself. It is an offer of peace. It is an offer of goodwill. It is a payment that He has made on our behalf.

A Powerful Message

The message is that "God made him who had no sin to be sin for us, so that in him we might become the righteousness of God" (2 Cor. 5:21). God sent His Son, Jesus, into the world to pay the debt for our sin. For those who are Christians, sometimes we hear this message so much that we become accustomed to it. We forget what it was like the first time we encountered the gospel.

I will never forget the day Gary walked into my office at church. I had never seen him before. He was distraught. Gary was a local transmission mechanic. He was a plain-talking, hard-working man. He told me that he had driven by the church many times. He told me his wife had just filed for divorce. It came completely unexpected for him. He had a young son. He was unsure what was going to happen to his son. His life was literally crashing in around him.

To be honest, I wasn't sure what to say. My words would not heal his marriage or fix his problems. My encouragement would only be a Band-Aid for his situation. I knew I could pray for him, which I did. As I sat there listening to his story, I had this deep impression in my spirit that I should share the gospel with him. I debated it in my own mind for a moment, but then I said, "Gary, do you mind if I share some good news with you?"

I pulled out a piece of paper and began to draw the bridge illustration for him. I told him how, despite how bad things look today, God still has a plan and purpose for his life. I told him that our sin problem means that people make bad decisions. I said that this sin problem is universal. The impact of it is devastating. I told him that because of our sin problem, not only do people get hurt, but ultimately we all deserve eternal separation from God. Gary listened intently.

When I got to the part of the story where Jesus paid the price for him on the cross, Gary stopped me. He started to cry. His reaction took me by surprise. He said, "You are telling me that God did that for me? You are telling me that God loved me that much?" I said, "Yes, Gary. God loves you. He wants to give you new life and a new purpose. Jesus paid for your sins so you can be forgiven from whatever you have done." I sat there amazed as this rough-handed, warmhearted mechanic was both broken and inspired by the message of the gospel. He said, "What do I do?" I told him that he needed to believe in Jesus and His payment on the cross, confess that belief, repent of his sins, and be baptized. That very day, that is exactly what Gary did.

I don't know why, but after all these years, I continue to be surprised by the impact of the gospel on people's lives. The message of salvation is a message of hope and healing. The message is about peace and forgiveness. The message that God so loved the world that He gave His only Son is a powerful, life-changing, world-altering message.

Why do we think we need to have all the answers?

I think one of the hesitations people have about being ambassadors is that they fear they need to have all the answers to someone's questions. Why do we feel that way? If you share the good news about a Super Bowl victory by your favorite team, do you believe you need to know all the stats from the game? If you share the good news about a new baby being born, do you believe you need to explain all the scientific intricacies of how the baby was created? If you share the good news about getting a new job, do you believe you need to know all the details of the position before you can share the news? No! You simply celebrate the victory. You tell everyone that the baby is happy and healthy and looks just like her mother.

You give the job title, the benefits package, and the fact that you are moving to Hawaii. Why do we feel we need to have all the answers before we tell the good news of Jesus coming to earth, dying for our sins, and giving us the promise of heaven?

In the Bible, we read story after story of people who told about God but did not have all the answers. The shepherds went home from the manger praising God and telling all the people. The woman at the well went into town and said to come and see a man who knows everything about me. After the resurrection, the two men on the road to Emmaus ran to the disciples and told them that the rumors are true—Jesus is alive!

In John 9, we read the story of a blind beggar. This man had been blind from birth. Jesus made some mud, put it on the man's eyes, and then told him to go and wash. When he did, he was able to see. The Pharisees heard about this miracle and questioned both this man and his parents. In fact, they summoned the man more than once. Read through the account, and you will see question after question from the Pharisees. They were accusing Jesus of being a sinner because He healed this man on the Sabbath. The man gave a very simple, good-news answer: "Whether he is a sinner or not, I don't know. One thing I do know. I was blind but now I see!" (John 9:25). This formerly blind man did not have all the answers, but he did have good news to share. The message we have been given is a good-news message. The message is about everlasting life in heaven, but it is also about life in Jesus today!

The Good News Is Now

There is a misconception that once you become a Christian, all the fun is over. People erroneously believe that when they decide to follow Jesus, they will be forced to follow a list of rules and regulations. While all their friends are off partying and enjoying life, the new believer will be forced to meditate in solitude. That is just not the case.

You can experience good news in your life right now. After all, the result of much of that "fun" behavior often leads to regret, disappointment, guilt, and even more tragic consequences. In John

10:10, Jesus said, "The thief comes only to steal and kill and destroy; I have come that they may have life, and have it to the full." The devil will tempt you by saying that the consequences won't be so bad. Just live it up, and no one will know. But the devil is a liar and thief. Sin is fun for a season, but the consequences are usually worse than we project.

On the other hand, Jesus came to give you life. The good news is that you can have peace now. You can have a peace that passes understanding. You can be completely at peace with yourself and with God. You can have joy now. You can have that deep, abiding joy that comes when you know your sins are forgiven. You can have love now. You can experience true love, the love of God. You don't have to worry about what other people think about you. You can find your self-worth in the fact that the God of the universe is on your side.

The message of the gospel is good news both now and for eternity. You have an inheritance waiting for you in heaven, and you get the benefit of being God's child now. He is on your side. He will never leave you. He will never let you down. When bad things happen, the Holy Spirit is there to comfort you. When you need to make a decision, His Word is there to instruct you. When you face temptation, He is there to protect you. When you don't know what to pray, the Spirit is there to speak on your behalf. Living as a Christian is your best life both now and forever. That is a message worth sharing!

Questions for Reflection

In your own words, what is the good news of Jesus?

How has this message impacted your life?

Do you think you need to have all the answers before you can tell the good news to someone else?

How is being a Christian good news for you right now?

Chapter 34

Method

How do you share the message of hope? Here is a brutal truth: most Christians never share their faith with another human outside of their family. That is not scientifically researched; it is simply my observation. Most people I talk to are reluctant to share their faith with anyone. I think we overcomplicate the method of sharing the message.

What I want to do in this section is walk you through a story in scripture and pull some principles out that I think will make sharing your faith much more tangible. In Acts 3 and 4, we read a story about how Peter and John, two of the apostles, healed a man who had been crippled from birth and how this encounter not only changed the man but also served as a platform for the gospel.

My Part

What is our part in evangelism? How can we learn from these early followers of Jesus? We cannot control the outcome, but we can do our part in sharing the good news message.

Look for Opportunities

Acts 3:1-2 says, "One day Peter and John were going up to the temple at the time of prayer—at three in the afternoon. Now a man who was lame from birth was being carried to the temple gate called Beautiful, where he was put every day to beg from those going into the temple courts." Peter and John were simply doing their regular routine. They were not going out of their way. They were not adding something else to their schedules. But they were aware of the opportunities in front of them.

One of the arguments people have against going to make disciples is that they just don't have the time. They are too busy. Maybe God is not expecting you to add to your schedule. What if He is just asking you to be more aware of people as you carry out your schedule? We all encounter people every day who have needs. The man Peter and John encountered was put at the temple gate every day. The need was there. Peter and John just needed to be aware.

Who is God putting in your path that is in need? Is it a coworker or a friend? Is it another parent at the soccer game? Is it someone in your book club or scout troop? Is it a guy on your softball team? Your part is to look for opportunities.

Listen to the Story

It seems almost too simple, doesn't it? Take time to simply listen to their story. Pay attention to their needs. Acts 3:3–5 says, "When he saw Peter and John about to enter, he asked them for money. Peter looked straight at him, as did John. Then Peter said, 'Look at us!' So the man gave them his attention, expecting to get something from them."

The beggar in this story had real needs. His real need wasn't money; it was healing for his legs. More than that, he needed the salvation that only Jesus could give. I like that Peter told the man to look at him. Peter could have done a drive-by healing. Instead, he took time to actually see the man. He heard his words.

Many times, the people we encounter will not be able to identify their deeper needs. Like the man in this story, they will tell us about their felt needs. They will tell us about something tangible. Our job is to listen to the story with empathy and compassion.

Lead with Love

I cannot emphasize this enough: the message is best received through relationship. Very rarely will someone respond to the gospel from a tract in a bathroom or a bullhorn on the corner of a downtown intersection. People respond when they know and trust the person sharing the message. We must always lead with love.

"Then Peter said, 'Silver or gold I do not have, but what I do have I give you. In the name of Jesus Christ of Nazareth, walk.' Taking him by the right hand, he helped him up, and instantly the man's feet and ankles became strong" (Acts 3:6–7). Peter took the man by the hand and, through the power of God, healed him. This act of kindness would forever change this man. There is something powerful in human touch. There is something meaningful that happens when one person notices another person.

Galatians 5:6 is one of the theme verses for my life. "The only thing that counts is faith expressing itself through love." This is not an overstatement on Paul's part. When your faith is expressed to others, through love, that is what matters. That is the only thing that counts. This verse is similar to the commands of Jesus to love God and love people. We are ambassadors of love, bringing the message of hope and salvation to the world. In their book *Lost in America*, Tom Clegg and Warren Bird write:

> *The inescapable conclusion is that we must throw out any notion that God is truly at the center of the church's heart in North America. The shift in society's view of the church has resulted in the marginalization of the church and the secularization of society. Christianity has lost its place at the center of American life. Christians must learn how to live the gospel as a distinct people who no longer occupy the center of society. We must learn to build relational bridges that win a hearing.*[27]

We must build relational bridges. That requires creativity and compassion. Mostly, it takes time.

Part of my living life on mission leads me to teach classes at a local university. The university has a Christian foundation, so the

---

27. Tom Clegg, and Warren Bird. *Lost in America: How You and Your Church Can Impact the World Next Door* (Loveland, CO: Group Publishing, 2001), 27.

students are required to take faith-based courses, even though many of them are not Christians. That has given me a unique opportunity to teach students from all walks of life and all types of faith.

I have learned that no matter the subject I am teaching—New Testament Survey, Old Testament Survey, Biblical Themes, Philosophy and Christian Life—I need to start with a basic rationale for Christianity. We begin by looking at questions like these: Does God exist? Is the Bible true? Who is Jesus? At the beginning of each class, we go around the room and get to know one another. I always ask the students to describe their faith background. In every class, I try very hard to build relational bridges with the students. We take extra time in every class to hear their stories.

In a recent class, I had a student named James. He described himself as agnostic. He wasn't sure if God existed or not, but if He did, James was pretty sure that God was not available. I could sense that James was interested in the class. He took the assignments seriously. His papers were filled with questions and thoughts but were very well written. During breaks, he would often come up, and we would talk about life and challenges. Sometimes he had a question about something in class.

On week four, we had a breakthrough. During break, James came up and described in detail his issues with God. He talked about his faith background. He talked about the church he tried to attend for a while. It was very dogmatic and judgmental. I began to understand that maybe James had an issue with the Jesus that other people had modeled for him instead of with the real Jesus. I tried as best I could to describe the Jesus of the Bible. I talked about what Jesus actually did. We walked through the characteristics of the fruit of the Spirit and how living in Christ brings joy, peace, patience, kindness, gentleness, and more.

During the next teaching segment, I noticed that James was on his phone. As a professor, you realize that is not generally a good sign. But at the next break, James came up to me and said, "Dr. Sams, I apologize for being on my phone. I was texting my wife." He had told me previously that she was also agnostic. He said, "I just asked her one question: "What if God is real?'" He went on to take his break. I sat in silent amazement. It wasn't long after this that James emailed me. He wanted to grab lunch, catch up, and update me on his life and spiritual journey. He wasn't going to church, but he was watching preachers online. He and his wife were praying together for the first time. He is taking steps from agnosticism to faith to growth.

Are you building relational bridges with people? Are you living authentically? Are you demonstrating God's love to the people you encounter? Are you looking for ways to turn your conversations toward God?

Let God Show You What's Next

This is where many of us struggle. We might be on the lookout for people. We probably have the desire to share this message of hope. We do want to love people sincerely. That is often the stopping point. Many of us do not know what to do next. I think it is helpful to remember that you do not need to have all the answers. God already has a plan. He is working ahead of you. Let God show you what is next. Here's what Acts 3:8–11 says:

> *He jumped to his feet and began to walk. Then he went with them into the temple courts, walking and jumping, and praising God. When all the people saw him walking and praising God, they recognized him as the same man who used to sit begging at the temple gate called Beautiful, and they were filled with wonder and amazement at what had happened to him. While the man held on to Peter and John, all the people were astonished and came running to them in the place called Solomon's Colonnade.*

This miraculous encounter garnered the attention of the town. The man ran off praising God. People took notice. They were filled with wonder and amazement. God used this story as a platform for Peter and John to share the good news. One of the best things to do when you are sharing the good news is to pray this simple prayer: "What's next, God?" For Peter and John, they first focused on this man's physical need, and it opened him up to something much more important. He went from begging to praising.

Everyone is at a different place spiritually. Too often, we put everyone we encounter at a similar place on a spiritual growth journey. We make assumptions about people. Rather than seeing people as individuals, we wrongly think that people move at the same pace. The question we should ask is this: "What is the next step for the person we are talking to now?" Our prayer should be, "God, what is next? How can I help them progress to the next step?" Or, for that matter, "God, what should I do to progress to the next step in my walk with you? How do I move closer to you?"

The Arrow Tool

We took this idea of the next step and developed a tool we call "the arrow." The arrow helps us assess where someone is in their spiritual journey and how we can support them in the next step in their growth.

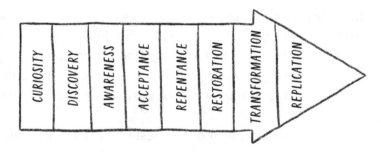

Curiosity Stage

In this stage, the person is beginning to ask questions. They are showing some interest in spiritual matters. During this stage, your job is to love and listen. It is good to ask questions. "How can I help you?" "How can I pray for you?"

"A great crowd of people followed him because they saw the signs he had performed by healing the sick" (John 6:2).

Discovery Stage

In the discovery stage, the person is exploring who God is and what His intentions are. The person is becoming a spiritual seeker. During this stage, your job is to tell your story and what God has done in your life. It is good to simply ask, "Can I share my story with you?"

"You will seek me and find me when you seek me with all your heart" (Jer. 29:13).

Awareness Stage

In this stage, the person has a growing awareness of their own sin and need for God. It is important during this stage to help them clearly understand the gospel. You can get this conversation going by asking, "Can I share God's story with you?" The bridge is a helpful tool as you explain the gospel.

"When the people heard this, they were cut to the heart and said to Peter and the other apostles, 'Brothers, what shall we do?'" (Acts 2:37).

"But God demonstrates his own love for us in this: While we were still sinners, Christ died for us" (Rom. 5:8).

Acceptance Stage

In this stage, someone understands and accepts the gospel. They respond. Again, the bridge is a very helpful tool here. Help the person clearly understand their part in accepting God's great gift.

"For God so loved the world that he gave his one and only Son, that whoever believes in him shall not perish but have eternal life" (John 3:16).

"If you declare with your mouth, 'Jesus is Lord,' and believe in your heart that God raised him from the dead, you will be saved" (Rom. 10:9).

"Peter replied, 'Repent and be baptized, every one of you, in the name of Jesus Christ for the forgiveness of your sins. And you will receive the gift of the Holy Spirit'" (Acts 2:38).

Repentance Stage

Repentance is needed both when they accept Christ, as they turn from their old way and embrace the way of Jesus, and as they grow in Christ. There may be many moments in a person's life when they return to this point. Your job is to balance grace and truth.

"'The time has come,' he said. 'The kingdom of God has come near. Repent and believe the good news!'" (Mark 1:15).

Restoration Stage

In this stage, the person begins to live in the peace of forgiveness. They have new hope in Christ. They begin to understand that this is the best life both now and forever. There is a newness and freshness in their relationship with God. This stage is often accompanied by pure joy. This is also the stage where someone can become disillusioned. They might believe that life in Christ is a life free of problems and challenges. They need support and encouragement.

"The thief comes only to steal and kill and destroy; I have come that they may have life, and have it to the full" (John 10:10).

Transformation Stage

This is the stage of continual growth and maturity. It is a lifelong pursuit to become more and more like Jesus. The person in this stage needs other believers close by in community. They need ongoing learning and mentoring. The person develops new life patterns. They discover new priorities.

"I am the vine; you are the branches. If you remain in me and I in you, you will bear much fruit; apart from me you can do nothing" (John 15:5).

Replication Stage

This is a stage that most believers in Jesus struggle to achieve, but it is of paramount importance to Jesus. His last command for us included marching orders to reproduce. That is where the person is making other disciples and helping others discover hope and new life in Christ.

"Therefore go and make disciples of all nations, baptizing them in the name of the Father and of the Son and of the Holy Spirit, and teaching them to obey everything I have commanded you" (Matt 28:19–20).

The arrow is merely a tool for you. It helps to understand where someone might be on their spiritual journey and how you can better facilitate their moving to "what's next?"

God's Part

When we do our part in sharing the good news message, God will take care of the results. When you look for opportunities, listen to their story and lead with love. Then, through prayer, let God show you what's next. God will do what He does best. God loves people and wants nothing more than to see every person come to know Him.

God Allows Changed Lives to Change Lives

We read earlier in Acts 3:9–11 that when the people saw the crippled beggar jumping and praising God, they took notice. The people were filled with wonder. You cannot underestimate the power of a changed life. God allows changed lives to change lives. When one person is wrecked and then changed by the power of God, people begin to take notice. They begin to ask, "What happened to that person? Why are they so different?"

It is so important for every Christian to learn to tell their spiritual story. Some Christians feel like they do not have a story to tell. They think their story is mundane and not dramatic. Never underestimate the power of a life-changing story. It may not be dramatic, but people are impacted by the simple as much as they are the dramatic. You have a story to tell.

God Opens Doors You Do Not Expect

In Acts 3:12–13, we see how God opened doors for Peter to share the good news message. "When Peter saw this, he said to them: 'Fellow Israelites, why does this surprise you? Why do you stare at us as if by our own power or godliness we had made this man walk? The God of Abraham, Isaac and Jacob, the God of our fathers, has glorified his servant Jesus.'" The formerly crippled man started to jump and praise God. The people took notice and came to Peter and John. Peter saw the open door and shared the good news message.

God will open doors for you that you do not expect. In Acts 4:4, we read, "Many who heard the message believed; so the number of men who believed grew to about five thousand." Peter and John probably did not expect that this simple miracle would lead to such an outcome.

We also learn that Peter and John were arrested and put in front of the Sanhedrin to be questioned by them. These apostles did not see this as a hardship; instead, they embraced it as another opportunity. God opened a door for them to share the good news message with an even greater number of people. Sharing the good news message can be intimidating, but sometimes a simple act of kindness will open the doors to much greater opportunities. You just need to be faithful to step through the door.

God Uses Your Uniqueness

After Peter courageously presents the gospel before his accusers, we find a sentence in the story that jumps off the page. Acts 4:13 says that when the members of the Sanhedrin "saw the courage of Peter and John and realized that they were unschooled, ordinary men, they were astonished and they took note that these men had been with Jesus." I love that. Jesus did not choose the wise or the accomplished. He did not select the best dressed or most likely to succeed. He chose the ordinary. That encourages me. God uses the unique you to share His good news message.

He uses introverts who prefer one-on-one conversations. He uses extroverts who grab the attention of a room. He uses PhD scientists who like to explain the intricacies of the universe. He uses the welder who talks to his buddy on their lunch break. He uses the Jr. high student who convinces his friend to go to camp. He uses my hard-of-hearing grandfather as he sells his woods mower. There is not one right way to share the message. God will use your own personality and experiences. Just be you and prayerfully ask God, "What's next?" Then do it.

Questions for Reflection

Of the four principles (look for opportunities, listen to their story, lead with love, and let God tell you what's next), which area is your best? Your worst? Specifically, what can you do to be more aware in each area?

Where do you spend the majority of your time? Who is God wanting you to love there?

Where are you on the arrow? What is the next step for you?

Write down and tell your spiritual story.

Conclusion

An Important Reminder

Stephen

I love to joke around and laugh with my children. Once when we were about to eat dinner, I noticed a plastic grenade that one of my children must have gotten from a toy army kit. I threw the grenade on the ground, leaped from the stool where I was sitting, landed squarely on the grenade and yelled, "Get back! I will save you! I will save you!" Without even a second of hesitation, my six-year-old son, Jason, jumped from his stool, laid full out on my back and at the top of his lungs yelled, "I'll die with you, Dad!"

That is a moment I will never forget. The action of my son taught me a lot about sacrifice. The essence of discipleship is a call to self-sacrifice. In many ways, it is a call to die.

In Luke 14, large crowds followed Jesus. It appeared that they were interested in what He could do for them. He had just healed a man who had unusual swelling and a crippled woman as well. Jesus saw through their self-interests and said, "If anyone comes to me and does not hate father and mother, wife and children, brothers and sisters—yes, even their own life—such a person cannot be my disciple. And whoever does not carry their cross and follow me cannot be my disciple" (Luke 14:26–27). The Son was teaching them a lot about sacrifice.

Jesus often deflected crowds and attention. He was not interested in having people join a political revolution or some popularity movement. He was concerned about things that were much more important. He understood that those who signed up to follow Him were soon in for utter hardship.

266

That brings up an obvious question: Why would anyone want to be a disciple of Jesus when the cost is so high? If you have ever wondered that, you are in good company. Even the Apostle Peter, in a moment of apparent risk-reward analysis, blurts out, "We have left everything to follow you!" (Matt. 19:27).

"Truly I tell you," Jesus replied, "no one who has left home or brothers or sisters or mother or father or children or fields for me and the gospel will fail to receive a hundred times as much in this present age: homes, brothers, sisters, mothers, children and fields—along with persecutions—and in the age to come eternal life. But many who are first will be last, and the last first."

—Mark 10:29–31

Jesus reminds Peter that there are rewards both now in this age and eternal life in the age to come. There are rewards in heaven and on earth. For the early disciples of Jesus, that was enough. The prize was worth the pain.

I think the greatest high school sport ever invented is cross-country. I say this as an experienced parent of four children who all participated in different sports. Why do I think cross-country is the best? The races almost always start on time. As a parent, you show up just before the beginning of the race. You snap a couple of pictures, which is very important to your social media–oriented teenager. You yell a hearty, "Go get 'em!" The gun sounds. I run straight to the kettle corn booth. I get my huge bag of delicious kettle corn and position myself somewhere in the middle of the course to wait for the runners to pass. I see my child in the distance. I get my phone camera ready. I take a blurry picture as she runs by me. I yell, "Get that girl in front of you! You pass her!" I catch a glare from the parent of the other girl. I eat a handful of kettle corn. I make my way over to the finish line for one final picture, and I cheer. I congratulate my child after the race. I tell her I will see her at home. I am back in my car in 30 minutes. What's not to love? That is how it usually goes. But there was one race that took an unexpected twist.

When my daughter was a senior in high school, I invited my 80-year-old mother to the race. She really enjoyed watching the girls run. She embraced every moment. She cheered gleefully when her granddaughter passed by. My daughter finished in less than 21 minutes. There were hundreds of spectators at the finish line cheering on the racers. After the race, my mom gave hugs and posed for photos with her family. Then my mom said, "Stephen, I want to go back to the finish line. There were a couple of girls who were at the end of the pack. I want to watch them finish." So we walked over to the finish line. We looked off into the distance. We could not see any runners. Thirty minutes had passed on the race clock. There were no longer hundreds of spectators. Only a few people remained at the finish line. Just then, I looked up and saw two girls running near each other. The parents and coaches who were left at the finish line were clapping and yelling, "You can do it! Keep going! Finish strong!" They crossed the line, exhausted but satisfied.

As we were standing there, we noticed a man who was still at the finish line. He was clearly looking intently into the distance. He had his phone in his hand, ready to take a video. I said, "Sir, what are you looking for? The race is over." He said, "Oh no, my daughter, she is still out there." I said, "Really? We will stay with you." He said, "My wife couldn't come today, so I am making sure I take this video for her." He continued. "My daughter does not run. This is the only athletic thing she has ever done in her life." He said, "She has asthma. It is a real challenge for her to even walk up the stairs at home without losing her breath. She is not athletic at all. We are so proud of her. I can't wait to show her mother this video." We are the only three people at the finish line.

Just then, this father stops talking to us because he sees his daughter coming across that field. She is a long way off. She is limping a bit as she runs. One moment she is jogging. The next moment she is walking. We are now at 38 minutes on the clock. She has been on the course a long time.

This father has his phone out taking a video. You can hear him say, "Come on, baby. Come on. You can make it, baby. Come on." He starts to yell out louder so she can hear. I am getting caught up in the moment. I am thinking, "Yeah, come on!" He is at the end of the roped-off area where the earlier runners all made their final push. "Come on, baby!" She hears him. She starts to pick up her pace a little bit. You can see that her eyes, instead of looking down at the ground, start to focus on the finish line where her father is waiting for her. "Come on, baby! You can do it! You can make it! I am with you!"

She is now getting close to that final finish, and her dad, who is also overweight, starts to run with her. He is taking that video and yelling, "Come on, baby! I am with you! You can do it, baby!" People start to take notice. Other parents and athletes start to come over to the finish line. More of us are now applauding and celebrating this girl.

When that daughter crossed the line, you have never seen a more proud father. She might as well have been the first-place runner. When she crossed that line, she fell in exhaustion. That father went under the rope line and put his arm on her shoulder. "You did it, baby! You did it!"

Here is what I want you to understand. You have a heavenly Father who runs with you! Yes, running requires sacrifice. It is difficult at times. You may find yourself wanting to give up. But be encouraged today. You are not alone!

When Jesus commissioned His followers to go make disciples, His purpose came with a promise. "I am with you always, to the end of the age" (Matt. 28:20).

There will be times when you are discouraged. I am with you.

There will be moments of exhaustion. I am with you.

There will be people who reject you. I am with you.

There will be times when the path takes an unexpected turn. I am with you. You are not alone!

Be encouraged by the truth that our God runs with you. He runs with you in this life and when your race on earth is complete. He runs with you to the other side. He puts His eternal arms around you, wipes every tear from your eyes, and says, "You did it, my child! You did it! Your race is over. Welcome home!" The prize is worth the pain. In Revelation 2:10, Jesus said it this way: "Be faithful, even to the point of death, and I will give you life as your victor's crown."

So go! Start running!

Go after the crown and discover a greater kingdom.

Give up your nets and embrace the call to follow Jesus.

Receive and give away the gift of salvation.

EAT the bread of life, the Word of God.

Drop the stones of judgment and relate to others with love.

Listen to God's voice and connect to Him in prayer.

Pick up a towel and be a servant.

Bear good fruit and develop deep roots that last.

Go with the message of good news! Go now!

Recommended Resources

- elementarydiscipleship.com

- exponential.org

- discipleship.org

- renew.org

- stadiachurchplanting.org

- Relational Discipleship Network – rdn1.com